BIRDWA

THE FAMILY LEISURE GUIDE

A comprehensive guide to RSPB and Wildlife Trust reserves in the United Kingdom and the major leisure attractions around them

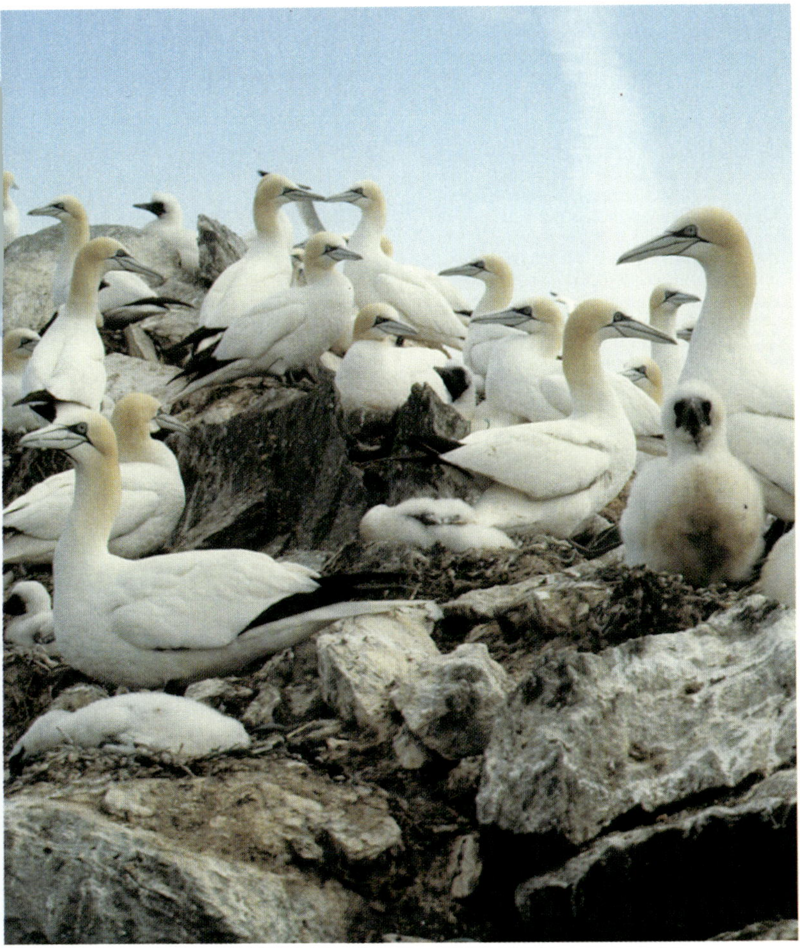

Published in association with the National Tourist Boards of England, Scotland, Wales and Northern Ireland

First published in 1992
by Charles Letts & Co Ltd,
Letts of London House,
Parkgate Road,
London SW11 4NQ

Published in association with the National Tourist Boards of England, Scotland, Wales and Northern Ireland.

© The Pen & Ink Book Company Ltd,
Whitwell Chambers, Ferrars Road, Huntingdon,
Cambs PE18 6DH.

All our rights reserved. No part of this publication may be reproduced, stored in a retrieval system, or transmitted, in any form or by any means, electronic, mechanical, photocopying, recording or otherwise, without the prior permission in writing of the publishers.

The information contained in this Guide has been published in good faith and every effort has been made to ensure its accuracy. Neither the publishers, copyright holders nor the National Tourist Boards can accept any responsibility for error or misinterpretation. All liability for loss, disappointment, negligence or other damage caused by reliance on the information contained in this Guide, or in the event of bankruptcy or liquidation or cessation of trade of any company, individual or firm mentioned is hereby excluded.

Research – James Tindall
Cartography – Lovell Johns Ltd., Oxford
Photographs
BTA/Britain in View
All Sport

Ian Johnson
Tim Pankhurst
Jo Thomas
Avon Wildlife Trust
Cuckmere Haven
Fingringhoe Wick
The Norfolk Naturalists Trust
Thorndon Country Park

Design and production – PEN & INK

Printed and bound in Great Britain

A CIP catalogue record for this book is available from the British Library.

ISBN 1 85238 327 5

'Letts' is a registered trademark of Charles Letts & Co Limited.

GUIDE TO SYMBOLS

- ☎ telephone
- *i* tourist information
- P car parking
- 🚌 guided tours
- 🏛 admission charged
- 🏛 no charge
- ♿ disabled access
- ♿ disabled facilities
- ♥ the reserve
- ✗ catering
- ⛳18 18-hole golf course
- ⛳9 9-hole golf course
- ➔A nearest 'A' road

INTRODUCTION

Welcome to the first edition of BIRDWATCHING – THE FAMILY LEISURE GUIDE. This is the latest title in the successful *Family Leisure Guide* series and it has been written to provide birdwatchers with practical information on major birdwatching centres and reserves around the country.

As with the rest of the series, this Guide is published in association with the National Tourist Boards of England, Scotland, Wales and Northern Ireland and has been produced to allow birdwatchers to work out how and where to combine enjoyment of their favourite pastime with a holiday or short break for the whole family.

This Guide has been produced with the help of the RSPB, RSNC and the Wildlife Trusts around the country.

The first part of the Guide contains detailed descriptions of more than 105 locations that welcome visiting birdwatchers. The entries are organised geographically for ease of use and each entry includes information on how to get to the reserve, what species to look for and when, what facilities it has and what restrictions, if any, are imposed. Where they are available there is also information on disabled facilities. Any fees that are payable are also noted.

The second part of the Guide is again organised geographically and contains information about the major leisure, recreational and sporting facilities that can be enjoyed within approximately 15 miles of each reserve. Up to 50 different leisure pursuits are covered ranging from historic houses and museums to microliting and hang gliding. Symbols (◀ ▶) at the top of each page refer to pages in the 'What to Do and See' section.

All the information on the birdwatching locations has been researched during 1991 and is as accurate as possible.

The information on leisure facilities around each establishment has also been researched during 1991. This information is not intended to be exhaustive, merely to show the range of leisure activities available around each location. If you feel that we have missed out a major attraction please let us know so that we may include it in the next edition of each Guide.

We are very grateful for the assistance we have received from the RSPB and RSNC and particularly the members of the individual Wildlife trusts whose reserves are included in this Guide. These enthusiasts have given us great help and we hope that this Guide will add to their enjoyment and make people more aware of the valuable service they give to the preservation of wildlife in their own areas of the country. We are particularly grateful to those who also supplied photographs or other illustrations for inclusion in this Guide.

CONTENTS

GUIDE TO SYMBOLS	2
INTRODUCTION	3

ENGLAND

NORTH DEVON
RESERVES	6
WHAT TO DO AND SEE	98, 99

DEVON
RESERVES	7, 8, 9
WHAT TO DO AND SEE	100, 101

DORSET
RESERVES	10, 11
WHAT TO DO AND SEE	102, 103

SOMERSET
RESERVES	12
WHAT TO DO AND SEE	104, 105

AVON
RESERVES	13, 14
WHAT TO DO AND SEE	106, 107

HAMPSHIRE
RESERVES	15
WHAT TO DO AND SEE	108, 109

HAMPSHIRE/SUSSEX BORDERS
RESERVES	16
WHAT TO DO AND SEE	110, 111

SUSSEX
RESERVES	17
WHAT TO DO AND SEE	112, 113, 114

EAST SUSSEX
RESERVES	18
WHAT TO DO AND SEE	115, 116

EAST KENT
RESERVES	19, 20
WHAT TO DO AND SEE	117, 118

WEST KENT
RESERVES	21, 22
WHAT TO DO AND SEE	119, 120

ESSEX
RESERVES	23, 24, 25
WHAT TO DO AND SEE	121, 122, 123

HERTFORDSHIRE
RESERVES	26
WHAT TO DO AND SEE	124

GLOUCESTERSHIRE
RESERVES	27, 28
WHAT TO DO AND SEE	125, 126

WEST MIDLANDS
RESERVES	29
WHAT TO DO AND SEE	127, 128

STAFFORDSHIRE/DERBYSHIRE
RESERVES	30
WHAT TO DO AND SEE	129, 130

BEDFORDSHIRE/CAMBRIDGESHIRE
RESERVES	31, 32, 33
WHAT TO DO AND SEE	131, 132

SUFFOLK
RESERVES	34, 35
WHAT TO DO AND SEE	133, 134

NORFOLK
RESERVES	36, 37, 38, 39, 40, 41, 42, 43
WHAT TO DO AND SEE	135, 136, 137, 138

CAMBRIDGESHIRE/LEICESTERSHIRE
RESERVES	44, 45
WHAT TO DO AND SEE	139, 140

EAST LINCOLNSHIRE
RESERVES	46, 47
WHAT TO DO AND SEE	141

WEST LINCOLNSHIRE
RESERVES	48
WHAT TO DO AND SEE	142, 143

SOUTH HUMBERSIDE
RESERVES	49
WHAT TO DO AND SEE	144, 145

HUMBERSIDE
RESERVES	50, 51, 52
WHAT TO DO AND SEE	146, 147

NORTH YORKSHIRE
RESERVES	53
WHAT TO DO AND SEE	148, 149

LANCASHIRE
RESERVES	54, 55
WHAT TO DO AND SEE	150, 151

CUMBRIA
RESERVES	56, 57
WHAT TO DO AND SEE	152, 153

DURHAM AND CLEVELAND
RESERVES	58
WHAT TO DO AND SEE	154, 155

TYNE AND WEAR
RESERVES	59
WHAT TO DO AND SEE	156, 157

NORTHUMBERLAND
RESERVES	60, 61
WHAT TO DO AND SEE	158, 159

WALES

WEST GLAMORGAN
RESERVES	62
WHAT TO DO AND SEE	160

DYFED (SOUTH)
RESERVES	63, 64
WHAT TO DO AND SEE	161

DYFED (NORTH)
RESERVES	65, 66
WHAT TO DO AND SEE	162

GWYNEDD/POWYS
RESERVES	67, 68, 69
WHAT TO DO AND SEE	163, 164, 165, 166

CLWYD
RESERVES	70
WHAT TO DO AND SEE	167

SCOTLAND

DUMFRIES AND GALLOWAY
RESERVES	71
WHAT TO DO AND SEE	168, 169

Contents

BORDERS
RESERVES	72
WHAT TO DO AND SEE	170

STRATHCLYDE AND LOTHIAN
RESERVES	73, 74
WHAT TO DO AND SEE	171, 172, 173, 174, 175

FIFE
RESERVES	75
WHAT TO DO AND SEE	176, 177

TAYSIDE (PERTH)
RESERVES	76
WHAT TO DO AND SEE	178, 179

TAYSIDE (ANGUS)
RESERVES	77
WHAT TO DO AND SEE	180, 181

TAYSIDE AND GRAMPIAN
RESERVES	78, 79
WHAT TO DO AND SEE	182, 183, 184, 185

GRAMPIAN AND HIGHLAND
RESERVES	80, 81
WHAT TO DO AND SEE	186, 187

EAST HIGHLANDS
RESERVES	82
WHAT TO DO AND SEE	188

WEST HIGHLANDS
RESERVES	83
WHAT TO DO AND SEE	189

WESTERN ISLES
RESERVES	84

ORKNEY ISLANDS
RESERVES	85, 86, 87, 88
WHAT TO DO AND SEE	190, 191

SHETLAND ISLES
RESERVES	89, 90
WHAT TO DO AND SEE	190, 191

NORTHERN IRELAND

COUNTY DOWN
RESERVES	91, 92
WHAT TO DO AND SEE	192, 193, 194

COUNTY ANTRIM
RESERVES	93, 94
WHAT TO DO AND SEE	195, 196

COUNTY LONDONDERRY
RESERVES	95
WHAT TO DO AND SEE	197, 198

COUNTY FERMANAGH
RESERVES	96
WHAT TO DO AND SEE	199, 200

VISITING RSPB RESERVES 201, 202, 203
INDEX MAP 207
MAP SECTION 208–222

NORTH DEVON

98, 99 ◀

LUNDY

NT/LANDMARK TRUST

An unspoiled island numbering just 17 inhabitants and measuring just over three miles long and half a mile wide. It has tall cliffs towards south and west with grass and heather on top, and steep sidelands with trees, shrubs and bracken in small hanging valleys on the east coast.

GETTING THERE

12 miles north of Hartland Point in the Bristol Channel; by MS Oldenburg from Bideford (all year) or Ilfracombe (summer only); for sailing times Telephone 0237 470422 (24 hr answering service); for reservations Telephone (Bideford) 0237 477676 (Ilfracombe) 0271 863001. Reservations advisable during summer. Sea crossing takes 2¼ hrs, leaving four hours to explore.

FACILITIES

Information Centre at the Linhay, refreshments and shop at the Marisco Tavern.

♿ Wheelchair access

Telephone in advance so that disembarkation arrangements may be made.

Admission charge

Ferry, adult £18.95, child (3–14) £9.95, child under 3 £1, landing charge £2.50 (waived for ferry passengers).

Opening times

Daily.

Top right Fulmar on nest

SPECIES TO LOOK FOR

Puffins

This is the best seabird breeding site in the south-west. Guillemots are the most numerous species, with over a thousand pairs. Razorbill, kittiwake, shag, fulmar, great and lesser black-backed gulls are also common. Puffins can be found in small numbers on the north-west of the island while buzzards, kestrels, ravens, manx shearwaters and storm petrels also breed here.

Best time to visit

Spring and autumn for a good variety of migrants.

DEVON

▶ 100, 101

SLAPTON LEY

Slapton Ley is the largest natural freshwater lake in the south-west. Streams and steep-sided valleys lead into the Ley through extensive reedbeds and a three-mile-long shingle barrier separates it from the seawater of Start Bay.

GETTING THERE

Slapton village, north of Torcross off A379 or north-east of Kingsbridge off A381.

FACILITIES

Information Centre, two hides, Nature Trails, Guided Walks mid-June to mid-September, picnic site, car parks.

♿ Wheelchair access

Information Centre (partial), one hide (at Torcross), wheelchair viewpoint on shingle ridge at Monument car park.

Admission charge

Opening times

Daily.

SPECIES TO LOOK FOR

This is the main Devon site for nesting great creasted grebe, joined in winter by red-breasted merganser and goldeneye. Breeding birds in the reed marsh and scrub include reed and sedge warblers and resident Cetti's warbler. Firecrests and chiffchaffs also spend the winter here. Offshore seabirds may include great northern divers and Slavonian grebes in winter and terns in summer. Moving inland scarce cirl buntings are resident in the valley hedgerows and coastal scrub.

Best time to visit

Spring and autumn for migrants.

Top right Great crested grebe

DEVON

EAST DARTMOOR

Parke, Yarner Wood, Dunsford Wood

Parke: 200 acres of parkland in the lush wooded Bovey Valley. Yarner Wood: rich oak wood with small areas of heathland. Dunsford Wood: 140 acres of river valley woodland, heath-covered rocky slopes and fertile flood plain scrub and grassland.

GETTING THERE

Park, 3 miles north-west of Bovey Tracey on B3344. Yarner Wood, 2 miles north-west of Bovey Tracey on B3344. Dunsford Wood, Steps Bridge 3 miles north-east of Moretonhampstead on B3212.

FACILITIES

Parke: Dartmoor Park Interpretation Centre (also National Park headquarters – open April–October 10am–5pm), see Dartmoor Visitor free newsheet for details of Guided Walks, refreshments, toilets, picnic site. Yarner Wood: waymarked paths. Dunsford Wood: mobile Information Centre (April–October 10am–5pm) refreshments, toilets. Car parks at all sites.

Wheelchair access
Footpath suitable at Dunsford Wood.

Admission charge

Opening times
All sites daily.

SPECIES TO LOOK FOR

Blue tit at nest hole.

Both Yarner and Dunsford include warblers, redstarts and pied flycatchers (in nestboxes at Yarner, best seen May–June). Yarner also attracts nuthatches and tree creepers, while tits, buzzard, dipper and woodlark have been recorded at Dunsford. The latter two are also at Parke plus grey wagtail and sparrowhawk. Woodpeckers are common to all three sites.

Best time to visit
Yarner: May, June; Dunsford: spring.

DAWLISH WARREN

The reserve covers over 500 acres on the spit at the mouth of the Exe and includes a wide variety of habitats. These include sandy foreshore, extensive mud flats, salt and freshwater marshes, sand dunes, dune grassland and heath plus scrub.

GETTING THERE

Access is from the A379 in Dawlish Warren village. Turn towards the estuary, drive under the railway and use the large pay-and-display car park.

FACILITIES

Visitor Centre (summer 10.30am–1pm, 2–5pm daily, winter weekends – same hours, winter weekdays – hours according to staff availability), hide, occasional Guided Walks. The car park has toilets and food kiosks.

Wheelchair access
Paths unsuitable.

Admission charge

Opening times
Daily.
Visitors should avoid walking on the fragile dune grasses; dogs banned May–September.

SPECIES TO LOOK FOR

Ringed plover

Over 180 species can be seen annually here though the reserve is most noted for its high tide roosts of waders and wildfowl both on the mud flats and along the sea shore. Common species include godwits, oystercatcher, brent goose, curlew, redshank and ringed plover. Divers, Slavonian grebe and sea duck, such as common scoter, are often seen.

Best time to visit
Autumn, winter for waders and wildfowl, spring and autumn for migrants.

DEVON ▶ 100, 101

AYLESBEARE COMMON

(RSPB)

450 acres of heathland, both dry and wet with valley bogs and streams, mature heather and gorse, birch, oak and Scots Pine woodlands and alder scrub.

Sunset

GETTING THERE

1 mile west of Newton Poppleford, to the north of the A3052 Lyme Regis–Exeter road.

FACILITIES

Waymarked Trail, car parking.

Wheelchair access
Metalled road through reserve.

Admission charge

Opening times
Daily.

SPECIES TO LOOK FOR

On the heath – Dartford Warbler, nightjar, stonechat, yellowhammer, tree pipit, grasshopper warbler and curlew. Buzzards, redpolls and green woodpeckers also breed here. Birds of prey on the common include kestrel, sparrowhawk, hobbies in summer, hen harrier in winter.

Best time to visit
Equal interest throughout year.

DORSET

102, 103 ◀

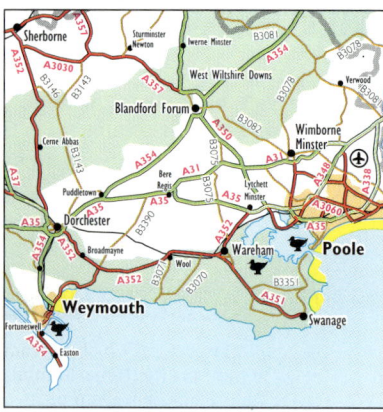

RADIPOLE LAKE

(RSPB)

192 acres of reedbeds and lakes with rough pasture, scrub and artificial lagoons.

Heron at dusk

GETTING THERE

Weymouth town centre, entrance beside Swannery car park.

FACILITIES

Information Centre with panoramic viewing windows overlooking the lake (daily 9am–5pm), three hides, toilets, non-RSPB car park (charge).

♿ Wheelchair access

Information Centre, hide and paths.

Admission charge

Reserve free, permit charge for two hides £1.50 (third hide free).

Opening times

Daily.

SPECIES TO LOOK FOR

Several warblers (including Cetti's) plus bearded tit, kingfisher, great crested grebe and mute swan breed in the reeds. The latter also come in number to moult. Heron, cormorant, shelduck and sparrowhawk visit regularly. Water rail, coot and uncommon species of gull, including Mediterranean, occur while shoveler, teal and pochard winter here.

Best time to visit

Spring and early summer. Autumn for migrants, waders.

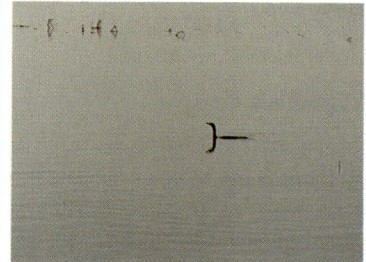

Cormorant

Top right *Mute swans*

DORSET

▶ 102, 103

ARNE

(RSPB)

1,258 acres of remote heathland extending into Poole Harbour, comprising heather, gorse clumps and scattered pines with valley bogs. On the edge of the harbour is mixed woodland, fen, saltings, creeks, tidal mudflats and a freshwater reedbed.

GETTING THERE

2 miles east of Wareham, off A351 Wareham–Swanage road. Head south of Wareham for half a mile, turn left in Stoborough and follow signs.

FACILITIES

Nature Trail (open end May–beginning September), toilets, car park.

♿ Wheelchair access

No facilities.

Admission charge

Opening times

Daily.

SPECIES TO LOOK FOR

Wigeon

Dartford warbler, nightjar and stonechat breed on the heath, other breeding birds include buzzard, sparrowhawk, redpoll and shelduck. Wildfowl include shelduck and Brent geese, and in winter red-breasted merganser, teal, wigeon and goldeneye. Wintering birds of prey include hen harrier, peregrine and merlin. On the mudflats are godwits, spotted redshank, curlew plus whimbrel and greenshank during migration.

Best time to visit

Equal interest throughout year.

BROWNSEA ISLAND NATURE RESERVE

(NT/DORSET TRUST)

This 500-acre heath and woodland estuary island comprises a wide variety of habitats – saltmarsh and mudflats, reedbeds, lakes and lagoons, carr, grassland, mixed woodland and shore.

GETTING THERE

Poole Harbour, only accessible by boat from Poole Quay (30 min) or Sandbanks (6 min). Ferry service daily 10am–5pm (6pm peak season), every half hour.

FACILITIES

Information Centre, shop and cafe in The Villa (daily Easter–September), Self-guided Trail, one public hide, Guided Tours (for naturalists and non-naturalists), summer events.

♿ Wheelchair access

Paths difficult but area around Quay accessible. Mainland car parking near Poole Quay. All boats will accept and help wheelchair users. Wheelchair toilet near Island Quay.

Admission charge

Ferry: from Poole, adult £3, OAP £2.75, child £2; from Sandbanks, adult £2, child £1.40. Landing fee – adult £1.80, child 90p, family (2 adults, 2 children) £4.50. Nature Trail – adult 50p, child 30p. Guided Tour – adult 90p, child 50p. (Trail and tour reductions for NT members.)

Opening times

April–June and September, Monday, Wednesday, Friday, Saturday. Nature Trail open 10.30–13.00. Guided tours 14.45.

SPECIES TO LOOK FOR

The main features are the large heronry, common and sandwich tern colonies and duck and wader roosts.

Best time to visit

Only open to public during certain times (see above).

104, 105 ◀ # SOMERSET

WEST SEDGEMOOR

(RSPB)

960 acres of extensive, open, low-lying wet meadows within the larger Sedgemoor, bordered by deciduous woodland.

GETTING THERE

1 mile east of Fivehead village on A378 Taunton–Langport road.

FACILITIES

Two hides and waymarked path. 'Willow and Wetlands Centre' to north of reserve (via North Curry and Mare Green), car park.

♿ Wheelchair access
Yes.

Admission charge
🐦

Opening times
Daily.

SPECIES TO LOOK FOR

Swell Wood features one of Britain's largest nesting heronries, counting some 70 pairs. Buzzard, blackcap, marsh tit and nightingale also breed in the wood. On the moor are redshank, curlew, lapwing, black-tailed godwit, yellow wagtail, sedge warbler, whinchat and kestrel and some 2,000 whimbrel are seen on spring migration. In winter there are large numbers of lapwing, golden plover, teal, wigeon and Bewick's Swan (dependent on the amount of flooding). Other birds of prey may include peregrine and hen harrier.

Best time to visit

April–early June for herons. Winter for large numbers of wildfowl (when flooding occurs).

AVON ▶ 106, 107

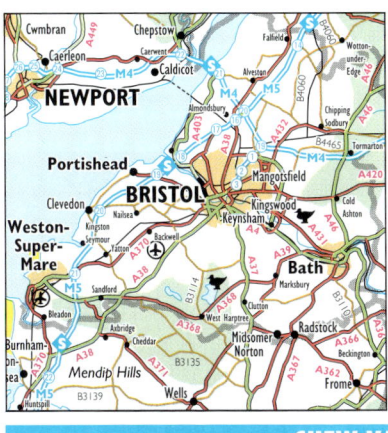

CHEW VALLEY LAKE

This is the third most important reservoir in Britain for wintering wildfowl and has one of the most extensive reedbeds in the south-west. Some 130,000 trees have been planted around the margins to blend into the lush wooded Chew Valley landscape.

GETTING THERE

To the north of the A368 Weston-super-Mare–Bath road, approx. 8 miles south of Bristol.

FACILITIES

Information Centre, including public toilets and cafe (open daily summer, weekends only at other times). Public Nature Trail and hide along the north-east shore and a further four hides for permit holders only (apply to Bristol Water Co., Woodford Lodge, Chew Stoke, Bristol BS18). Two landscaped picnic areas.

♿ Wheelchair access

Along part of public Trail to hide and Visitor Information Centre. Good views from surrounding roads.

Admission charge

Public Trail and hide free ✻. Permit to use other hides, ✻£1 per day, ✻£6 per year, under-16 half-price.

Opening times

Permit holders, throughout light hours.

SPECIES TO LOOK FOR

Ducks (up to twelve different species including large numbers of shoveler and gadwall); great crested grebes (autumn); migrating tits, warblers, swallows, terns and gulls; a multitude of waders (lapwing, dunlin, snipe) in the autumn, roosting gulls (common and black-headed); nesting reed and sedge warblers plus grebes and coots.

Best time to visit

August–December.

Shoveler

13

AVON

WILLSBRIDGE VALLEY

The valley contains several habitats with woodlands, three ponds (man-made to replace the old mill pond), a wildlife garden and meadows being replanted with native trees.

GETTING THERE

Willsbridge Hill, off the A431 Bristol–Bath road, turn into Long Beach Road.

FACILITIES

Visitor Information, cafe, shop and Wildlife and Historical Exhibition in Willsbridge Mill, open Easter–October, Tuesday–Friday and Sunday, admission to exhibition £1.50 adult, £1 child (under 5), £4 family (2 adults, 2 children); Avon Wildlife Trust members free. Nature Trails, Guided Walks and regular events (April–October).

Wheelchair access

Mill Exhibition, toilet, cafe, events, ponds and gardens. For parking details Telephone 0272 326 885.

Admission charge

Mill Exhibition only (see above).

Opening times

Reserve open daily.

SPECIES TO LOOK FOR

Good variety of commoner birds, redpolls and siskins in winter, dippers and various warblers breeding.

Best time to visit

Early May.

Siskin

HAMPSHIRE ▶ 108, 109

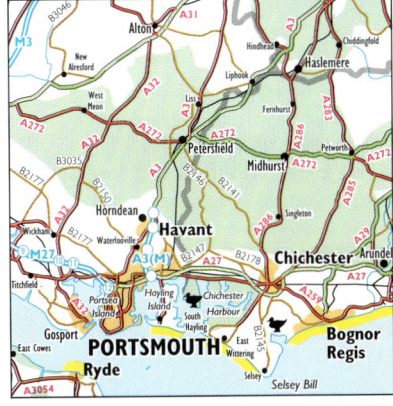

NEW FOREST

Some 60,000 acres of countryside are open to the public and few forests in Britain have such a rich variety of trees. Beeches, oaks and birches predominate and there is abundant hawthorn, blackthorn and every kind of shrub and plant. There are also great stretches of heathland, covered in gorse or heather plus bogs and ponds, grazing land and farmland.

GETTING THERE

South-west of Southampton.

FACILITIES

Enquire at the Tourist Information Centre at Lyndhurst for Waymarked Trail details.

♿ Wheelchair access
No special facilities (enquire at Lyndhurst).

Admission charge

Opening times
Daily.

SPECIES TO LOOK FOR

The Forest is renowned for its birds of prey with significant numbers of buzzard, sparrowhawk, hobby and kestrel. Woodpeckers, nuthatch, treecreeper, tits, redstart and wood warbler flourish in the middle of the woods while nightjar and woodcock may occasionally be seen on the edges. Oak and conifers attract crossbill and goldcrest and sometimes firecrest and siskin. Stonechat and Dartford warbler may be seen on heathland while curlew nest in the wet areas.

Best time to visit
Avoid peak holiday periods.

Nightjar

◀ 110, 111

HAMPSHIRE/SUSSEX BORDERS

CHICHESTER HARBOUR/ LANGSTONE HARBOUR

Divided by Hayling Island these two harbours form one of the largest areas of estuarine mudflats on Britain's south coast, also including low islands, saltings and disused gravel pits.

GETTING THERE

Chichester Harbour: five miles west of Chichester, off A27 or A286 and B179; Langstone Harbour: ¼ mile south of Havant, viewing points on A27.

FACILITIES

Access to Chichester Harbour is by public footpath only and there is no entrance to Langstone Harbour Reserve. Recommended viewing points for the latter are from the car park close to the A3/A27 roundabout and at the car park off the Hayling island road by the Esso garage.

Wheelchair access

No facilities.

Admission charge

Opening times

Daily.

SPECIES TO LOOK FOR

Both harbours are outstanding for wintering wildfowl and waders with up to 5,000 dark-bellied Brent geese, 20,000 dunlin and up to 1,000 knots. Large numbers of mallard, teal, wigeon, shelduck, oystercatcher, curlew, bar-tailed and black-tailed godwit, redshank, greenshank, grey plover, sanderling. One of Britain's largest little tern colonies, plus common and Sandwich terns, black-headed gull, reed bunting and heron breed in the area. Outside the breeding season black-necked grebe, red-breasted merganser and greenshank occur regularly.

Best time to visit

Autumn and winter for wildfowl and waders.

FERRY FIELD

Ferry Field covers 46 acres of pastureland developed by the accumulation of silt in the channel that once separated Selsey Bill from the Sussex mainland. In addition to large brackish mudflats it contains a freshwater pool.

GETTING THERE

B2145, 1 mile south of Sidlesham (five miles south of Chichester), two miles north of Selsey.

FACILITIES/RESTRICTIONS

Interpretive Centre and hide (daily summer, weekends only winter). Note – no entrance to the reserve in order to avoid disturbance to the birds.

Wheelchair access

Nature Trail along edge of reserve.

Admission charge

Opening times

Daily.

SPECIES TO LOOK FOR

Short-eared owl
The muddy margins attract a large number of waders and waterfowl, including shelduck, mallard, teal and coot. Redshank and lapwing breed in summer.

Best time to visit

Spring and autumn.

SUSSEX   ▶ 112, 113, 114

ARUNDEL WILDFOWL & WETLANDS CENTRE

Set on the Sussex Downs, the Centre has been developed from water meadows, drained by ditches full of rush and sedge, with a natural reedbed.

GETTING THERE

1 mile north Arundel, signposted from A27 and A29.

FACILITIES

Exhibition Area, viewing gallery, seven hides, binoculars for hire, shop, licensed restaurant, picnic tables, activity days during school holidays.

♿ Wheelchair access

Throughout Centre: includes all hides, toilets, free wheelchair loan. Other facilities for disabled visitors: talks and tactile exhibits by prior arrangement.

Admission charge

Adult £3.50, OAP/single parent/claimant £2.50, child £1.75, family (2 adults, 2 children) £8.75.

Opening times

Daily. Summer 9.30am–6pm, winter 9.30am–5pm (last admission one hour before closing), closed 25 December.

SPECIES TO LOOK FOR

Wild birds include breeding reed and sedge warblers, common sandpiper, water rail, reed bunting. New Zealand blue duck, Bewick's swan, whistling duck and a flock of some 60 eider are some of the captive collection's main attractions. Mandarins may be seen on the adjacent Swanbourne Lake.

Best time to visit

Greater variety of wildfowl in winter. Note – Feeding the ducks, 3.30pm in summer, 4pm in winter in front of the viewing gallery is always popular.

Common sandpiper   *Sedge warbler*

EAST SUSSEX

115, 116 ◀

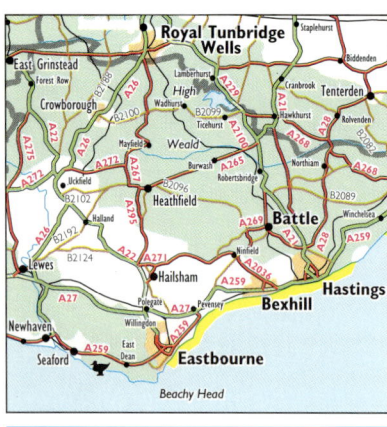

CUCKMERE HAVEN

The area around Cuckmere Haven comprises the Seven Sisters Country Park and Seaford Head Nature Reserve. The former includes part of the famous sheer white chalk cliffs, shingle, open water, salt marsh, meadowland, downland and scrub. The latter covers over 300 acres of similar habitat including cliff downland.

GETTING THERE

6 miles west of Eastbourne off A259 Eastbourne–Seaford road.

FACILITIES

(At Seven Sisters Country Park) Visitor Centre (Good Friday–October 10.30am–5.30pm, November–Good Friday weekends only 11am–4pm), 'The Living World' Natural History Exhibition Area (charge), Park Trail, Guided Walks by prior arrangement, toilets, car park.

♿ Wheelchair access
Park Trail, Visitor Centre (inc. toilets).

Admission charge

Opening times
Daily.

Little ringed plover

SPECIES TO LOOK FOR

Mute swan

The Cuckmere river meanders support cormorant, heron, mute swan, shelduck and many winter wildfowl including little grebe, mallard, teal, tufted duck and wigeon. Plovers and terns nest on the lagoon, fulmar, herring gull and jackdaw nest on cliff ledges, while meadow pipit and skylark breed on the grassland. At Seaford Head nightingale and stonechat are resident while migrants include willow warbler, chiffchaff, whitethroat and redstart. Ring ouzel, pied flycatcher and rarities such as hoopoe, bluethroat and wryneck have also been seen.

Best time to visit
Equal interest throughout year.

EAST KENT ▶ 117, 118

DUNGENESS

(RSPB)

Extensive shingle, part of which has been excavated to form flooded pits of high value to waterfowl, plus natural ponds, marshy depressions and scattered clumps of gorse and bramble.

Goldeneye

GETTING THERE

From Lydd take the road south-east to Dungeness and the reserve is signposted after almost one mile.

FACILITIES

Information Centre (April–September daily 9am–5pm, October–March weekends only), five hides, waymarked path.

♿ Wheelchair access

Information Centre, four hides.

Admission charge

Non RSPB members: adult £2.50, child £1.50.

Opening times

Wednesday–Monday 9am–9pm or sunset.

SPECIES TO LOOK FOR

Dungeness is a famous landfall for small migrants including many rarities. Large flocks of teal, shoveler, mallard, pochard and tufted duck occur outside the breeding season; other winter visitors include goldeneye, smew, goosander and both Slavonian and red-necked grebes. Wheatear, great and little grebes plus a large colony of common and Sandwich terns, with black-headed gulls, nest here.

Best time to visit

Migrants end March–late May, otherwise of equal interest throughout year.

EAST KENT

117, 118 ◀

BLEAN WOODS

(RSPB)

765 acres of the extensive Blean Forest, mainly deciduous woodland on clay and gravel soil. Mature oakwood contrasts with open sweet chestnut coppice and areas of silver birch, crossed by several rides.

GETTING THERE

From Canterbury take the A290 west to Whitstable, turn left after 1½ miles to Rough Common.

FACILITIES

Three waymarked paths.

♿ Wheelchair access

Paths partially accessible.

Admission charge

Opening times

Daily.

SPECIES TO LOOK FOR

Great and lesser spotted woodpecker

Green, great spotted and lesser spotted woodpecker, nightingale, tree pipit, willow warbler, blackcap, garden warbler and nuthatch are some of the commoner breeding species. Redstart, hawfinch and wood warbler also breed here and crossbill sometimes occurs.

Best time to visit

Spring.

SANDWICH BAY

100 acres of dune pasture, 100 acres of saltmarsh and 900 acres of beach and tidal mudflats to the north and south of the river Stour estuary.

GETTING THERE

2 miles north of Sandwich off A256 Ramsgate road.

FACILITIES

Picnic site at Stonelees.

♿ Wheelchair access

No facilities.

Admission charge

Access to reserve south of the river Stour is via Sandwich Bay Estate property, toll £2 per car. Otherwise free.

Opening times

Daily.

SPECIES TO LOOK FOR

Wigeon

Migrants are the main attraction here. In spring waders and terns, garganey, black redstart and firecrest arrive and scarce birds such as Kentish plover and golden oriole have been recorded regularly. During autumn, chats, warblers, flycatchers and other passerines return. Other birds of passage at this time include black-tailed godwit, common, wood and curlew sandpipers, greenshank, ruff, little stint, whimbrel, greenshank, terns and short-eared owl. Teal, wigeon, bar-tailed godwit, dunlin, redshank, sanderling, grey plover, snow buting and hen harrier occur in winter. Residents and summer visitors at Stonelees include reed, sedge and grasshopper warblers, spotted flycatcher, nightingale and redpoll.

Best time to visit

Late spring and particularly late autumn for rarities; bulk of spring passage occurs April–May, autumn waders mid-July to September, passerines August to late autumn.

WEST KENT ▶ 119, 120

BOUGH BEECH RESERVOIR

Set in a farmland valley the reserve comprises some 54 acres of water (in winter) with adjacent fields and wood. As the water level falls shallow water pits, islands, spillways and a stream become exposed.

GETTING THERE

Northern end of Bough Beech Reservoir, 2 miles south of Ide Hill, five miles south-west of Seven Oaks, off B2042 or B2027.

FACILITIES/RESTRICTIONS

Information Centre (April–October, Wednesday and weekends 11am–4.30pm). No access to lake margins, view from public roads.

♿ Wheelchair access
Toilets in Information Centre.

Admission charge

Opening times
See above.

Top right Wigeon

Spotted sandpiper

SPECIES TO LOOK FOR

Mallard

Large flocks of wildfowl winter here including mallard, teal, shoveler, tufted duck and Canada geese, while smaller numbers of goldeneye and pochard also occur. In summer lapwing and little ringed plover nest and migrants on passage include greenshank, green and common sandpipers. Unusual visitors spotted here include garganey, osprey and red-necked phalarope.

Best time to visit
Winter.

21

WEST KENT

ELMLEY MARSHES

(RSPB)

700 acres of coastal grazing marshes with freshwater fleets and shallow floods, bordered by saltmarsh on the north side of the Swale estuary.

Short-eared owl hunting.

GETTING THERE

Isle of Sheppey. ½ mile south of junction of A249 and A250, one mile north of Kingsferry Bridge.

FACILITIES

Five hides, toilet.

Wheelchair access

Elderly and disabled visitors are permitted to drive the mile-long track from the reserve car park to the hides.

Admission charge

Non-RSPB members: adult £2.50, OAP & concessions £1, child 50p.

Opening times

Wednesday–Monday 9am–9pm or sunset.

SPECIES TO LOOK FOR

The Spit-end peninsula is a major refuge for thousands of wigeon, teal, mallard, shelduck and roosting white-fronted geese in winter. Winter waders include black-tailed godwit, grey plover, curlew, dunlin and redshank. Hen harrier, merlin and short-eared owl also occur regularly in winter, Redshank, pochard, shoveler, lapwing and mallard are numerous in the breeding season and are joined by nesting avocet and little tern. Curlew sandpiper, little stint, greenshank, spotted redshank and rarities such as Kentish plover also use the reserve on passage.

Best time to visit

January, February for peak wildfowl, late May, June for breeding birds (including ruff in summer plumage), September for passage waders.

ESSEX ▶ 121, 122, 123

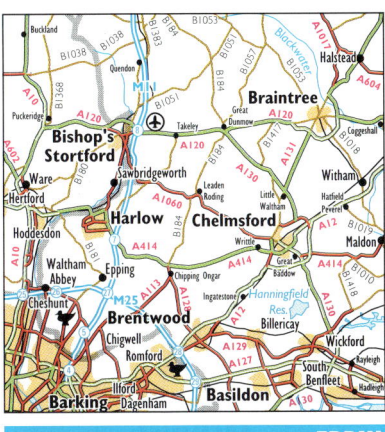
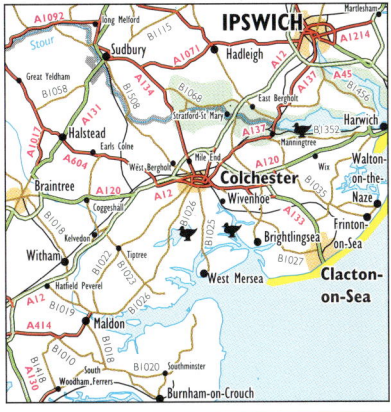

EPPING FOREST

At 6,000 acres one of the largest near-continuous blocks of woodland in England comprising hornbeam pasture (some pollarded) beech pasture and oak pasture, acid grassland, wet lowland heathland and around 150 ponds and lakes.

GETTING THERE

North of Woodford and Chingford, to either side of A104.

Below: Queen Elizabeth the 1st Hunting Lodge.

FACILITIES

Epping Forest Conservation Centre (High Beach, signposted west off A104). Visitor Centre, with book shop and library.

♿ Wheelchair access

No facilities.

Admission charge

Opening times

Daily during summer. Closed winter.

SPECIES TO LOOK FOR

Woodland species include all three types of woodpecker, nuthatch, tree creeper, tits and finches. Sparrowhawk, tree pipit and the occasional redstart and nightingale also occur. In winter redpoll, siskin, chaffinch, greenfinch and hawfinch may be seen. Connaught Water and the lakes in the southern part of the forest attract large flocks of Canada geese plus great crested grebe, gadwall, wigeon, shoveler and even mandarin.

Best time to visit

Late November–January and April–July.

Greenfinch

23

121, 122, 123 ◀ ESSEX

THORNDON COUNTRY PARK

400 acres of woodland and parkland comprising extensive conifer plantations, mixed deciduous woodland (including pollarded ancient oaks and hornbeams) three artificial ponds, an abundance of birch and bracken and large open grass areas.

GETTING THERE

3 miles south of Brentwood, on the A127.

FACILITIES

Information Centre, shop, picnic area, toilets, car park (charge at weekends April–October).

♿ Wheelchair access

Information Centre, toilet, paths.

Admission charge

Opening times

Daily.

SPECIES TO LOOK FOR

All three species of woodpecker breed in the woods, goldcrest and coal tit are common residents in the conifers and the occasional crossbill may also be spotted here. During summer, whitethroats and spotted flycatcher occur and large numbers of swallow, martin and swift can be seen over the pond.

Best time to visit

Autumn, winter, early spring.

ABBERTON RESERVOIR

The reservoir and its adjacent farmland cover 1,200 acres. Thickets of blackthorn and hawthorn, patches of grassland and clumps of gorse dominate the reserve.

GETTING THERE

6 miles south west of Colchester on B1026, just outside Layer-de-la-Haye.

FACILITIES

Visitor Centre/observation room with panoramic windows, Nature Trail, daily information board, three hides, children's play area, car park.

♿ Wheelchair access

Visitor Centre, wheelchair toilets, some bird hides (with assistance).

Admission charge

Suggested donation, adult £1, child 50p.

Opening times

Reserve and Visitor Centre, Tuesday–Sunday 9am–5pm, closed 25, 26 December.

SPECIES TO LOOK FOR

This is one of the country's top bird reservoirs: huge gatherings of wigeon, mallard and tufted duck may run into thousands. There are also large numbers of teal, pochard, shoveler, gadwall, pintail, goldeneye and coot. Canada geese, mute swan and moorhen nest while goosander, smew, ruddy duck, Bewick's swan and white-fronted geese also visit. Black terns pass through in spring and autumn and are joined across the water by yellow wagtail and sandpipers. In summer up to 500 mute swans find safety (during their flightless period) on the reservoir and in the breeding season Britain's only tree-nesting colony of cormorants can be seen.

Best time to visit

Early in the year for large numbers of wildfowl. Warm days in spring when swallows, swifts and martins chase the enormous, hatching insect population. Late summer for passage birds.

ESSEX

▶ 121, 122, 123

FINGRINGHOE WICK

A 125-acre site beside the mudflats and salt marshes of the Colne estuary, comprising mostly worked-out gravel excavations with scattered pockets of grassland, trees and numerous ponds.

GETTING THERE

South of Colchester via Abberton on B1025, signposted on unclassified roads to Fingringhoe, the South Green.

FACILITIES

Information Centre/observation tower, nine hides, two Nature Trails, children's Nature Trail, toilets, car park.

♿ Wheelchair access

Two hides, one trail.

Admission charge

Suggested donation, adult £1, child 50p.

Opening times

Tuesday–Sunday, 9am–7pm summer, 9am–4.30pm winter (check). Closed 25, 26 December.

SPECIES TO LOOK FOR

Wintering wildfowl may include up to 1,500 Brent geese and large populations of other wildfowl and waders, including mallard, tufted duck, wigeon and goldeneye. In spring some 30 pairs of nightingale and many warblers, finches, buntings and tits breed. Kingfisher, red-legged partridge, pheasant, fieldfare, redwing and goldcrest are seen, while birds of prey include hen harrier, sparrowhawk and kestrel.

Best time to visit

Good all year round – winter for waders, May for nightingale song.

STOUR WOOD & COPPERAS BAY

(RSPB)

Stour Wood comprises 134 acres of oak and sweet chestnut with extensive chestnut coppice. Copperas Bay is mudflats fringed by some saltmarsh, reedbed and scrubby fields.

GETTING THERE

1 mile east of Wrabness village, off the B3152 Manningtree–Ramsey road. Nearest town Colchester 10 miles west.

FACILITIES

Waymarked path (round trip of 4 miles) including three hides, car park.

♿ Wheelchair access

No facilities.

Admission charge

Opening times

Daily.

SPECIES TO LOOK FOR

Mute swans and cygnets

In summer, all three species of woodpecker, nightingale and warblers. Whitethroats and reed warblers breed by the estuary. In autumn and winter up to 1,000 black-tailed godwit, thousands of dunlin and redshank and large numbers of grey plover, wigeon, curlew, pintail and Brent geese. A good number of shelduck stay on to breed and a flock of mute swan can be seen around Mistley.

Best time to visit

Autumn, winter for waders; summer for woodland birds.

25

HERTFORDSHIRE

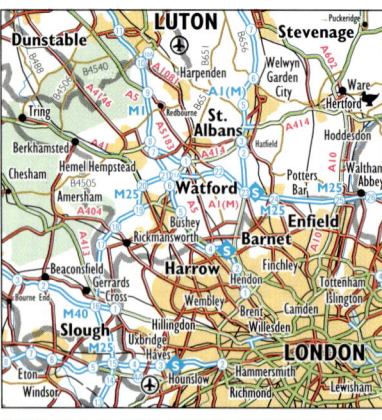

RYE HOUSE MARSH

(RSPB)

A 13-acre riverside marsh comprising flood meadows, shallow pools and mud fen, stands of reed and reed sweet-grass, willow and alder scrub and wet woodland.

Long-tailed tit

Top right Juvenile snipe

GETTING THERE

Rye House, Rye Road (towards Marlow), 1 mile north-west of Hoddesdon, off the B180 Ware road.

FACILITIES

Information Centre (9am–5pm daily), five hides, observation platforms, Nature Trail.

♿ Wheelchair access

Information Centre, most of Trail and some hides.

Admission charge

Non-RSPB members: adult £1.50, child 50p.

Opening times

Daily.

SPECIES TO LOOK FOR

Kingfisher, mallard, tufted duck, coot, moorhen, cuckoo, reed and sedge warblers breed regularly and common tern nest on rafts on the adjacent lakes. Green and common sandpipers, swallows, martins and warblers occur on migration. Cetti's warbler, snipe and teal are here in winter and water rail, jack snipe, siskin and occasionally bittern and bearded tit are recorded.

Best time to visit

Of equal interest throughout year (greatest number of birds in winter).

GLOUCESTERSHIRE ▶ 125, 126

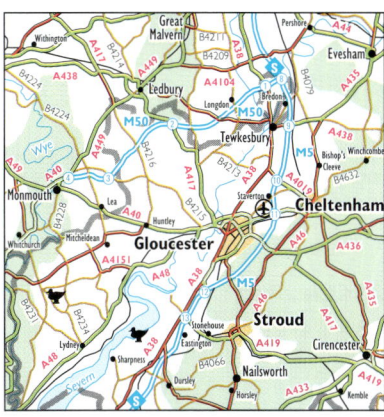 

NAGSHEAD
(RSPB)

761 acres of mature oakwood with beech, birch, rowan and holly, including a rocky stream, a pool and clumps of alder and firs.

Robin

GETTING THERE

West of Parkend village, two miles south east of Coleford; signposted off B4331 Coleford/Monmouth–Yorkley road.

FACILITIES

Information Centre (mid-April–August, weekends only 9.30am–4.30pm), two waymarked paths, two hides, car park.

♿ Wheelchair access

Information Centre, partial access to reserve (hilly).

Admission charge

Opening times

Daily.

SPECIES TO LOOK FOR

A large population of pied flycatcher nest, mainly in boxes, as do some of the redstart, great and blue tit and nuthatch. Other breeding species include warblers, chiffchaff, tree pipit, blackcap, tree creeper and the three species of woodpecker. Buzzard, sparrowhawk, crossbill, the elusive hawfinch and, in winter, raven occur regularly.

Best time to visit

Mid-April to June for nesting birds, otherwise of interest throughout year.

GLOUCESTERSHIRE

SLIMBRIDGE WILDFOWL & WETLANDS CENTRE

(WILDFOWL AND WETLANDS TRUST)

The headquarters of the Wildfowl Trust, Slimbridge occupies 800 acres on the south shore of the river Severn.

GETTING THERE

Slimbridge, 10 miles south of Gloucester, off A38 (signposted from M5, junctions 13, 14).

FACILITIES

Exhibition Hall with panoramic viewing windows, 'Swan Lake' observatory (floodlit from sunset), Salt Marsh observatory, screened walkways, hides, Nature Trails, binoculars for hire, licensed restaurant, picnic tables, shop, mothers' nursing room, activity days during school holidays, tropical house and aviary.

Wheelchair access

Easy paths, access throughout the Centre including hides and toilets, free wheelchair loan. Other facilities for disabled visitors – loan of audio cassettes and players, talks and tactile exhibits by prior arrangement.

Admission charge

Adult £4, OAP/single parent/claimant £3, child £2, family (2 adults, 2 children) £10.

Opening times

Daily, summer 9.30–5pm, winter 9.30–4pm. Closed 24, 25 December.

SPECIES TO LOOK FOR

Slimbridge boasts the world's largest collection of ducks, geese and swans and includes Bewick's swans from Siberia, large flocks of wigeon, pochard, tufted duck and teal, greylag geese, pintail, thousands of white-fronted geese and all six species of flamingo. Summer visitors include curlew, kingfisher and little grebe. Redshank, greenshank and several species of sandpiper occur during migration periods. Peregrine falcons are attracted in winter.

Best time to visit

Winter (but excellent all year).

Black swans at Slimbridge

WEST MIDLANDS ▶ 127, 128

SANDWELL VALLEY

(RSPB)

An area of 25 acres around the end of a lake comprising an island bordered by a marsh with willows, reed sweet-grass and shallow pools.

Little ringed plover

Top right Great crested grebe

GETTING THERE

Sandwell Valley Country Park, Hamstead, Great Barr, four miles north-west of Birmingham city centre; entrance off Tanhouse Avenue via Hamstead Road (B4167) or via A4041 Sutton Park–West Bromwich road.

FACILITIES

Information Centre with panoramic views (9am–5pm Monday–Thursday, 10am–5pm weekend), four hides, shop, toilets, car park.

♿ Wheelchair access
Information Centre, toilet, Trail.

Admission charge

Opening times
Daily.

SPECIES TO LOOK FOR

Mallard, tufted duck, coot, moorhen, little ringed plover, lapwing, snipe, warblers, whitethroat and willow tit breed while common tern and great crested grebe visit in summer. Curlew, dunlin, ringed plover, sandpipers and greenshank drop in on migration. The lake attracts wigeon and pochard in winter, with teal in the marsh, where snipe, jack snipe and water rail are seen daily. There is also a good number of heron plus the opportunity to see green woodpeckers.

Best time to visit
Spring.

29

129, 130 ◀ STAFFORDSHIRE/DERBYSHIRE

COOMBES VALLEY

(RSPB)

A steep-sided secluded valley of 263 acres with a rocky stream and slopes covered by oak woodland, bracken clearings, heath and pasture.

Redstart

GETTING THERE

3 miles south-east of Leek; turn off the A523 Leek–Ashbourne road to Apesford, continue for one mile.

FACILITIES

Information Centre, Nature Trail, two hides (one elevated), toilets, car park.

♿ Wheelchair access

No facilities.

Admission charge

Non-RSPB members; adult £1.50, child 50p.

Opening times

Wednesday–Monday, 9am–9pm or sunset.

SPECIES TO LOOK FOR

From the stream hide, dipper, kingfisher, woodpeckers and grey wagtail are visitors while from the tree hide redstart, pied flycatcher and tree pipit form part of the breeding bird community. Wood warbler also occurs. Other birds include sparrowhawk, tawny and long-eared owls, the three species of woodpecker and large flocks of fieldfare, redwing, tits and finches occur in winter.

Best time to visit

Avoid early July–end September; equal interest throughout remainder of year.

BEDFORDSHIRE/CAMBRIDGESHIRE ▶ 131, 132

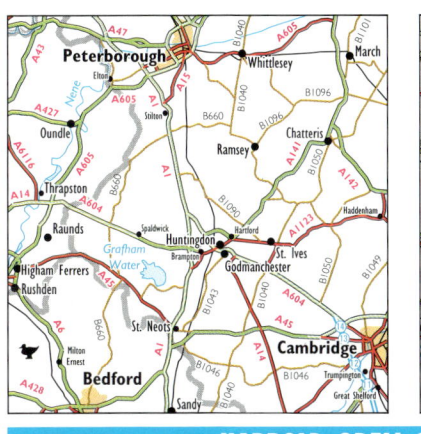
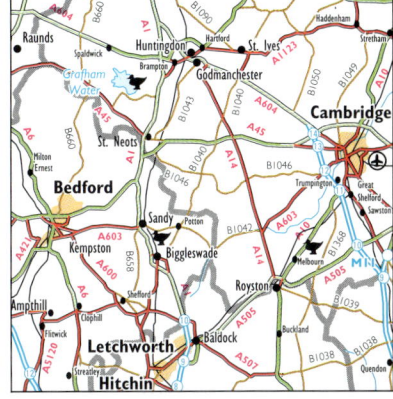

HARROLD–ODELL COUNTRY PARK

144 acres of old sand and gravel workings adjacent to the River Ouse comprising one large lake with an island, two smaller lakes, water meadows, reedbeds and woodland, including willow thickets.

GETTING THERE

Village Road, Harrold, 100 yards north of Harrold Bridge; 10 miles north-west of Bedford, between Harrold and Odell on Harrold–Poddington road.

FACILITIES

Visitor Centre with large observation windows and shop (November–Easter weekends only 1–4.30pm, weekends and bank holidays 1–6pm), toilets, car park.

♿ Wheelchair access

Information Centre, toilet, lake, Trail. Wheelchair available for free use.

Admission charge

Opening times

Daily.

SPECIES TO LOOK FOR

Large numbers of wildfowl are present in winter with some 5,000 ducks (mostly mallard and some tufted duck) plus great crested grebe, greylag and Canada geese. Mute swans regularly breed on the main lake. Coot and moorhen also occur. Other breeding birds include terns and reed and sedge warblers.

Best time to visit

January, February.

31

131, 132 ◀ BEDFORDSHIRE/CAMBRIDGESHIRE

GRAFHAM WATER

The nature reserve occupies an area of mixed woodland and rough grassland/meadow just to the west of the large 2½-acre reservoir.

Cormorant

GETTING THERE

West Perry, six miles south-west of Huntingdon. Follow A45, then B661 to West Perry.

FACILITIES

Three hides, Guided Walks, Nature Trail (work in progress) regular events, toilets, car park.

♿ Wheelchair access

One hide (work in progress).

Admission charge

Opening times

Daily.

SPECIES TO LOOK FOR

Wintering waders including dunlin, roosting duck, gulls, cormorants, divers and grebes, goldeneye (particularly early March), goosanders (peak numbers in February – best seen from north shore), golden plover (on meadowland).

Best time to visit

Winter and autumn.

BEDFORDSHIRE/CAMBRIDGESHIRE ▶ 131, 132

THE LODGE

(RSPB)

The Lodge, a Victorian mansion, is the headquarters of the RSPB and is surrounded by 100 acres of mature woodland, pine plantations, birch and bracken slopes with some heath and an artificial lake.

GETTING THERE

1 mile east of Sandy on B1042 Sandy–Cambridge road.

FACILITIES

Information Centre and shop (open 9am–5pm Monday–Friday, weekends 10am–5pm. Weekends Christmas–Easter 12–4.30pm). Four Nature Trails and hide overlooking the lake, toilets, car park.

♿ Wheelchair access

Information Centre and one Trail, disabled parking spaces.

Admission charge

Non-RSPB members: adult £2, OAP £1, child 50p.

Opening times

Daily 9am–9pm or sunset.

SPECIES TO LOOK FOR

Breeding birds include kestrel, green and great spotted woodpecker, nuthatch, treecreeper, blackcap, garden warbler, moorhen and tree pipit. Kingfisher, sparrowhawk, crossbill and heron occasionally visit, while winter brings siskin, redpoll and brambling. Look for coal tit and goldfinch in coniferous areas.

Best time to visit

Spring and early summer.

FOWLMERE

(RSPB)

With a combination of reeds and spring fed pools; also an adder copse and some hawthorn scrubland. This isolated fen provides a varied habitat for a large variety of birds.

GETTING THERE

Near Fowlmere village. Turn off the A10 Cambridge–Royston road by Shepreth. Nearest village Melbourn, 1.5 miles south.

FACILITIES

Nature Trail, four hides, (one elevated), car park.

♿ Wheelchair access

One hide and boardwalk.

Admission charge

Donation requested from non-RSPB members, adult £1.

Opening times

Daily.

SPECIES TO LOOK FOR

Kingfisher

The reedbeds attract large numbers of reed and other warblers, reed bunting and water rail. Kingfishers are frequently spotted while green sandpipers call in on autumn migration. Lesser whitethroat and turtle dove nest in the scrub and in autumn and winter large flocks of fieldfare, redwing and corn bunting roost.

Best time to visit

Spring and summer, when the reedbeds are at their liveliest.

133, 134 ◀ # SUFFOLK

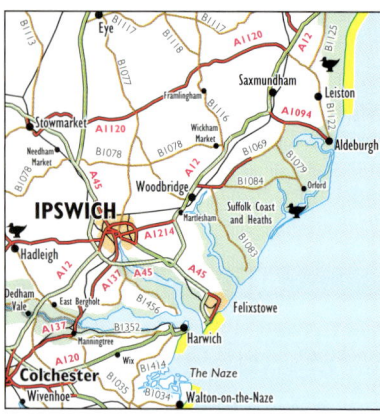

WOLVES WOOD
(RSPB)

92 acres of mixed deciduous ancient woodland comprising oak, ash, birch, hornbeam, aspen and hazel with an area of coppiced scrub.

Long-tailed tit

GETTING THERE

Two miles east of Hadleigh, 8 miles west of Ipswich on A1071.

FACILITIES

Information Centre (weekends only April–September), Waymarked Trail, car park.

♿ Wheelchair access
No facilities.

Admission charge

Opening times
Daily.

SPECIES TO LOOK FOR

Nightingales are the major attraction here and favour the scrub and coppiced rides. Other breeding birds include blackcap, chiffchaff, warblers, nuthatch, woodpeckers, tits, woodcock and sometimes in the hornbeams, hawfinch.

Best time to visit
May–June to hear nightingales in full song.

SUFFOLK ▶ 133, 134

HAVERGATE ISLAND

(RSPB)

An island of 267 acres containing shallow brackish lagoons with islands, saltmarsh and shingle beaches.

GETTING THERE

Island in the River Ore; by boat from Orford Quay, south of Orford (16 miles east of Ipswich). Tickets/Permits only obtainable by writing in advance to The Warden, 30 Munday's Lane, Orford, Woodbridge IP12 2LX (enclose SAE).

FACILITIES

Information Centre on island, eight hides, picnic area and basic toilets.

♿ Wheelchair access

No facilities.

Admission charge

RSPB members £3, non-members £5 (payable on arrival)

Opening times

Boat departs April–August, Saturday–Monday & Thursday 10am. September–March alternate Thursdays and Saturdays (enquire with warden). 1992 only – September–March, first Saturday of each month only; April–August first weekend of each month only).

SPECIES TO LOOK FOR

The main attraction is Britain's largest nesting colony of avocet, numbering around 120 pairs. Sandwich and common terns, oystercatcher, ringed plover, redshank and shelduck also breed here. Regular migration visitors include godwits, whimbrel, spotted redshank and little stint. In winter avocet, teal, wigeon, pintail, shoveler, mallard and occasionally Bewick's swan and hen harrier occur.

Best time to visit

Migration time, for spotting unusual species.

Avocet

MINSMERE

(RSPB)

One of the RSPB's premier reserves, this 2,000-acre site includes the renowned Scrape – a man-made area of shallow brackish lagoons, mud and island inside the shingle beach. In addition there are some 400 acres of reedbeds with meres, heathland and deciduous woodland.

GETTING THERE

South of Dunwich on coast. Access either from Dunwich–Westleton road to National Trust car park, or from Westleton (2 miles west of Dunwich), signposted off B1125 Blythburgh–Middleton road, or from East Bridge south of the reserve, signposted off the B1122 Theberton–Leiston road.

FACILITIES

Information Centre and shop (summer 9am–5pm, winter 9am–4pm), Nature Trail, ten hides (one elevated), toilets, car park.

♿ Wheelchair access

Information Centre, one hide specially adapted, most others accessible, most of trail accessible.

Admission charge

Reserve free, charge to use trail hides, Non-RSPB members £3 (two public hides on beach always free).

Opening times

Wednesday–Monday 9am–9pm or sunset (public hides on beach always open).

SPECIES TO LOOK FOR

A huge variety of breeding birds includes common tern, a large avocet colony, little tern, bittern, marsh harrier, bearded tit, water rail, stonechat, nightjar, nightingale and redstart. Visitors and residents on the Scrape also include godwits, spotted redshank, dunlin, knot, snipe, gulls, little stint, Bewick's swan, wigeon, gadwall, teal and rarities such as the occasional spoonbill.

Best time to visit

April–September to see activity on the Scrape.

35

135, 136, 137, 138 ◀ NORFOLK

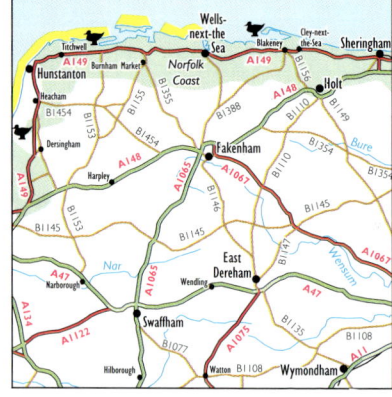

STRUMPSHAW FEN/SURLINGHAM CHURCH MARSH

(RSPB)

Strumpshaw Fen; 427 acres of fen with reed and sedge beds, alder and willow stands, damp woodlands and broads alongside the river Yare plus wet grazing marshes. Surlingham Church Marsh, a former grazing marsh of 68 acres containing dykes and pools with reed, sedge, and some alder and willow scrub.

GETTING THERE

Strumpshaw Fen: Strumpshaw/Brundall; from A47 Great Yarmouth–Norwich road turn south to Brundall, turn sharp right beyond the railway bridge and right again into Low Road. Take care walking across level crossing to reception. Surlingham Church Marsh: on the south bank of the river Yare adjacent to Surlingham Church off the A146 Norwich–Lowestoft road.

FACILITIES

Strumpshaw Fen: Information Centre, waymarked path, two low hides, one tower hide, fen Nature Trails (late June–September), toilets, car park. Surlingham: (shares Strumpshaw Fen Information Centre) two hides.

♿ Wheelchair access

Strumpshaw Fen only: one hide, limited access to paths.

Admission charge

Strumpshaw Fen only: non-RSPB members: adult £2.50, OAP & concessions £1, child 50p.

Opening times

Daily 9am–9pm or sunset.

SPECIES TO LOOK FOR

Marsh harrier

Strumpshaw Fen: typical Broadland birds include marsh harrier, bittern, bearded tit, Cetti's warbler, pochard, water rail, great crested grebe, gadwall, tufted duck and reed warbler in the fen, with redshank, snipe and yellow wagtail in the marshes. Woodland inhabitants are cuckoo, woodcock, nuthatch, treecreeper plus all three woodpecker species. In winter Britain's largest flock of bean geese, a roost of hen harriers plus mallard, wigeon and pochard occur. Migrating ospreys occasionally fly in. Surlingham: many of the above birds plus kingfisher, common tern, little ringed plover, shoveler, sedge and grasshopper warblers.

Best time to visit

Late December to early February to watch bean geese and wigeon, late May–June for swallowtail butterflies.

NORFOLK ▶ 135, 136, 137, 138

SNETTISHAM

(RSPB)

Over 3,000 acres of tidal sand and mudflats with saltmarsh, a shingle beach and flooded pits.

GETTING THERE

West of Snettisham village; off the A149 King's Lynn–Hunstanton road, 12 miles north of King's Lynn.

FACILITIES

Information Centre (all year weekends 9am–5pm; summer, autumn, Monday–Wednesday according to staff availability), four hides, photographer's hide, toilets, car park (charge). Monthly programme of high-tide Guided Walks (non-RSPB members: adult £1, others 50p, contact warden for details, Telephone 0485 542589).

♿ Wheelchair access

Cars with disabled visitors may drive through the reserve gate. Access to paths, Information Centre, free use of all-surface wheelchair and pusher available given notice, Telephone 0485 542689.

Admission charge

Opening times

Daily.

TITCHWELL MARSH

(RSPB)

510 acres of tidal and freshwater reedbeds, sea aster, saltmarsh, brackish and freshwater pools with sand dunes and a shingle beach.

GETTING THERE

Titchwell, six miles east of Hunstanton on the A149 Hunstanton–Brancaster road. Car park to west of village.

FACILITIES

Information Centre and shop (April–October 10am–5pm; November–March, 10am–4pm), three hides, picnic area, toilets, car park.

♿ Wheelchair access

Information Centre, two hides, wheelchair for hire.

Admission charge

Parking charge for non-RSPB members.

Opening times

Daily.

Bearded tit

SPECIES TO LOOK FOR

Spectacular numbers of waders (up to 100,000 birds in winter) roost on the lake, in front of the hide, and mudflats at high tide. These include large numbers of oystercatcher, knot, ringed and grey plovers, bar-tailed godwit, dunlin, redshank, curlew and turnstone. Up to 30,000 geese including large numbers of pink-footed geese plus shelduck, mallard, wigeon and pintail roost and feed on the foreshore. In the pits common terns nest and diving ducks frequently occur. Large numbers of sanderling and several passerines rest on migration.

Best time to visit

For large numbers of wildfowl avoid June, otherwise of equal interest throughout year.

SPECIES TO LOOK FOR

Over 40 avocet nest on the marsh alongside gadwall, tufted duck, shoveler and black-headed gull. Bearded tit, water rail, bittern and marsh harrier frequent the reedbeds. Terns, ringed plover and oystercatcher nest on the beach. During autumn wigeon, black-tailed godwit and curlew sandpiper are migrants to the marsh and during the high tides of September–October large numbers of knot and bar-tailed godwit occur. Winter visitors include Brent geese and goldeneye; offshore are divers, grebes and seaduck while snow buntings occur on the beach.

Best time to visit

Last week May, first week October.

135, 136, 137, 138 ◀ 　　　　**NORFOLK**

BLAKENEY POINT

(NATIONAL TRUST)

A 3½ mile long sand and shingle spit of dunes, salt marsh and mudflats, protected on its northern side by a shingle beach.

GETTING THERE

North of Blakeney village, nine miles east of Wells-next-the-Sea off the A149 Cromer–Hunstanton road. Access on foot from Cley Beach (3½ miles) or by ferry from Morston and Blakeney (tidal).

FACILITIES

Information Centre (generally open during tidal period April–September), three hides, light refreshments at the Old Boathouse, public toilets, car park (charge non-NT members).

♿ Wheelchair access

Local boatmen will assist wheelchairs (telephone warden in advance April–September 0263 740480, October–March 0328 830401). An all-surface wheelchair is provided at the Lifeboat House (where there is an adapted toilet), then a wooden walkway leads to the main hide.

Admission charge
Boat charge.

Opening times
Daily.

SPECIES TO LOOK FOR

Caspian tern

The Point is renowned for its tern colonies where common, little, Sandwich and occasionally even Arctic breed, alongside ringed plover and oystercatcher. Large numbers of linnet and black-headed gull also nest. Large falls of migrants often include hordes of robin and goldcrest and redstart, warblers, pied and spotted flycatchers are usual in autumn.

Best time to visit

Early August to early November particularly when easterly or northerly winds are blowing, for migrants including many rare species.

NORFOLK ▶ 135, 136, 137, 138

HOLME DUNES

Holme comprises some 90 acres of dunes plus scrub, saltmarsh, grazing marsh, brackish and freshwater pools with Corsican pine trees.

GETTING THERE

3 miles north-east of Hunstanton, off A149 Holme road, signposted 'beach'.

FACILITIES

Holme Bird Observatory and seven hides, toilets, car park.

♿ Wheelchair access

No facilities.

Admission charge

Non-members of the Norfolk Naturalists' Trust £3.

Opening times

Daily 10am–5pm.

SPECIES TO LOOK FOR

During winter thousands of oystercatchers, bar-tailed godwits and knot roost along with grey plover, dunlin, turnstone and sanderling. Up to a thousand Brent geese and wigeon graze on the pasture. At sea, divers, grebes, scoter, eider, mergansers, goldeneye and long-tailed duck are usually present. Raptors are attracted to the flocks of skylark, twite and other finches or redwing and fieldfare. Snow bunting are frequent while Lapland bunting and shore lark also occur. Spring migrants include firecrest, ring ouzel and black redstart. In May pied flycatcher, redstart and wood warbler are seen. Spotted redshank and ruffs are on the pools and Temminck's stint also regularly appears. September and October sees large movements of lapwing, starling, rook, skylark and finches by day while redwing and other thrushes pass by night. In winter falls of goldcrest appear and thousands of gulls include the occasional glaucous and Iceland gulls while hordes of Bewick's and whooper swans fly west.

Best time to visit

Spring and autumn migrations with over 280 species recorded. Summer for breeding migrants.

Black-winged stilt

135, 136, 137, 138 ◀

NORFOLK

RANWORTH & COCKSHOOT BROADS

The reserve lies within the Bure Valley, comprising open water and unreclaimed fen with some restored sedge beds. Ranworth Broad covers some 95 acres.

GETTING THERE

Ranworth, north of B1140.

FACILITIES

The Broadlands Conservation Centre is a unique floating building of timber and local reed thatch with an upstairs gallery allowing superb views through dormer windows (binoculars available). Other facilities include a wooden boarded Nature Trail to the Centre from Ranworth village, a wooden boarded Trail to Cockshoot Broad (from the car park at the Horning Inn) plus hide.

Wheelchair access

Along boardwalk.

Admission charge

Cockshoot Broad
Ranworth Broad: adult £1, child 50p, OAP/student 75p. NNT members free.

Opening times

Cockshoot Broad, daily all year. Ranworth/ Broadland Conservation Centre Sunday–Thursday 10am–5pm, Saturday 2–5pm April–October.

SPECIES TO LOOK FOR

Vast numbers of winter waterfowl include wigeon, tufted duck, pochard, shoveler, gadwall, mallard, teal, goldeneye and Bewick's swan. As many as 400 cormorants roost in the trees and up to 20,000 gulls roost on Ranworth Broad. Finches, linnets, redpoll and siskin frequent the woods. In spring herons return and several species of grebe and geese are seen. Summer sees terns and hirundines, and swans, coot, waterhen and water rail breed. Waders include woodcock, snipe, redshank and common sandpiper. Kingfishers and cuckoos are seen regularly while in the sedge and reed warblers and buntings are numerous. Woodland varieties include willow warbler, blackcap, chiffchaff and spotted flycatcher. Pheasants and jays forage in the autumn and tits are common. Nuthatch, tree creeper and all three woodpeckers occur.

Best time to visit

Equal interest throughout year.

Barn owl

40

NORFOLK ▸ 135, 136, 137, 138

CLEY MARSHES

The oldest bird-watching reserve in the country and still one of the most popular. Stretching over 400 acres it comprises sand flats, shingle ridges, spits, dunes, fresh and brackish marshes, grazing lands and saltings.

GETTING THERE

East of Cley-next-the-Sea village, north of A149.

FACILITIES

Information Centre, eight hides, car parks, toilets.

Wheelchair access

One hide.

Admission charge

Non-members of the Norfolk Naturalists' Trust: adult £3, junior (under 16) £1, family £7 (one public hide freely accessible).

Opening times

April–October, 10am–5pm Tuesday–Sunday.

SPECIES TO LOOK FOR

Winter wildfowl numbers are impressive with abundant wigeon plus teal, mallard, shoveler and pintail. Brent geese, whooper swan, goldeneye, red-breasted merganser and long-tailed duck also appear. Spring migrants include chiffchaff, wheatear and Sandwich tern. The marsh holds an abundance of warblers, and swallows, ruffs, reeves and black-tailed godwit may be seen. Kentish plover and Temminck's stint are regular May visitors plus marsh harriers. Spoonbills appear among late migrants and breeding birds include bearded tit, avocet, bittern and black-tailed godwit, ringed plover, oystercatcher, garganey, gadwall and shelduck. Early autumn waders include greenshank, whimbrel, little ringed plover and golden plover. During autumn storms all four skuas appear plus gannet, guillemot, razorbill, kittiwake, shearwater and petrel. October's varied visitors include hundreds of snow bunting. December sees a variety of ducks and water rail.

Best time to visit

Spring (April, May) and autumn (September, October) for outstanding rarities.

Wigeon

135, 136, 137, 138 ◀

NORFOLK

HICKLING BROAD

Hickling is the largest of the Norfolk Broads and its reserve covers 1,360 acres. In addition to some 300 acres of open water, special pools have also been created. Other habitats are reedbeds, dykes and ponds, grazing marsh, sedge and mixed fen and old oak woodland.

GETTING THERE

3 miles south east of Stalham, off A149 Potter Heigham road, turning to Hickling village.

FACILITIES

Information Centre and shop, hides, wildlife gardening demonstration area, car park, toilets. Nature Trails, Water Trail including tree tower and hides (2 hr 30 min boat trip – departs from Pleasure Boat Inn, Staithe 10am and 2pm Tuesday–Thursday May–September and Monday–Friday June–August. Booking essential, Telephone Hickling 276).

♿ Wheelchair access
Limited access to Nature Trail, toilets.

Admission charge
Nature Trail: adult £2, OAP, child £1; Water Trail adult £4, OAP, child £2.

Opening times
Wednesday–Monday, April–October 10am–5pm, November–March 10am–4pm.

SPECIES TO LOOK FOR

The open water is home to nesting great crested grebe, pochard and tufted duck and a feeding ground for swan, coot, greylag and Canada geese. Bittern, marsh harrier, bearded reedling and water rail inhabit the reedbeds and kingfisher can be seen on the ponds. Snipe and lapwing are the commonest nesting waders, while water rail, reed bunting, grasshopper and sedge warbler are found in the sedge and mixed fen. Oaks support heron nesting and woodcock, willow warbler and chiffchaff find cover on the woodland floor. Winter birds include Bewick's and whooper swans, smew, merlin, hen harrier, merganser and goosander in hard weather. Summer sees breeding common and little terns, warblers and many passage migrants including unusual species such as spoonbill, whimbrel, Caspian tern, red-necked phalarope and the occasional osprey. Savi's warbler is also seen.

Best time to visit
Winter for waders and wildfowl, autumn and spring for migrants, summer for visiting species.

NORFOLK ▶ 135, 136, 137, 138

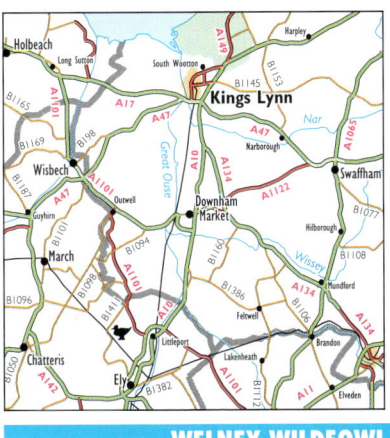

WELNEY WILDFOWL & WETLANDS CENTRE

850 acres in the Ouse Washes of original Fen vegetation and Fenland dykes (see also Ouse Washes).

Mute swans

GETTING THERE

Welney village, 12 miles north of Ely, signposted from A10.

FACILITIES

Reception Centre/Exhibition Area, observatory, information room, hides, binoculars for hire, lagoon floodlit in winter, shop, tea room, picnic tables. 'Swans under floodlight' one hour winter evening visit 6.45pm early November–March, booking required.

♿ Wheelchair access

Reception centre, main hide, toilet.

Admission charge

Adult £2.70, OAP/student/single parent/claimant £2, child £1.35, family (2 adults, 2 children) £6.75.

Opening times

Daily 10am–5pm, closed 24, 25 December.

SPECIES TO LOOK FOR

Winter brings thousands of migrating birds, principally Bewick's and whooper swans, wigeon, pochard, pintail, mallard and teal. Black-tailed godwit and ruff are also seen (see also Ouse Washes).

Best time to visit

Winter, light best for birdwatching in afternoon.

Bewick swans in winter wheat

139, 140 ◀ CAMBRIDGESHIRE/LEICESTERSHIRE

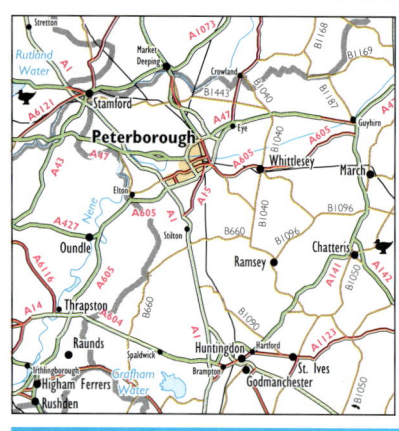

RUTLAND WATER

In total the reserve covers 350 acres. Egleton features three man-made lagoons, a number of islands with specially created areas of shallow water and muddy shoreline, willow thicket plantations, hay meadows, a small reedbed and at Lax Hill, mature woodland. The Lyndon site also comprises mature woodland, willow thicket, two ponds and a purpose-made scrape. Rutland Water itself is one of Europe's largest man-made lakes with a shoreline stretching some 24 miles.

GETTING THERE

Two entrances to the nature reserve. Egleton, one mile south-east of Oakham, off A6003 Oakham–Uppingham road; Lydon, off minor road from Manton–Edith Weston off the A6003.

FACILITIES

Egleton – small Information Centre, Nature Trail, ten hides, toilets, car park. Lyndon – Information Centre, Nature Trail, three hides, car park.

♿ Wheelchair access

Egleton – one hide, toilets, wheelchair available at car park. Lyndon – Information Centre.

Admission charge

Egleton day permit, adult £2, accompanied child (under 16) 50p, disabled visitor £1; Lyndon, adult £1, OAP 75p, child 30p.

Opening times

Egleton – weekends, Wednesdays and bank holidays.
Lyndon – weekends all year plus Tuesday–Thursday, Easter–October, 10am–4pm.

SPECIES TO LOOK FOR

The reserve is one of Britain's most important year-round wildfowl sanctuarys, and the prime inland site for passage waders. In winter rarer species such as smew, long-tailed duck, scoter, Bewick's swan, several grebes and the occasional wild geese join divers and large flocks of wigeon. Short-eared owl, hen harrier, sparrowhawk and kestrel are regulars while hobbies hunt the huge flocks of swallows and martins on the water in summer. Summer migrants include wheatear, whinchat, large flocks of yellow wagtail, terns and many waders. Breeding ducks include shoveler, shelduck, teal, occasionally garganey, pochard and North American ruddy duck plus large numbers of gadwall. Moulting flocks of tufted duck have reached 5,000 with pochard in excess of 1,000.

House martin

Best time to visit

Late summer for flocks of moulting ducks and autumn for migratory wildfowl; however there are large numbers of wildfowl present all year.

CAMBRIDGESHIRE/LEICESTERSHIRE ▶139, 140

TITCHMARSH LOCAL NATURE RESERVE

This 180-acre reserve, adjacent to the River Nene, is based on two lakes, formerly used for gravel extraction. The smaller lake features a heronry on the site of an old duck decoy, the larger has seven islands which are undisturbed nesting areas.

GETTING THERE

Lowick Lane, Aldwincle; take the A605 about one mile north from Thrapston, turn left at Thorpe Waterville, then turn left (just past the church) into Lowick Lane.

FACILITIES

Four hides and a picnic area.

Wheelchair access
No facilities.

Admission charge

Opening times
Daily.

SPECIES TO LOOK FOR

Oystercatcher

The heronry has a large breeding population and in some years over 40 occupied nests have been counted. Other breeding birds include shelduck, oystercatcher and sparrowhawk. Wintering wildfowl include wigeon, teal, pochard, goosander and tufted duck. Other birds seen regularly are kingfisher, plovers, cormorants, Canada and greylag geese, yellow wagtail. Rarer visitors such as little egret, manx shearwater, marsh warbler and red-necked grebe have occurred.

Best time to visit
Heron nesting February–March, young from May onwards (do not enter the heronry). Large colony of common terns in summer.

OUSE WASHES

(RSPB/WILDFOWL AND WETLANDS TRUST/ THE WILDLIFE TRUST)

One of the most important wetland sites in Europe, the Washes comprise a strip of grassland up to half a mile wide and 20 miles long between the Old and New Bedford Rivers. Part of the fens drainage system, they are flooded in autumn and winter creating a huge area of open water. In summer the water drains away leaving rich pasture.

GETTING THERE

Welches Dam, Manea. South of Manea village off the B1093/A141 March–Chatteris road and follow signposts.

FACILITIES

Information Centre (weekends and bank holidays only, 10am–5pm or dusk) ten hides, toilets, car park. Escorted walk and boat trips by prior arrangement.

Wheelchair access
Information Centre only.

Admission charge
£1 donation requested from non-RSPB members.

Opening times
Open all year (Sundays preferable to Saturdays during September–January when wildfowling on adjacent non-reserve washes may cause disturbance).

SPECIES TO LOOK FOR

The largest concentration of black-tailed godwits in Britain breed here, alongside yellow wagtail, garganey, redshank, snipe and the occasional ruff. In the winter flood up to 30,000 wigeon, 5,000 Bewick's swans and thousands of teal, mallard, pintail and pochard congregate. Small flocks of greylags and other geese may also be seen. Birds of prey include kestrel, merlin, sparrowhawk and hen harrier.

Best time to visit
Winter, especially when shallow flooding conditions prevail, when wildfowl numbers increase dramatically.

EAST LINCOLNSHIRE

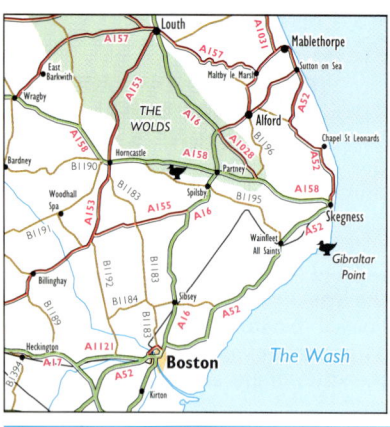

SNIPE DALES COUNTRY PARK

Snipe Dales is situated on the southern edge of the Wolds and consists of steep-sided valleys fretted by streams which have cut through the soft sandstone into the clay below. It is one of the few surviving substantial wet valley systems. The higher slopes are covered by rough grassland and the valley bottoms have a dense tall herb flora in summer. The Country Park comprises 90 acres of mostly coniferous woodland (mainly Corsican pine).

GETTING THERE

North of the A115 between Spilsby and Horncastle.

FACILITIES

Six different waymarked walks of varying lengths (⁴⁄₅ to 3 miles) with information boards, picnic area in country park.

Wheelchair access
Along metalled track.

Admission charge

Opening times
Daily.

SPECIES TO LOOK FOR

Wood pigeon

The most abundant species in the Country Park are chaffinch, redpoll, willow warbler and wood pigeon. There are several tits and tree-creeper and goldcrests forage in the woodland, particularly in autumn and winter. Finches, including siskin, may be common in the woods in winter together with small numbers of bramblings, other finches and crossbills. Tawny and barn owls are regularly seen while jay, chiffchaff, lesser whitethroat and great spotted woodpecker may be heard. Woodcock is a regular winter visitor. The reserve is home to blackcap, sedge warbler, spotted flycatcher, snipe, meadow pipit, grasshopper warbler, whitethroat, willow warbler, linnet, yellowhammer and reed bunting. Barn owl and kestrel hunt regularly on the Wolds and the green woodpecker may be heard.

Best time to visit
Equal interest throughout year.

EAST LINCOLNSHIRE ▶ 141

GILBRALTAR POINT NATIONAL NATURE RESERVE

An outstanding unspoilt area of some 1,000 acres, comprising sandy and muddy sea-shore, an extensive complex of sand-dune and saltmarsh and freshwater habitats.

GETTING THERE

Gibraltar Road, 3 miles from Skegness, signposted from town centre.

FACILITIES

Field Centre, Visitor Centre (open daily May–October, weekends and bank holidays at other times). Guided Walks during summer. Wash Viewpoint (also contains displays about the natural features and wildlife of the Wash (open for most of year). Observation platform and two public hides. Walkabout Guide co-ordinated with trail marker posts, car parking.

♿ Wheelchair access

Ramp access to Wash Viewpoint, access to Visitor Centre.

Admission charge

Free, car park charge during summer.

Opening times

Daily.

SPECIES TO LOOK FOR

Little grebe, shelduck, wigeon, teal, mallard, shoveler, pochard, tufted duck, goldeneye, sparrowhawk, oystercatcher, plovers, knot, dunlin, ruff, black-tailed godwit, spotted redshank, greenshank, common sandpiper, gulls, little tern, cuckoo, short-eared owl, sand martin, swallow, wagtails, wheatear, fieldfare, warblers, whitethroat, pied flycatcher, linnet, buntings.

Best time to visit

The high tides of spring and autumn see huge flocks of waders either on passage or as winter visitors.

Short-eared owl

47

WEST LINCOLNSHIRE

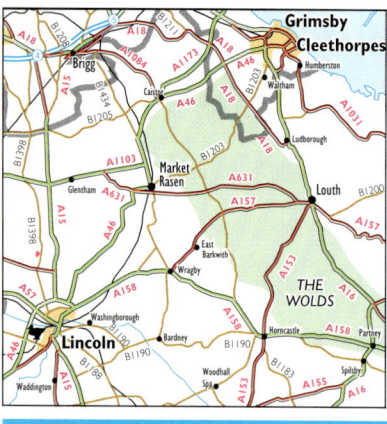

WHISBY NATURE PARK

The Nature Park is an area of 160 acres of lakes, ponds, woodlands (including oak wood), scrub and grassland, created by the quarrying of sand and gravel.

GETTING THERE

Moor Lane, Whisby, west of Lincoln town centre. From Lincoln take the A57 north west, head south on the Lincoln by-pass and turn left into Moor Lane.

FACILITIES

Three waymarked walks (two of 1¾ miles, one of 3 miles) with interpretive boards and three hides, toilets.

Wheelchair access

The Coot Walk (1¾ miles) and access to the first hide is possible in dry weather with assistance. Disabled toilet facilities are available for RADAR key holders.

Admission charge

Opening times

Daily.

SPECIES TO LOOK FOR

Great crested grebe, tufted duck and less common waterfowl can usually be seen from the hides and common tern, sand martin and reed warbler are summer visitors to the lake. Elsewhere nightingales and several species of warbler sing in the scrub and great spotted woodpecker, sparrowhawk and kingfisher are frequently seen.

Best time to visit

Winter for wildfowl; spring, summer for breeding birds.

Great crested grebes

SOUTH HUMBERSIDE ▶ 144, 145

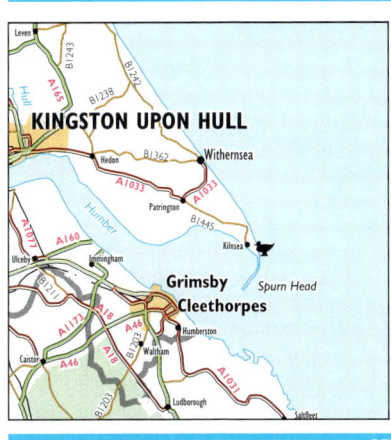

SPURN

A 4-mile-long sand and shingle spit projecting into the mouth of the river Humber. 280 acres lie above high water mark with another 477 below. These comprise saltmarsh, extensive mudflats, beaches and sand dunes plus an old lighthouse and a lifeboat house and an old overgrown First World fort, both disused.

Common and arctic terns

GETTING THERE

Kilnsea, 18 miles south-east of Hull. From Hull take the A1033 to Patrington, the B1445 to Easington, then unclassified roads to Kilnsea and Spurn.

FACILITIES

Information Centre/observatory (open 10am–5.30pm Monday–Thursday during holiday season, weekends at other times plus bank holidays and Good Friday), two hides, car park.

♿ Wheelchair access

One hide, no other facilities but good views from roadside.

Admission charge

Cars £1.80 April–October, £1 November–March, free to pedestrians.

Opening times

Daily.

SPECIES TO LOOK FOR

Spurn is a major European site for observing bird migration. In August–September wheatear, whinchat, redstart and flycatchers plus great numbers of thrushes, starling, fieldfare and redwing. Waders include dunlin, knot, redshank, curlew and oystercatcher. Among the large number of ducks are mallard, shelduck and Brent geese. Sandwich, common and Arctic terns migrate in large numbers and little terns are also seen. Disoriented wryneck, bluethroat, shrike and barred and icterine warblers have also been seen during adverse weather conditions.

Best time to visit

September, October.

Top right Ringed plover

HUMBERSIDE

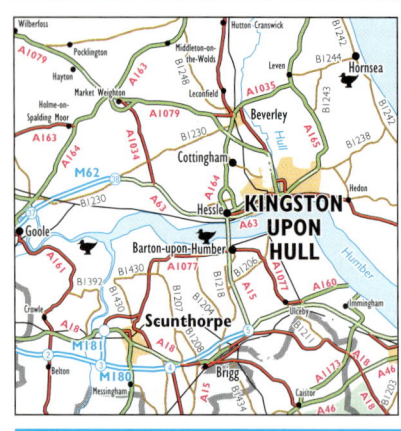

BLACKTOFT SANDS

(RSPB)

Some 460 acres comprising a large tidal reedbed, fringed by saltmarsh, with an area of man-made brackish lagoons, pasture fields and a willow plantation, situated at the confluence of the rivers Ouse and Trent on the Inner Humber Estuary.

GETTING THERE

1/2 mile east of Ousefleet; 6 miles east of Goole on the A161 Goole–Scunthorpe road.

FACILITIES

Basic Information Centre (open according to staff availability, closed Tuesday), five hides, toilets, picnic site.

Wheelchair access

Information Centre, toilets, some hides, paths suitable for wheelchairs.

Admission charge

Non-RSPB members: adult £2.50, OAP and concessions £1.50, child 50p.

Opening times

Wednesday–Monday 9am–9pm or sunset.

Above Barn owl

SPECIES TO LOOK FOR

Great crested grebe, shoveler, gadwall and pochard nest on the lagoon. Stints, greenshank, spotted redshank, godwits, sandpipers and the occasional avocet visit on passage. Reed, sedge and grasshopper warblers, bearded tit, water rail and occasionally marsh harriers are found in the reedbeds. Short-eared owl, hen harrier and many wildfowl visit in winter. Other birds of prey include merlin, sparrowhawk and barn owl.

Best time to visit

Good bird watching throughout year but especially the passage periods for rare wading birds (autumn for passerines) and the breeding season.

Barn owl nesting box.

HUMBERSIDE ▶ 146, 147

FAR INGS AND BARTON REEDBED

The reserve occupies a chain of flooded clay pits and extensive reedbeds on the bank of the River Humber. It comprises the open water of Ness Lake, large areas of reedbed, recently made scrapes with shallow water, grassland, hedgerow and scrub and estuarine saltmarsh.

GETTING THERE

Far Ings Road, Barton-on-Humber; just west of Humber Bridge on south bank, signposted to Barton-on-Humber, then follow brown tourist signs.

FACILITIES

Visitor Centre, five hides.

Wheelchair access
No facilities.

Admission charge

Opening times
Daily.

SPECIES TO LOOK FOR

Nesting species include bearded tit, great crested grebe, water rail, shoveler and pochard. Scrub and reed warblers are abundant and willow, sedge and grasshopper warblers, lesser whitethroat, whitethroat and blackcap have recently been recorded. The scrapes have breeding lapwing and redshank, the lakes provide for diving ducks and sawbills – goosander, merganser and occasionally smew – while bittern is a fairly frequent winter visitor.

Best time to visit
Winter for wildfowl, spring and summer for breeding birds.

HORNSEA MERE

(RSPB)

The largest natural freshwater lake in the county, reed-fringed and bordered by mixed woodland and farmland, close to the sea.

GETTING THERE

Hornsea, take the road west signposted to The Mere.

FACILITIES

Information Centre on Kirkholme Point. Cafeteria, toilets. (Note: this is not part of the reserve therefore visitors should not leave their cars here while visiting the reserve.) Car park. No access into reserve itself – use public footpath along the south side of the Mere, starting in Hull Road.

Wheelchair access
No facilities.

Admission charge

Opening times
Daily.

SPECIES TO LOOK FOR

Hundreds of reed warbler nest here alongside sedge warbler, reed bunting, coot and great crested grebe. Cormorants roost in the lakeside trees. Little gulls and black terns are often numerous on summer passage and wheatear, whinchat and various warblers pass through during spring. Winter brings large numbers of gadwall, goldeneye, mallard, coot, wigeon, teal, pochard and tufted duck. The woodlands boast great spotted woodpecker, treecreeper, tawny owl and jay. Good numbers of waders on the fringe of Kirkham Point or on the south side of mere.

Best time to visit
May for spring migrants, August/early September for waders, terns and little gulls.

Flock of wigeon

146, 147 ◀ HUMBERSIDE

BEMPTON CLIFFS
(RSPB)

The reserve stretches over two miles of spectacular coastline featuring the highest chalk cliffs in Britain, rising up to 400 ft in places and covered with grass and scrub.

Great skua

Great skua chick

GETTING THERE

1 mile north of Bempton village, north of the B1229 Flamborough–Bridlington Road.

FACILITIES

Information Centre (open only during breeding season April–September 10am–5pm daily), five observation barriers overlooking the seabird colonies, toilets.

♿ Wheelchair access

Two wheelchair viewpoints, access along cliff-top path, wheelchair toilet, wheelchair hire.

Admission charge

Opening times

Daily.

SPECIES TO LOOK FOR

Among the enormous numbers of seabirds is the only gannetry on mainland England with some 1,250 pairs counted. This is England's largest seabird colony and other residents include guillemot, razorbill, puffin, kittiwake (over 100,000 pairs in total on the headland), fulmar, herring gull and shag – the latter at the boulder base. Offshore migrants may include terns, skuas and shearwaters while wheatear, ring ouzel, peregrine and bluethroat frequent the cliff-top. Corn bunting breed on the grassland.

Best time to visit

May, June for gannets and puffins (gone by August).

Top right Gannet

NORTH YORKSHIRE ▶ 148, 149

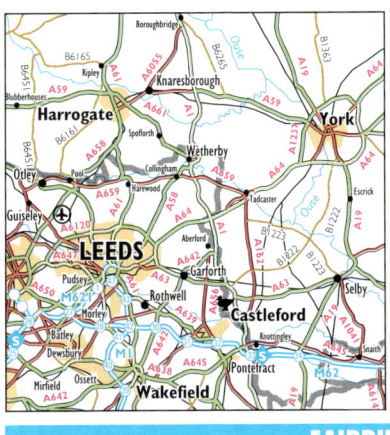

FAIRBURN INGS

(RSPB)

680 acres of large shallow lakes, marsh, scrub and flood pools formed by mining subsidence with deciduous woodland by the River Aire.

Yellow wagtail

GETTING THERE

West of Fairburn village; Fairburn lies 2 miles north of Ferrybridge on the A1.

FACILITIES

Five hides, Information Centre (weekends and bank holidays only), raised boardwalk through marsh, toilets, car parks.

♿ Wheelchair access

Information Centre, raised boardwalk, partial access to reserve (telephone in advance to arrange, Telephone 0977 673257).

Admission charge

Opening times

Daily.

SPECIES TO LOOK FOR

Wintering wildfowl are the main attraction here and include mallard, teal, shoveler, pochard, tufted duck, goldeneye, goosander, smew, coot and in winter up to 100 whooper swans. In spring and autumn terns, little gull, yellow wagtail and swallow stop off. Pied wagtail gather in autumn roosts with large numbers of swallows. Yellow wagtail pass through in autumn while lapwing, redshank, snipe, little ringed plover, common tern, mute swan, grebes and several species of duck nest. In summer blackcap, lesser whitethroat and warblers are common. Spectacular hirundine roosts occur in September.

Best time to visit

Spring (raptors) and autumn (waders) for migrants, winter for greatest variety of wildfowl, whooper swans and large flocks of gulls.

150, 151 ◀

LANCASHIRE

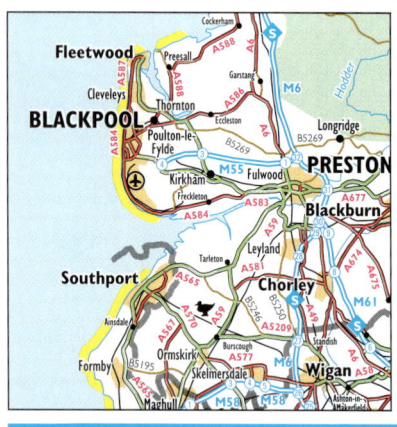

MARTIN MERE WILDFOWL & WETLANDS CENTRE

364 acres of flat peat, drained mere land; dry in summer, re-flooded in winter.

GETTING THERE
Burscough, six miles north of Ormskirk, off A570 (signposted from M61, M58, M6, off A59).

FACILITIES
Visitor Centre, Nature Trail, nine hides, licensed cafe, shop, picnic tables, play area.

Wheelchair access
Throughout the Centre including hides and toilets. Free wheelchair loan, special parking area. Other facilities for disabled visitors: Braille Trail, loan of audio cassettes and players, talks and tactile exhibits by prior arrangement.

Admission charge
Adult £3.50, OAP /single parent/claimant £2.50, child £1.75, family (2 adults, 2 children) £8.75.

Opening times
Daily. Summer 9.30–5.30pm, winter 9.30am–4pm, closed 24, 25 December.

SPECIES TO LOOK FOR

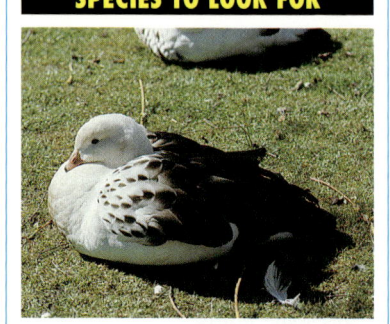

Among the more unusual tame birds are Chilean flamingo, flightless steamer ducks from the Falkland Islands and the extremely rare Recherche Island cereopsis. Wild visitors include ruff, black-tailed godwit and little ringed plover. In winter thousands of pink-footed geese, over a thousand whooper swans from Iceland, and Bewick's swans from Siberia, all fly in.

Best time to visit
End September–early March.

LANCASHIRE ▶ 150, 151

LEIGHTON MOSS

(RSPB)

A 300-acre reedswamp with meres and willow and alder scrub in a quiet and scenic valley with woodland on its limestone slopes.

GETTING THERE

Silverdale, three miles north-west of Carnforth; exit from the A6 at either Carnforth, Yealand Conyers or Yealand Redmayne. Leighton Moss is signposted off the M6 (Junction 35).

FACILITIES

Information Centre with live video link for bird watching, shop, tea room (10am–5pm Wednesday–Monday), five hides, toilets, car park.

♿ Wheelchair access

Information Centre (downstairs), three hides.

Admission charge

Non–RSPB members: adult £3, OAP £2, child 50p, (one hide on public causeway permanently open free of charge).

Opening times

Wednesday–Monday 9am–9pm or sunset.

SPECIES TO LOOK FOR

Britain's largest concentration of up to five pairs of bittern breed here, together with bearded tit, various warblers, teal, shoveler, pochard, tufted duck and marsh harrier. Black tern and osprey often pass through in spring and greenshank and various sandpipers in autumn. Large flocks of mallard, teal, wigeon, pintail and shoveler are among the wintering wildfowl and thousands of starlings, swallows and wagtails roost seasonally in the reeds, often attracting hunting sparrowhawks.

Best time to visit

March–early June for bitterns, otherwise of equal interest throughout year.

Tufted duck

MORECOMBE BAY

(BSRSPB)

The estuary comprises extensive sheep-grazed saltmarsh and inter-tidal sandflats with some artifical brackish water pools on the inner side.

GETTING THERE

Leave the M6 at junction 34 or 35. The A5105 runs from Morecambe to Carnforth along the estuary. A car park across the level crossing at Hest Bank, just off the A5105, and another car park off the Carnforth–Silverdale road (near Leighton Moss Reserve) provide vantage points.

FACILITIES

Shares Information Centre with the adjacent reserve of Leighton Moss (see entry for details). Two hides at the Carnforth–Silverdale road car park. (Beware dangerous channels and quicksands on the foreshore.)

♿ Wheelchair access

Hest Bank car park, one hide.

Admission charge

Opening times

Daily.

SPECIES TO LOOK FOR

In winter this estuary supports more waders than any other site in Britain. Knot, dunlin, oystercatcher, curlew, bar-tailed godwit and redshank are among them. Peregrines frequently hunt the waders in winter when shelduck, pintail, wigeon, red-breasted merganser and greylag are present. Sanderling occur on May migration and oystercatcher, redshank and wheatear nest on the saltings. Lagoons excellent for wintering wildfowl and passage waders.

Best time to visit

Winter and late summer. Late July–late May for waders.

Red-breasted merganser

152, 153 ◀

CUMBRIA

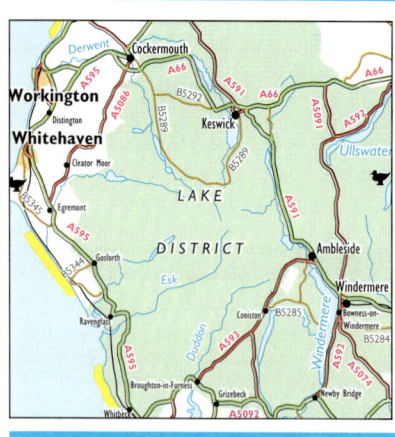

ST BEES HEAD

(RSPB)

A famous 3-mile stretch of red sandstone cliffs, towering up to 300 ft high and looking over to the Isle of Man. Several ledges and grassy tops with gorse patches.

GETTING THERE

The cliff headland lies south of Whitehaven and west of the B5345 road to St Bees.

FACILITIES

Four safe observation points on the steep public footpath north along the cliffs, toilets.

♿ Wheelchair access

Cars with disabled visitors may use the private road to the lighthouse from Sandwith (2 miles due north of St Bees).

Admission charge

Opening times

Daily.

SPECIES TO LOOK FOR

This is the largest seabird colony on the west coast of England and the only place in England where the black guillemot breeds. There are large numbers of guillemot, also razorbill, kittiwake, herring gull, fulmar and a small number of puffins. Rock pipit, raven, peregrine, stonechat, whitethroat, shag and cormorant also frequent the cliffs. Gannets, skuas, terns, shearwaters and eider may sometimes be spotted offshore.

Best time to visit

Late summer and autumn for arctic and great skuas and Manx and sooty shearwaters on passage.

Above Herring gull

Black guillemot nesting.

CUMBRIA

▶ 152, 153

HAWESWATER

(RSPB)

Situated in the Lake District National Park, Haweswater is a reservoir in a quiet, rugged valley surrounded by steep oak and birch woodland with rocky streams and some heather moor.

GETTING THERE

Take the A6 to Shap (M6 Junction 39/40) follow the signs to Bampton then turn left in the village and follow the road beside Haweswater. Park at the southern end.

FACILITIES

Wardens run an observation post 8am–6pm April–August when the reserve's golden eagles are nesting.

♿ Wheelchair access

No facilities.

Admission charge

Opening times

Daily.

SPECIES TO LOOK FOR

England's only pair of golden eagles nest here on the high crags near the head of the reservoir. Other upland breeding birds include peregrine, raven, ring ouzel, golden plover, curlew, redshank and snipe. Pied flycatcher, wood warbler, tree pipit, redstart, buzzard and sparrowhawk may be seen in the woodland.

Best time to visit

Spring–midsummer when the golden eagles are nesting and raising their young.

154, 155 ◀ **DURHAM AND CLEVELAND**

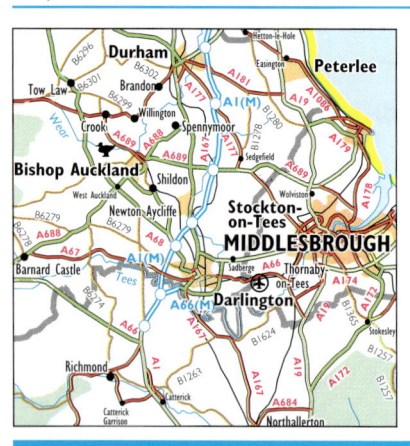

LOW BARNS

100 acres of grassland, scrub, young and mature woodland, ponds, streams and a large lake with several islands, formerly worked as a gravel pit.

Great crested grebes

GETTING THERE

1½ miles east of Witton-le-Wear, just off the A689 road to Bishop Auckland.

FACILITIES

Visitor Centre (April–September open daily, October–March closed Saturday), Nature Trail, five hides, toilets, car park.

♿ Wheelchair access

Visitor Centre, including wheelchair toilets, one hide.

Admission charge

Opening times

Daily.

SPECIES TO LOOK FOR

Resident wildfowl including tufted duck, mallard, coot and mute swan. In winter, numbers are augmented by teal, wigeon, pochard, shoveler and greylag geese. Heron are often seen in the shallows; kingfisher, dipper, goosander, yellow wagtail and common sandpiper also visit. In the woods are great spotted woodpeckers, tits and finches in winter while in summer blackcap, whitethroat and garden warblers can be heard.

Best time to visit

Winter.

Top right Magpies

58

TYNE AND WEAR

▶ 156, 157

WASHINGTON WILDFOWL & WETLANDS CENTRE

A hillside site of 100 acres on the river Wear with areas of mature woodland and ponds.

GETTING THERE

East of Washington, three miles west of Sunderland, signposted off A195 and A1231.

FACILITIES

Visitor Centre with picture windows, Exhibition Area, hides, shop, tea room, picnic areas, play areas.

Wheelchair access

Most of the Centre, hides, toilets, level paths. Other facilities for disabled visitors: braille map, tactile exhibits by prior arrangement.

Admission charge

Adult £2.95, OAP/single parent/claimant £2.20, child £1.50, family (2 adults, 2 children) £7.50.

Opening times

Daily. Summer 9.30am–5pm, winter 9.30–one hour before dusk, closed 24, 25 December.

SPECIES TO LOOK FOR

The 40-plus varieties of wild bird here include the largest concentration of mallard in the north-east, wigeon, pochard, tufted duck, teal, redshank, heron and lapwing. A woodland feeding station attracts great spotted woodpecker, sparrowhawk, brambling and bullfinch during winter. The Central Collection of captive wildfowl features over 1,200 birds of 105 species including ducks and swans from all over the world and a flock of Chilean flamingos.

Best time to visit

Autumn, winter.

Wigeon

NORTHUMBERLAND

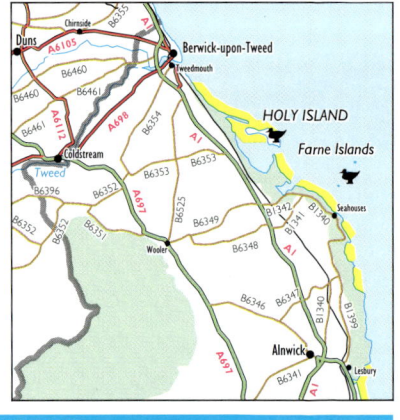

DRURIDGE BAY

Druridge Bay stretches five miles from Hauxley to Cresswell and encompasses four main sites. Hauxley consists of five large islands used for roosting, Druridge Bay Country Park includes a lake, Druridge Pools comprises a deep lake with adjacent wet fields, Cresswell Pond is a shallow brackish lagoon created by mining subsidence. Offshore to the north is Coquet Island, low and flat-topped with rocky and shingle shores.

GETTING THERE

From Alnwick take the A1068 south through Amble, and Hauxley is signposted (on the left). To visit the other sites rejoin the A1068 and continue south.

FACILITIES

Hauxley – Visitor Centre, four hides and toilets in car park; Druridge Bay Country Park – Visitor Centre; Druridge Pools – three hides, Walking Trail; Cresswell Pond – Visitor Centre, hide, toilets. Car parks at all sites; Coquet Island – RSPB North of England office arranges seasonal boat trips, (Telephone 091 232 4148).

♿ Wheelchair access

Hides, toilet and tracks at Hauxley, viewpoint at Cresswell Pond.

Admission charge

Day permit (covers all reserves), adult £1.50, child 75p, family £2.50, permits from Hauxley or Druridge Bay Country Park. Admission free to Northumberland Trust Members.

Opening times

Daily.

SPECIES TO LOOK FOR

Wigeon

Hauxley – waders, gulls, cormorant and terns; Druridge Bay Country Park – large flocks of overwintering wildfowl including smew and red-breasted merganser; Druridge Pools – large flocks of winter wildfowl, mostly wigeon and teal, but also goldeneye and whooper swan. In summer great crested grebe nest and waders feed along the shores. Snipe, redshank and teal breed; Cresswell Pond – wading birds all year, large numbers of wildfowl overwinter; Coquet Island – large tern colonies, good numbers of puffins and eider ducks.

Best time to visit

During the spring and autumn passage both Hauxley and Cresswell Pond are well known for rare birds; winter for wildfowl on Druridge Bay Country Park lake.

NORTHUMBERLAND ▶158, 159

LINDISFARNE

(NATIONAL NATURE RESERVE)

The reserve comprises in total over 8,000 acres of marshes, dunes and mudflats along the Northumberland coast from Budle Bay to Goswick Sands and includes Holy Island/Lindisfarne.

GETTING THERE

9 miles south-east of Berwick-upon-Tweed, off A1. Access to Holy Island is via a causeway which is impassable at high tide.

FACILITIES

Toilets, car parks.

Wheelchair access

No facilities.

Admission charge

Opening times

Daily.

SPECIES TO LOOK FOR

In winter up to 3,000 pale-bellied geese arrive from Spitzbergen, and from Iceland, Russia and Siberia whooper swans and great flocks of wigeon fly in. Dunlin and bar-tailed godwit occur in their thousands and grey plover, curlew, oystercatcher and redshank in smaller numbers. Eiders are common along the shoreline and red-breasted merganser along Budle Bay. In late autumn the thrush migration also involves hundreds of thousands of fieldfare, redwing and blackbird. Breeding birds include shelduck and fulmar.

Best time to visit

October–March for large numbers of wildfowl and waders, autumn for migrants.

Dunlin

FARNE ISLANDS

(NATIONAL TRUST)

A group of 15–28 small islands of which only Inner Farne (the largest) and Staple Island are open to visitors. Most of the islands are simply bare rock with no vegetation but there are large areas of peaty soil on Inner Farne and Staple Island which support a variety of plants.

GETTING THERE

2–5 miles off Bamburgh, daily boat from Seahouses (enquire about sailing times at National Trust Information Centre, Telephone 0665 721 099).

FACILITIES

National Trust Information Centre and shop (Easter–September), cafe (not National Trust) at Seahouses, nature walks on islands.

Wheelchair access

Wheelchair toilet on Inner Farne but islands are difficult for disabled or visually handicapped visitors and unsuitable for wheelchairs.

Admission charge

Enquire for boat charge (see above). Landing charge, May–July adult £2.80, child £1.40, August–April adult £2, child £1. Car park charge at Seahouses (inc. National Trust members).

Opening times

Easter–April, August–September daily 10am–6pm, during breeding season (May–July) Staple 10.30am–1pm, Inner Farne 1.30–5pm.

SPECIES TO LOOK FOR

The stacks and cliffs are inhabited by nesting kittiwake, shag, guillemot, fulmar and razorbill with good numbers of puffins (particularly on Staple) and eider. Between 650 and 1,350 nest on Inner Farne in May and June. Inner Farne also attracts hundreds of terns while on Staple the occasional ringed plover and oystercatcher are seen.

Best time to visit

During breeding season May–July (visitors are advised to wear hats!).

WEST GLAMORGAN

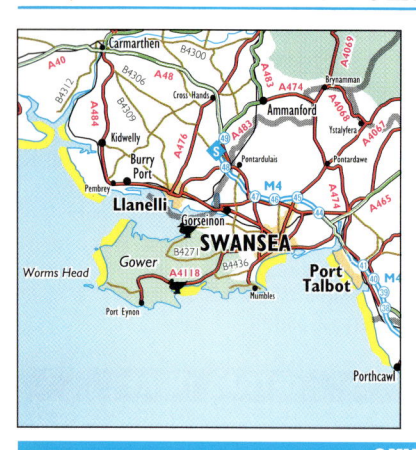

OXWICH

(NNR)

A tremendously varied range of habitats includes rocky and sandy shores, sloping headlands and cliffs, sand dunes, salt and freshwater marsh including reedbeds, open water and mixed fen, oak and alder scrub and mature woodlands, all in a fine setting on the south coast of the Gower Peninsula.

Reed bunting

GETTING THERE

Oxwich, 12 miles south-west of Swansea, signposted from A4118 Port-Eynon road.

FACILITIES

Very basic Information Centre (all year, Monday–Friday 9am–1pm; August, open all day; April–October also open 10am–noon at weekends), marsh boardwalk, lookout and hide (obtain permit from Information Centre), regular guided walks during summer (Telephone 0792 390320 for details), car park (charge).

Wheelchair access
Information Centre only.

Admission charge

Opening times
As above.

SPECIES TO LOOK FOR

A high density of breeding birds in the woods includes all three British species of woodpecker, nuthatch, treecreeper, buzzard, marsh and willow tit. Along the shoreline are occasional turnstone, purple sandpiper, oystercatcher, ringed plover, sanderling and a gull and wader roost. The freshwater marsh attracts little grebe, pochard, shoveler, teal and grey heron while the woodlands are used by many passerines for nesting. Water rail, Cetti's warbler and reed bunting frequent the reedbeds.

Best time to visit
Equal interest throughout year.

DYFED

▶ 160

LLANELLI WILDFOWL & WETLANDS CENTRE

150 acres of saltmarsh, man-made pools and scrapes near the seawall on the north side of the Burry Inlet, plus 80 acres inland with freshwater pools.

GETTING THERE

Parc Gitto, Llanelli; off A484 Loughor/Gorseinon road (by Llwynhendy Stores).

FACILITIES

Visitor Centre/observatory, hides, Guided Tours, cafe, shop, baby room.

♿ Wheelchair access

Most areas including hides and toilets. Special parking area.

Admission charge

Adult £2.95, OAP/student/single parent/claimant £2.20, child £1.50, family (2 adults, 2 children) £7.50.

Opening times

Daily. Summer 9.30am–5pm, winter 9.30am–4pm (grounds close one hour later), closed 24, 25 December.

Bewick's swan

SPECIES TO LOOK FOR

Large flocks of curlew, oystercatcher and redshank frequent the marsh and are supplemented by wintering pintail, wigeon and teal. Other wild inhabitants include short-eared owl and peregrine. Among the population of several hundred captive wildfowl are white-winged wood duck (from the world's threatened rain-forests) and Caribbean flamingos.

Best time to visit

Late autumn, early winter for waders on migration, mid-winter for hunting short-eared owl, late spring for breeding and young birds.

DYFED (SOUTH)

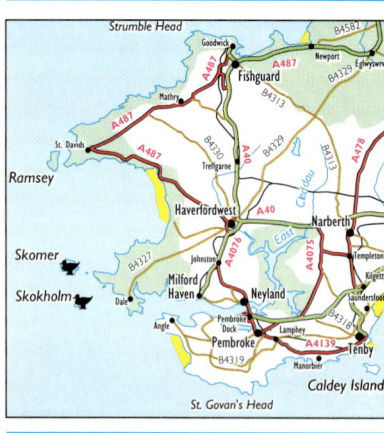

SKOMER ISLAND/SKOKHOLM ISLAND

Skomer is a spectacular wild island covering 720 acres and is internationally renowned for the finest seabird colonies in south-west Britain. Most of the island is a windswept plateau intersected by ridges of rock. Round the perimeter there are cliffs and steep slopes and at several places there are small rocky beaches. Footpaths lead to all the best sites. Skokholm comprises 240 acres of rabbit-grazed turf, made famous by the books of naturalist, Ronald Lockley.

GETTING THERE

Off the Marloes Peninsula, nr Haverfordwest.
Cars can be left for a fee at the National Trust Car Park, Martin's Haven beyond the village of Marloes. Weather permitting, the Skomer boat crosses Tuesday–Sunday (and Bank Holiday Monday) at 10am, 11am and noon, or more frequently from 10am onwards if demand exists. Return from around 3pm. Skokholm open April–September, Saturday–Saturday on weekly basis only (contact Dyfed Wildlife Trust, Telephone 0437 765 462). On daily basis sailing to Skokholm early June to mid-August, one boat per week Monday 10am. Reservations essential Telephone (Broad Haven) 0437 781 412 or (Dale Sailing) 0646 601 636.

FACILITIES

Dyfed Wildlife Trust Information Centre in Martin's Haven (open daily Easter–October). Toilets at Martin's Haven. Skomer – Self-guiding Trail and limited toilet facilities. Skokholm – shop, hides, portable hides for hire, natural history library.

Wheelchair access

No special facilities.

Admission charge

Return boat fare, adult £4, child (under 16) £2. Landing fees, adult £5, children free.

Opening times

Skomer – 10am–6pm Tuesday–Sunday and Bank Holiday Monday (see boat times). The island is closed for seabird survey and other management tasks for four days in June each year. Skokholm – see above.

SPECIES TO LOOK FOR

Skomer is famous for its 6,000 pairs of puffins and its 100,000 plus pairs of nocturnal Manx shearwaters. Other seabirds include fulmar, guillemot, kittiwake, oystercatcher, razorbill and large gulls. Land birds include chough, little and short-eared owls, raven, skylark and wheatear. Mallard and pheasant breed on the island. Skokholm is also important for its breeding seabird population. In addition to the above varieties it includes some 7,000 pairs of storm petrels.

Best time to visit

Skomer – resident seabirds April, May (June and July for seabirds feeding chicks). Puffins leave early August. Migrant birds, April, May and August to end of September. Rare birds late April to late May is good, late August to late September is best.
Skokholm – similar (day visits only possible June to mid-August).

Top right Razorbill

DYFED (NORTH)

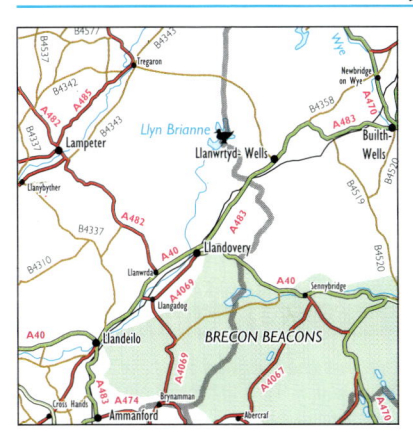

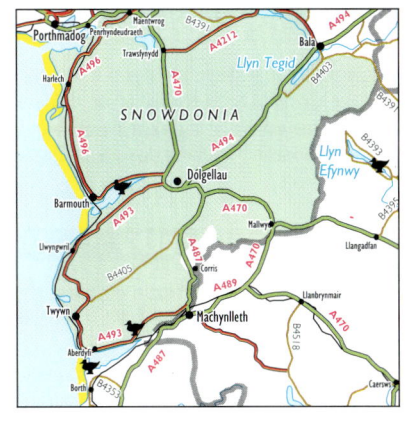

▶ 162

DINAS & GWENFFRWD

(RSPB)

Over 1,700 acres of hillside oakwoods with rocky outcrops, streams and bracken slopes rising to heather and grass moorland with valley fields and riverside woodland.

Grey wagtail

GETTING THERE

2½ miles north of Rhandirmwyn village, off road to Llyn Brianne dam.

FACILITIES

Dinas Nature Trail accessible at all times, Information Centre and Gwenffrwd Trail open Easter–end August 10am–5pm, toilets at Llyn Brianne, car park.

♿ Wheelchair access

No facilities.

Admission charge

Opening times

Daily (see facilities).

SPECIES TO LOOK FOR

Pied flycatchers are the commonest woodland nesting birds, mostly seen using nesting boxes. Other breeding species include redstart, wood warbler, nuthatch, woodcock, tits and woodpeckers. Buzzard, sparrowhawk, kestrel, raven and red kite are seen over the surrounding valleys. Grey wagtail, common sandpiper, goosander and dipper visit the rivers, tree pipit and whinchat frequent the hillsides and wheatear and red grouse are seen on the moors.

Best time to visit

Spring, early summer.

DYFED (NORTH)

YNYSLAS DUNES

The principal feature of this 5,000-acre reserve in the Dyfi estuary is its dunes, much planted with marram to protect against erosion. There is also a large wetland bog.

GETTING THERE

10 miles north of Aberystwyth, on unclassified road off B4353 Borth to Tre'r-ddol road.

FACILITIES

Information Centre and shop (daily, 9.15am–5.30pm March–September), Nature Trail, toilets, car park (charge).

Wheelchair access

Information Centre, toilets, Trail partially accessible.

Admission charge

Opening times

Daily.

SPECIES TO LOOK FOR

Birds breeding on the dunes include meadow pipit, skylark and wheatear. Terns arrive on passage during July, August and numbers of Sandwich tern can reach over 200. Wintering ducks include flocks of mallard, wigeon, teal, pintail and Greenland white-fronted geese; dunlin are present throughout the year. In the wetland bog golden plovers may often be seen in winter.

Best time to visit

Spring to September for migrants and waders on high tide.

Golden plover

YNYS-HIR

(RSPB)

981 acres of grazed saltmarsh at the head of the Dyfi estuary bordered by freshwater marsh and some remnant peat bogs. Mixed deciduous and conifer woodlands, with a river gorge, rise to a rocky hillside with bracken slopes.

GETTING THERE

Eglwys-fach, five miles south-west of Machynlleth, off A487 Machynlleth–Aberystwyth road.

FACILITIES

Information Centre (daily 9am–5pm), Nature Trail, eight hides (two elevated), toilets, car park.

Wheelchair access

Information Centre, toilets, main Trail, one hide – strong pusher required.

Admission charge

Non-RSPB members: adult £2.50, OAP & concessions £1.50, child 50p.

Opening times

Daily 9am–9pm or sunset.

SPECIES TO LOOK FOR

The saltmarsh attracts some 3,000 wigeon, a small flock of Greenland white-fronted geese, mallard and teal in winter. The woodlands' rich breeding community includes pied flycatcher, redstart, wood warbler, nuthatch and woodpeckers. Goldcrest and coal tit frequent the conifers and sedge, reed and grasshopper warblers are found in the marshes. Other breeding species include buzzard, kestrel, sparrowhawk, raven, grey heron, barn owl, tree pipit and whinchat. Large numbers of curlew use the estuary.

Best time to visit

Equal interest throughout year. Winter for large numbers of waders and also birds of prey.

GWYNEDD/POWYS ▶ 163, 164, 165, 166

MAWDDACH VALLEY

(RSPB)

The two reserves lie to north and south of the Mawddach Estuary. Coed Garth comprises 114 acres of hillside; sessile oak and birch wood with open areas above a river gorge. Arthog Bog is 12 acres of willow and alder scrub with pasture beside an extensive raised mire.

GETTING THERE

Comprises two major sections: Coed Garth Gell, on A496 Barmouth–Dolgellau road; Arthog Bog, 6 miles south-west, off A493 Fairbourne–Dolgellau road.

FACILITIES

Penmaenpool Wildlife Centre and hide with telescope and binoculars (open daily late May–September; April, May, October weekends only), limited car parking ½ mile south of Coed Garth Gell reserve in lay-by on A496; use Wildlife Centre car park in season. For Arthog Bog use the Morfa Mawddach station car park. Toilets at Penmaenpool, (summer only).

♿ Wheelchair access

The 'railway walk' at Arthog Bog, toilet at Penmaenpool (summer only).

Admission charge

Opening times

Daily.

Chiffchaff

SPECIES TO LOOK FOR

Buzzard, raven, pied flycatcher, redstart, wood warbler, tree pipit, lesser spotted woodpecker, grey wagtail and dipper breed at Coed Garth Gell. Whitethroat, warblers, and redpoll breed at Arthog Bog and water rail visit in winter. Cormorant, common sandpiper and redshank often appear on the estuary.

Best time to visit

Mid-April to June when woodland species are nesting.

LAKE VYRNWY

(RSPB)

The largest of the RSPB-managed reserves at over 17,500 acres, this comprises extensive heather moorland with conifer plantations, mixed deciduous woodland and sessile oakwoods, meadows and rocky streams surrounding the Lake Vyrnwy reservoir.

GETTING THERE

Llanwddyn; 10 miles south-east of Bala via the B4391 and B4396.

FACILITIES

Information Centre and shop (most hours during summer, weekends during winter), two woodland Nature Trails, two hides, toilets, car park.

♿ Wheelchair access

One hide (all visitors may travel round the reservoir by car).

Admission charge

Opening times

Daily.

SPECIES TO LOOK FOR

The lake supports a small breeding population of goosander and great crested grebe while common sandpipers frequent the shoreline. Dipper, grey wagtail and kingfisher nest by the lake and rocky streams. Deciduous woodland inhabitants include nuthatch, treecreeper, sparrowhawk, chiffchaff, redstart, pied flycatcher, warblers and woodpeckers, and crossbill and siskin nest in the conifers. Raven, buzzard, merlin and hen harrier frequent the moorland where wheatear, ring ouzel, curlew and golden plover breed.

Best time to visit

Spring and summer.

67

GWYNEDD

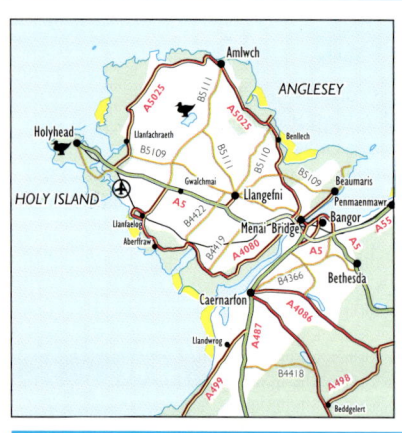

163, 164, 165 ◀

SOUTH STACK CLIFFS
(RSPB)

High cliffs with caves and offshore stacks, backed by the maritime heathland of Holyhead Mountain.

Gannet colony

GETTING THERE

Western headland of Anglesey, three miles west of Holyhead (signposted).

FACILITIES

Information Centre in Ellin's Tower (Easter–mid-September) with panoramic views and closed-circuit television pictures of the seabirds. Binoculars and telescopes also provided, refreshments adjacent to reserve, toilets, car park.

Wheelchair access
No facilities.

Admission charge

Opening times
Daily.

SPECIES TO LOOK FOR

Guillemot, razorbill and kittiwake congregate on the cliff in their thousands. Some 40 pairs of puffins and six pairs of choughs breed on or close to the reserve. Raven, jackdaw, shag and one or two pairs of peregrine also nest here, with whitethroat and stonechat on the heath. This is an important migration post with Manx shearwaters, gannets and large movements of passerines flying past. Rare species recorded include red-footed falcon, honey buzzard, dotterel, hoopoe, wryneck and bee-eater.

Best time to visit
April to mid-July for breeding seabirds. Migration times for others.

Top right Guillemot colony

GWYNEDD ▶ 163, 164, 165

LLYN ALAW

This reservoir, Anglesey's largest at 3 miles long by 1 mile wide and covering 777 acres, was formed by damming the Afon Alaw in 1966.

GETTING THERE

1½ miles north-west of Llanerchymedd, towards Ceidio, then Gwredog. Park and walk for ten minutes to hide (signposted).

FACILITIES

Information Centre (at west end of lake, signposted from B5111 Rhos-y-Bol and B5109 at Trefor), hide, picnic areas, toilets, car parks.

♿ Wheelchair access

Information Centre, toilet, wheelchair viewpoint.

Admission charge

Opening times

Daily.

SPECIES TO LOOK FOR

East end of lake – In winter there are good numbers of mallard, wigeon, tufted duck, pochard, goldeneye and teal, while Bewick's and whooper swans are recorded regularly, with occasional visits from white-fronted and pink-footed geese, long-tailed duck and even scaup. Kestrel, barn owl, short-eared owl and hen harrier search the lakeside for prey. In summer, wood, green and pectoral sandpipers have been recorded regularly as well as lapwing, curlew, dunlin, little stint, warblers, ruff and golden plover. Peregrine falcons hunt the lake.

Best time to visit

At low water level in early summer, autumn, also in winter for wildfowl when there are fewer people about.

CLWYD

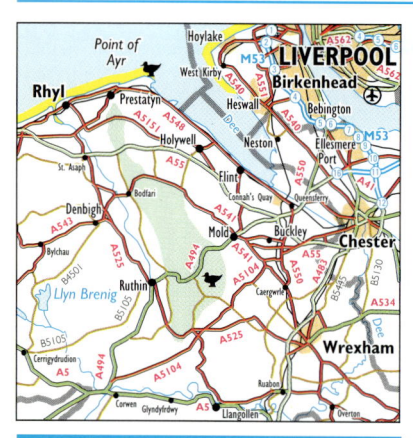

POINT OF AYR

(RSPB)
600 acres of inter-tidal mudflats at the mouth of the Dee Estuary with a single spit and a small area of saltmarsh.

GETTING THERE
Talacre, 2 miles east of Prestatyn, off A548 Prestatyn/Rhyl–Flint road.

FACILITIES
Limited car parking.

♿ Wheelchair access
No facilities.

Admission charge

Opening times
Daily.

SPECIES TO LOOK FOR
Huge numbers of waders feast on the mudflats here. Up to 20,000 roost in winter comprising mostly oystercatcher, knot, dunlin, curlew and redshank, with ringed plover and sanderling on migration. Winter also sees mallard, shelduck, teal, wigeon, pintail, red-breasted merganser, auks and great crested grebe while snow bunting, twite and the occasional Lapland bunting and shorelark visit the shingle spit. Terns gather in numbers in autumn and summer.

Best time to visit
Autumn or winter (beach popular with holidaymakers in summer). One to two hours before high water when waders are flying in to roost.

LOGGERHEADS COUNTRY PARK

The park is set on a limestone escarpment with craggy cliffs, river and woodlands, overlooked by the 1,818 ft high Moel Famau.

GETTING THERE
3 miles south-west of Mold on A494 Mold–Ruthin road.

FACILITIES
Information Centre (summer 10am–5pm daily), shop, restaurant, tea rooms and garden, Water Mill, Industrial Trail, Nature Trail.

♿ Wheelchair access
All facilities (Nature Trail partially accessible).

Admission charge
Car park charge.

Opening times
Daily.

SPECIES TO LOOK FOR
Dipper and grey wagtail can be seen by the shallow, fast-flowing river and pied flycatcher, chiffchaff, tree creeper, green and great spotted woodpecker breed in the woodlands. On the hills red grouse are present all year, the occasional ring ouzel and birds of prey may be seen. Summer visitors include meadow pipit, skylark, stonechat, wheatear and curlew.

Best time to visit
Spring and autumn.

DUMFRIES & GALLOWAY ▶168, 169

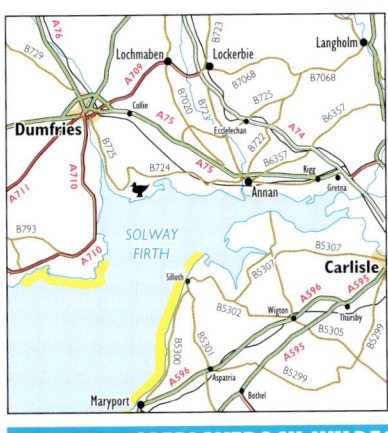

CAERLAVEROCK WILDFOWL & WETLANDS CENTRE

1,400 acres on the Solway Firth comprising huge tracts of intertidal mud and sand, with large areas of saltmarsh and fields along the coast.

GETTING THERE

Caerlaverock, 8 miles south of Dumfries off B725 (signposted from A75 in Dumfries).

FACILITIES

Visitors Centre/observatory with picture windows, three tower hides, 20 hides, binoculars for hire, screened approaches, 'Summer Walk' Trail (May–August), sheltered picnic area, refreshments, car parking.

Wheelchair access

Visitor Centre/observatory, Trails, one tower hide, some low hides.

Admission charge

Adult £2.70, OAP/single parent /claimant £2, child £1.35, family (2 adults, 2 children) £6.75.

Opening times

Daily, 10am–5pm, closed 24, 25 December.

SPECIES TO LOOK FOR

The entire population of some 12,000 barnacle geese from Spitzbergen (far beyond the Arctic Circle) winter here each year. Other regular visitors include pink-footed and greylag geese, whooper and Bewick's swan plus waders such as oystercatcher and golden plover. Peregrine, merlin, hen harrier and short-eared owl are also seen from time to time.

Best time to visit

Winter.

71

BORDERS

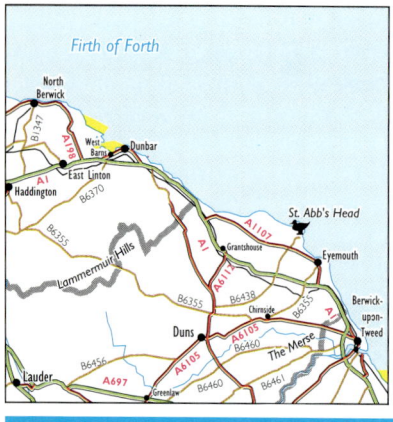

ST ABB'S HEAD

240 acres of high sea cliffs, freshwater and coastal grassland.

Puffin leaving the colony

GETTING THERE

12 miles north of Berwick-upon-Tweed, 1 mile north of Coldingham, off B6438.

FACILITIES

Information Centre (daily all year 9am–5pm, longer hours during summer) coffee shop (summer only), car park.

Wheelchair access
No facilities.

Admission charge

Opening times
Daily.

SPECIES TO LOOK FOR

This is one of the largest mainland seabird breeding sites on the north-east coast with important breeding populations of guillemot and kittiwake plus shag, razorbill, fulmar and puffin. Non-breeding purple sandpiper and turnstone are here most of the year. It is also a notable migration point in spring and autumn, with wryneck, red-breasted flycatcher and red-backed shrike passing through.

Best time to visit
May–October, good seawatching in autumn.

Top right Shag

171, 172 ◀ STRATHCLYDE AND LOTHIAN ▶ 173, 174, 175

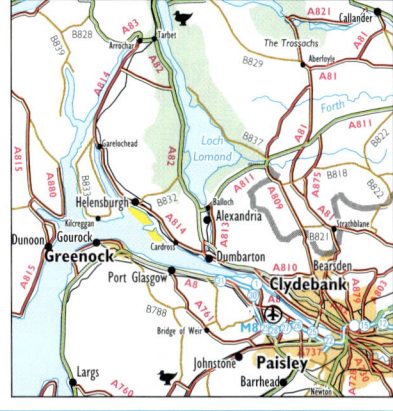

FALLS OF CLYDE

(SWT)

An ancient narrow woodland gorge set in 170 acres of broadleaved woodland and including the famous falls.

GETTING THERE

1 mile south of Lanark, signposted New Lanark off A73.

FACILITIES

Information Centre (mid-March–mid-October Monday–Thursday 11am–5pm, Friday 11am–4pm, weekends 1–5pm; mid-October–December and February–mid-March weekends only 1–5pm; closed January), slide show (adult £1, child 50p), Nature Trail, picnic site, toilets.

♿ Wheelchair access

Information Centre, toilet, limited access to reserve, telephone ranger in advance (Telephone 0555 65262).

Admission charge

Opening times

Daily.

SPECIES TO LOOK FOR

Breeding birds in the woodlands include spotted flycatcher, great spotted and green woodpeckers, garden warbler, chiffchaff. Crossbill also occur in summer. Dipper and grey wagtail can be seen feeding and nesting on the river. Kingfisher, cormorant and goosander are winter visitors.

Best time to visit

On special open days when the river is in full flow (usually controlled by Scottish Power). These vary but generally include Easter bank holiday and September bank holiday. Dates for 1992: 19 April, 25 June, 26 July, 27 September.

STRATHCLYDE AND LOTHIAN

LOCHWINNOCH

(RSPB)

Some 400 acres comprising a shallow loch, sedge marsh, alder and willow scrub and deciduous woodland.

GETTING THERE

½ mile east of Lochwinnoch, off A760 Largs–Paisley road.

FACILITIES

Information Centre including observation tower (with telescopes) and shop, (Friday–Wednesday 10am–5pm), refreshments at weekends, Nature Trails, four hides, toilets, car park.

Wheelchair access

Downstairs Information Centre and toilet, two Nature Trails including one designed specifically for wheelchair users with adapted hide, wheelchair available for free use.

Admission charge

Non-RSPB members: adult £1.50, child 50p.

Opening times

Reserve, daily 9am–9pm or sunset.

SPECIES TO LOOK FOR

Great crested grebes are the predominant breeding species alongside snipe, black-headed gull, sedge and grasshopper warblers, water rail and the occasional shoveler and tufted duck. Whooper swan, goosesander, greylag geese and goldeneye appear with large numbers of commoner ducks in winter while whimbrel and greenshank occur on autumn passage. Kestrel, sparrowhawk, and sometimes peregrine are seen throughout the year.

Best time to visit

Winter for greatest variety.

INVERSNAID

(RSPB)

923 acres of ground rising steeply from the loch through deciduous woodland to a craggy ridge, beyond which lies grass and heather moorland. Several mountain burns run down into the loch.

GETTING THERE

East side of Loch Lomond, off B829 west from Aberfoyle.

FACILITIES

Nature Trail, toilets (Inversnaid Hotel, summer only), car park. A passenger ferry operates across to the west bank of the loch (just north of Inveruglas) mainly in summer.

Wheelchair access

No facilities.

Admission charge

Opening times

Daily.

SPECIES TO LOOK FOR

Summer migrants, such as wood warbler, redstart, pied flycatcher and tree pipit augment the resident woodland birds. Buzzards are common on the crags and in the woods, blackcock frequent the lower slopes and sightings of eagles are possible. The loch is home to many wildfowl and dipper, grey wagtail and common sandpiper breed on the shore and along the burns.

Best time to visit

Mid-April to end June, particularly May.

Greylag goose

FIFE/TAYSIDE ▶ 176, 177

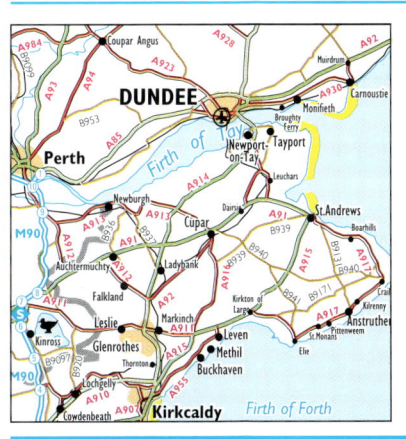

LOCH LEVEN & VANE FARM
(NNR/RSPB)

The reserve in total comprises nearly 4,000 acres. Vane Farm Nature Centre is the best place from which to view the loch and comprises 570 acres of marsh, shallow lagoons, mixed farmland and heather moorland with birch and bracken slopes and rock outcrops.

GETTING THERE

Access to Loch Leven NNR at Kirkgate Park, Findatie, Burleigh Sands and Loch Leven Castle. Vane Farm – southern shore of Loch Leven, off B9097 road to Glenrothes, 2 miles east of junction 5 on the M90.

FACILITIES

Information Centre with observation room and shop (daily Christmas–April 10am–5pm, January–March 10am–4pm), refreshments at weekends, Nature Trail, two hides, toilets, car park.

Wheelchair access

Information Centre and observation room, special wheelchair Trail, toilet.

Admission charge

Vane Farm: non–RSPB members: adult £1.50, OAP & concessions £1, child 50p. Rest of reserve free.

Opening times

Vane Farm 10am–5pm daily, rest of reserve always open.

SPECIES TO LOOK FOR

In autumn large numbers of pink-footed geese arrive at the loch alongside goosander, tufted duck and pochard. Greylag geese occasionally graze the fields and wigeon, teal, mallard, curlew, shoveler, Bewick's and whooper swans also occur. In summer gadwall, shelduck, great crested grebe and redshank frequent the scrape and tree pipit, redpoll and willow warbler can be seen in the birchwoods.

Best time to visit

Equal interest throughout year, autumn for wildfowl.

Looking out onto the loch.

178, 179 ◀ TAYSIDE

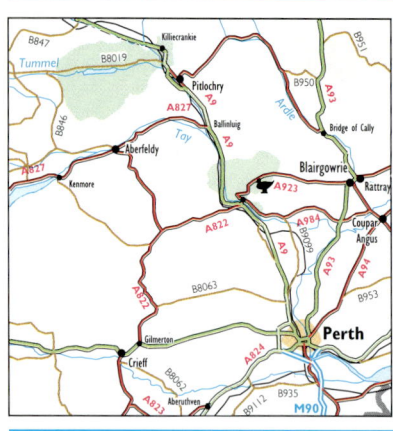

LOCH OF THE LOWES AND LOCH CRAIGLUSH

242 acres of lochs with woodland fringes.

GETTING THERE

Off A923 north-west of Dunkeld.

FACILITIES

Information Centre (April–September), hide (with binoculars), toilets.

♿ Wheelchair access
Hide.

Admission charge
✗

Opening times
Daily.

SPECIES TO LOOK FOR

Breeding ospreys are the speciality here. Woodland species include redstart, garden warbler, redpoll and siskin. Water birds include goldeneye, goosander and great crested grebe.

Best time to visit
April–June for breeding birds, October–March for wildfowl.

TAYSIDE

▶ 180, 181

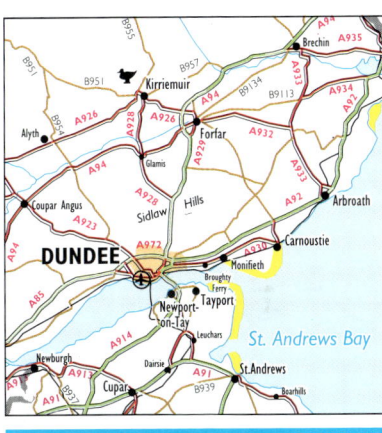

LOCH OF KINNORDY

(RSPB)

200 acres encompassing freshwater marsh with some open water, containing willow and alder scrub, fringed by woodland and set in a farming landscape.

GETTING THERE

1 mile west of Kirriemuir, off the B951.

FACILITIES

Three hides, car park.

♿ Wheelchair access

One hide.

Admission charge

Opening times

9am–9pm (closed Saturdays during September and October).

SPECIES TO LOOK FOR

In summer several thousand black-headed gull nest here alongside mallard, teal, shoveler, tufted duck, gadwall, grebes, ruddy duck, sedge warbler, reed bunting and redshank. Winter brings a large roost of greylag geese, a variety of ducks and hunting short-eared owl and hen harriers. Sparrowhawk and long-eared owl occur and greenshank, ruff and osprey are often seen on migration.

Best time to visit

Equally good throughout year (note opening times).

77

182, 183, 184, 185 ◀ TAYSIDE AND GRAMPIAN

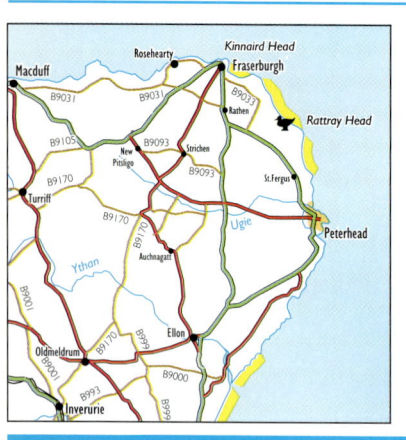

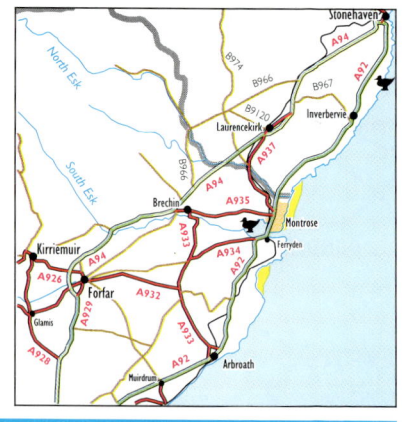

LOCH OF STRATHBEG

2,400 acres comprising a large shallow loch separated from the sea by wide sand dunes and bordered by freshwater fen and marsh, saltmarsh, woodland and farmland.

Ruff (winter plumage)

GETTING THERE

Immediately north of Crimond village, off the A952 Peterhead–Fraserburgh road.

FACILITIES

Information Centre/observation room (9am–5pm or dusk all year), boardwalk through fen woodland, three hides, toilets, car parks. Access to the loch is across MOD property, therefore visitors must obtain a permit from the warden (enquire at the Information Centre), £1 charge for non-RSPB members.) Other parts of the reserve are freely accessible.

♿ Wheelchair access
One hide.

Admission charge
Free to all areas except loch.

Opening times
Daily.

SPECIES TO LOOK FOR

Tens of thousands of greylag and pink-footed geese, plus hundreds of whooper and mute swans join tufted duck, pochard, and goldeneye on the loch in winter. Breeding birds include eider, shelduck, tufted duck, water rail, sparrowhawk and sedge warbler. A large colony of Sandwich terns nests on an island in the loch. This is also a migratory staging post with regulars such as green sandpiper, ruff, black-tailed godwit, osprey and marsh harrier plus unusual sightings including cranes, spoonbills and glossy ibis.

Best time to visit
Mid-September–April for waterfowl.

TAYSIDE AND GRAMPIAN ▶ 182, 183, 184, 185

MONTROSE BASIN

2,500 acres of tidal mudflats.

GETTING THERE

West of Montrose, views from A92, A934 and A935. Footpath from Old Montrose to Bridge of Dun along river or unclassified road to Bridge of Dun provides access to western flank of basin.

FACILITIES

Four hides (keys from ranger, £5 deposit) information boards sited around reserve.

Wheelchair access
No facilities.

Admission charge

Opening times
Daily.

FOWLSHEUGH

(RSPB)
1½ miles of red sandstone grass-topped cliffs with nooks and ledges.

GETTING THERE

Crawton, 4½ miles south of Stonehaven, signposted off A92 Inverbervie road.

FACILITIES

Car park. (Take great care on cliffs.)

Wheelchair access
No facilities.

Admission charge

Opening times
Daily.

Razorbill colony

SPECIES TO LOOK FOR

Large numbers of wintering waders and wildfowl include redshank, oystercatcher, knot and dunlin plus whooper and mute swans, greylag and pink-footed geese, wigeon, eider, shelduck, mallard, teal, pintailed and red-breasted merganser. Unusual waders on autumn passage may include spotted redshank and curlew sandpiper.

Best time to visit
April–May and July–early September (avoid mid-winter).

SPECIES TO LOOK FOR

This is one of the largest seabird colonies in mainland Britain including tens of thousands of guillemots, kittiwakes and razorbills in summer. Puffin can be seen at very close quarters and also fulmar, herring gull and shag. Eiders and peregrine can be seen offshore and along the cliffs.

Best time to visit
May–August.

186, 187 ◄ GRAMPIAN AND HIGHLAND

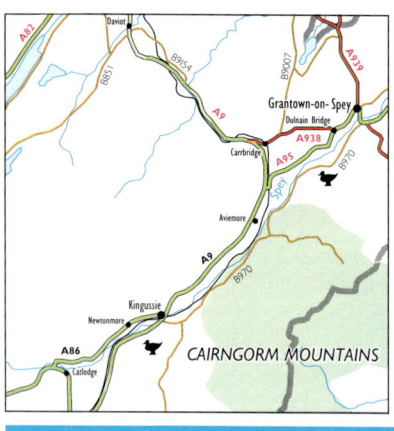

INSH MARSHES

(RSPB)

Over 2,000 acres including extensive marshes in the floodplain of the River Spey (usually flooded in winter), sedge meadows with pools and willow scrub bordered by birch and juniper woodland and moorland.

Hooded crow

GETTING THERE

1½ miles west of Kingussie, off B970 road to Insh village.

FACILITIES

Information Centre (April–June Wednesday, Sunday 10am–4pm; July–August Sunday 10am–4pm) Waymarked Trail, two hides.

♿ Wheelchair access

Information Centre, hides, views of rest of reserve from perimeter road.

Admission charge

Donations requested from non-RSPB members.

Opening times

Daily 9am–9pm or sunset.

SPECIES TO LOOK FOR

Wetland breeders include wigeon, teal, tufted duck, shoveler, goldeneye, native greylag, snipe, curlew, redshank and warblers. The woodland attracts nesting great spotted woodpecker, tree pipit, hooded crows, redstart and the occasional pied flycatcher. Osprey, hen harrier and buzzard are seen regularly and large numbers of whooper swans visit the marshes in winter.

Best time to visit

Spring, early summer for woodland species, winter for swans and wildfowl.

GRAMPIAN AND HIGHLAND ▶ 186, 187

ABERNETHY FOREST

Nearly 3,000 acres of Scots pine forest with an understorey of juniper in parts, forest bogs, lochs, some crofting land and a fringe of heather moorland. (Access only to Loch Garten section of reserve.)

Sparrowhawk

GETTING THERE

East of Boat of Garten, signposted off B970 north to Nethy Bridge.

FACILITIES

Information Centre/hide with shop, also equipped with powerful telescopes and binoculars (late April to late August, early September daily 10am–8.30pm), waymarked woodland walks, car parks.

♿ Wheelchair access
Information Centre/hide.

Admission charge
Non-RSPB members: adult £2, OAP & concessions £1, child 50p.

Opening times
Daily.

SPECIES TO LOOK FOR

Famous for its breeding ospreys, the reserve is also a showcase for breeding loch, marsh and Caledonian pine forest birds such as goldeneye, Scottish crossbill, crested tit, black grouse, redstart, siskin, sparrowhawk, teal, wigeon and little grebe. Greylag and goosander visit in winter.

Best time to visit

Ospreys can usually be seen from the end of April until mid-August. February to early March is the best time for the rest of the reserve. June and November–March are also good.

EAST HIGHLANDS

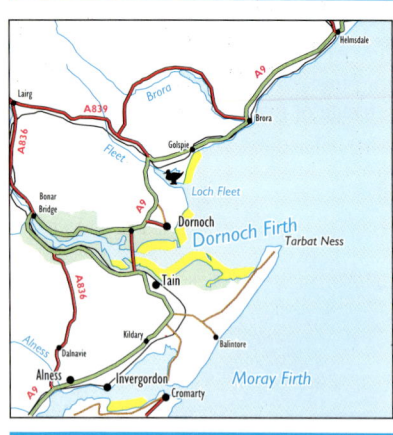

LOCH FLEET

(SWT)

1,750-acre tidal basin with sand dunes, coastal heath and pine woods. At low tide several square miles of mud and sand are exposed.

Red-necked grebe

GETTING THERE

5 miles north of Dornoch, entrance to Balblair Wood off unclassified road from Golspie to Littleferry, view across tidal basin from A9.

FACILITIES

Hide, nature trails.

Wheelchair access

Hide.

Admission charge

Opening times

Daily.

SPECIES TO LOOK FOR

Ducks and waders, including long-tailed duck, eider, king eider, common and velvet scoters, shelduck and wigeon. Offshore are small numbers of overwintering divers, Slavonian and red-necked grebes and white-winged gulls in winter – glaucous and, less commonly, Iceland. Woodland species include siskin, redstart goldcrest, coal tit and Scottish crossbill. Skylark and meadow pipit nest in the dunes and ringed plovers breed at the water's edge.

Best time to visit

Autumn and winter, when some 2,000–3,000 eiders congregate on the sea near the entrance to the loch.

WEST HIGHLANDS ▶ 189

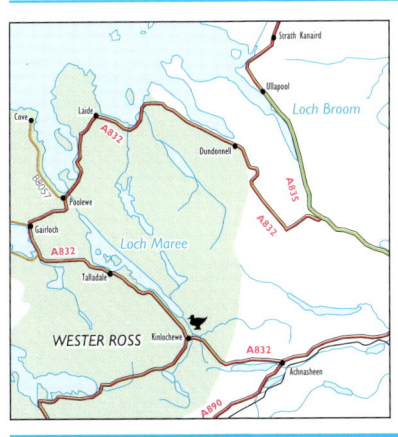

BEINN EIGHE

(NNR)

11,757 acres of mountain slopes including a significant remnant of the Caledonian pinewood forest, superb tracts of mountain and moorland scenery and a lochside strip.

Black-throated diver

GETTING THERE

1 mile north-west of Kinlochewe, off the A832.

FACILITIES

Information Centre (June–September), two Nature Trails, picnic site.

♿ Wheelchair access

Information Centre accessible (no ramp), no other facilities.

Admission charge

Opening times

Daily.

SPECIES TO LOOK FOR

Some fifteen species of moorland and mountain bird have been recorded here. Among the breeding birds are red-throated and black-throated divers, black grouse, ptarmigan and Scottish crossbill. Golden eagle, buzzard and merlin hunt for prey.

Best time to visit

Late May–early June.

83

WESTERN ISLES

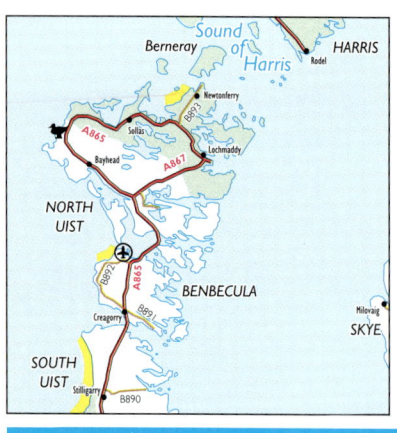

BALRANALD, NORTH UIST

(RSPB)

Over 1,600 acres comprising sandy beaches and a rocky foreshore separated from the machair and marshes by sand dunes. Much of the reserve is worked as crofting land.

GETTING THERE

3 miles north of Bayhead off A865 Bayhead–Balmartin road, signposted to Hougharry. Getting to the Western Isles: daily ferry from Uig on Skye to Lochmaddy or from Oban to Lochboisdale, South Uist. Ferry enquiries, Telephone 0475 33755. By air from Glasgow to Benbecula, British Airways, Telephone 041 332 9666.

Above Dunlin

FACILITIES

Visitor reception cottage at Goular (April–August). Please do not enter cemetery.

♿ Wheelchair access
No facilities.

Admission charge

Opening times
Daily.

SPECIES TO LOOK FOR

Corncrake, lapwing, snipe, oystercatcher, ringed plover and dunlin nest on the machair while teal, shoveler, gadwall, wigeon and mute swan prefer the marshes. Other breeding species include terns, twite, wheatear, eider and black guillemot. Whooper swans, greylags and several raptors visit in winter.

Best time to visit
May, June for breeding waders.

Lapwing

84

ORKNEY ISLANDS ▶ 190, 191

MAINLAND ORKNEY

Birsay Moors & Cottascarth (RSPB), Copinsay (RSPB), Hobbister (RSPB), The Loons (RSPB), Marwick Head (RSPB), Mull Head (Orkney Islands Council)

Birsay Moors & Cottascarth are mostly undulating heather moorland with bog and marsh. Hobbister, too, is predominantly heather moorland with bogs and fen and also includes low sea-cliffs. The Loons is a loch-side marsh while Marwick Head and Mull Head are cliff sites. Copinsay is a small island, 5 miles to the south, accessible by boat from Skail (Telephone 0856 74252).

GETTING THERE

Mainland Orkney: by daily ferry from Scrabster in Caithness to Stromness (Telephone P&O Ferriers 0224 572 615); by air, from Edinburgh etc (Telephone British Airways 0856 3356, Telephone Loganair 0856 3457).

FACILITIES

One small hide at Cottascarth plus main hide at Burgar Hill (northern part of reserve) and one at The Loons (no entry into reserve), no other facilities at other reserves apart from car parking.

♿ Wheelchair access

Burgar Hill hide at Cottascarth.

Admission charge

Opening times

Daily.

SPECIES TO LOOK FOR

Right nesting gannets

Birsay Moors & Cottascarth boast a high density of nesting hen harriers, with a few merlins and ground-nesting kestrels. Skuas and gulls and a fine variety of waders and ducks are present. Hobbister is home to typical Orkney moorland species such as hen harrier, short-eared owl, merlin, red grouse, curlew, snipe, red-throated diver and twite. Gulls, nesting cliff birds, divers and sea-ducks also occur. The Loons, too, holds a variety of breeding waders and ducks. Marwick Head is Mainland's most spectacular seabird reserve with tens of thousands of breeding guillemots and kittiwakes, plus large numbers of razorbill. Similar species can be seen at close quarters at Mull Head.

Best time to visit

All reserves late April–mid July.

ORKNEY ISLANDS

NOUP CLIFFS/NORTH HILL, PAPA

Noup Cliffs: 1½ miles of high sandstone sea cliffs with numerous ledges, backed by maritime heath. North Hill: 510 acres of maritime heath bordered by a rocky coastline with some low sandstone cliffs.

Shags on their colony.

GETTING THERE

Noup Cliffs: north-western promontory of Westray; North Hill: northern part of Papa Westray. Passenger ferry to both islands from Kirkwall (Orkney Island Shipping Company, Telephone 0856 2044), also by air to both (Loganair, Telephone 0856 2494), plus option of ferry to Papa Westray from Westray.

FACILITIES

North Hill: arrange in advance with the warden (mid-April to mid-August only) an escorted tour to view the nesting colonies (Telephone 085 74240); no facilities at Noup Cliff. Take great care on the cliff-top.

♿ Wheelchair access
No facilities.

Admission charge

Opening times
Daily.

SPECIES TO LOOK FOR

Noup Cliffs is one of the largest seabird colonies in the British Isles, with enormous numbers of guillemots and kittiwakes. Other nesting species include fulmar, rock pipit, raven, razorbill, puffin and shag. Many of the same species are present at North Hill together with an exceptionally large colony of arctic terns, arctic skua, eider, ringed plover, oystercatcher, dunlin, wheatear and gulls.

Best time to visit
Late April–mid-July. Arctic terns arrive mid-May.

ORKNEY ISLANDS ▶ 190, 191

NORTH HOY

Almost 10,000 acres in total, comprising a large plateau of moorland, dissected by glacial valleys, and varying from heather and deer grass to mountain heath and sub-Arctic vegetation on the summit. There are also several miles of spectacular cliffs, rising over 1,000 ft at St John's Head.

GETTING THERE

North-west part of Hoy, around Ward Hill. Passsenger ferry from Stromness to Moaness pier, then a short walk; car ferry from Houton to Lyness then along the B9047 to Rackwick.

FACILITIES

Information Centre (in progress) plus Information display at The Hoy Inn near the Moaness pier. Take special care on the cliff-tops, which are crumbly.

♿ Wheelchair access

No facilities, but a road runs through the reserve.

Admission charge

Opening times

Daily.

SPECIES TO LOOK FOR

Large populations of great and arctic skuas breed on the moorland with red grouse, golden plover, dunlin, curlew, hen harrier, merlin, short-eared owl, twite and great black-backed gull. Guillemot, razorbill, kittiwake, shag, peregrine and raven nest on the cliffs, with a colony of Manx shearwaters nearby.

Best time to visit

Late April–mid-July.

Shag

ORKNEY ISLANDS

TRUMLAND, ROUSAY

1,070 acres of mostly heather moorland rising up to 800 ft, dissected by small valleys and containing a small inland loch and crags.

GETTING THERE
Above Trumland House in the south of the island. Passenger ferry from Tingwall, off the A966 in the north-east of Mainland Orkney.

FACILITIES
Nature Trail (shop and public toilet in village near the pier).

Wheelchair access
No facilities.

Admission charge

Opening times
Daily.

SPECIES TO LOOK FOR

Red-throated diver, hen harrier, kestrel and golden plover breed, and short-eared owl, merlin and both great and arctic skuas may be seen. A mixed colony of herring and lesser black-backed gulls is located on the moorland where both great black-backed and common gulls also nest.

Best time to visit
Late April–mid-July.

Herring gull

SHETLAND ISLES ▶ 190, 191

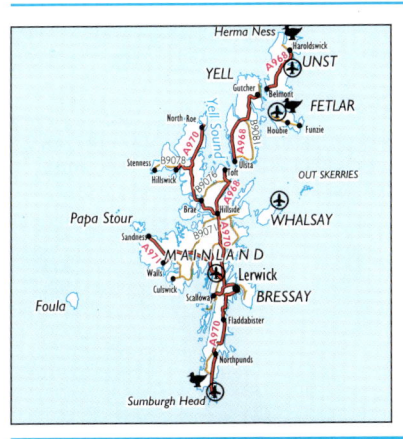

FETLAR (RSPB), HERMANESS (NNR)

Fetlar consists of grassy heathland, bordered by high sea cliffs and crofting areas. In addition there are heather moors, bogs, lochs, pools and marsh. Hermaness comprises nearly 2,400 acres of rough moorland plus one of the finest pieces of sea-cliff coastline in Britain, including the outlying stacks of Muckle Flugga.

GETTING THERE

(See p. 90 for Mainland Shetland.) Yell is connected to Mainland Shetland by ferry. The island of Fetlar is reached by car ferry from Yell and Unst. Hermaness occupies the northern point of Unst.

FACILITIES

Fetlar – one hide. Reserve may not be entered in summer other than by arrangement with the warden, present April–September at Baelance, just south of reserve. Telephone in advance to arrange guided walks (non–RSPB members £1) and to see the snowy owls, Telephone 09505 246).

♿ Wheelchair access

No facilities but good roadside viewing at Fetlar.

Admission charge

Opening times

Daily.

SPECIES TO LOOK FOR

Great skuas

Gannets

Fetlar is famous for snowy owls. Breeding birds include an important number of whimbrel plus red-necked phalaropes, Manx shearwater, storm petrel, eider, red-throated diver, golden plover, dunlin, snipe, curlew, raven and twite. Hermaness is one of the major seabird breeding stations in Europe and its main attraction is its gannetry of some 6,000 pairs plus its puffins and great skuas. In addition there are large colonies of guillemot and fulmar plus kittiwake, dunlins and golden plovers.

Best time to visit

(Both islands) end May–early August.

190, 191 ◀   MAINLAND SHETLAND

SUMBURGH HEAD

Loch of Spiggie (RSPB), Noss

Sumburgh Head: cliff-top with ledges; Loch of Spiggie: a shallow freshwater loch separated from the sea by dunes and from a neighbouring loch by marsh; Noss: 774-acre island formed of horizontally bedded planes of Old Red Sandstone.

Great skua

GETTING THERE

Car ferry from Aberdeen or Orkney (P&O Ferries, Telephone 0224 572 615), or by air from Edinburgh, Aberdeen, Inverness and Orkney (British Airways, Telephone 031 225 2525). Sumburgh Head, southern point of Mainland; Loch of Spiggie, southern end of Mainland; Noss, 2 miles east of Lerwick: ferry from Lerwick to Bressay, cross Bressay by car or on foot, dinghy to Noss May–August.

FACILITIES

Sumburgh Head – car park only. Loch of Spiggie – no access but excellent views from roadside. Noss – Information Centre on island.

♿ Wheelchair access
No facilities.

Admission charge

Opening times
Daily.

SPECIES TO LOOK FOR

Sumburgh Head offers excellent close views of puffins, razorbills and guillemots, plus shags and kittiwakes. Loch of Spiggie is a winter home to as many as 300 whooper swans as well as greylag, long-tailed duck, tufted duck, pochard, goldeneye and wigeon. Arctic tern, great and arctic skuas, and kittiwake use the loch while several species of wader nest in the area. Noss is one of the most spectacular seabird colonies in Europe with thousands of guillemots, kittiwakes and gannets plus a wide variety of other seabirds. A colony of some 200 greater black-backed gulls breed on the reserve while the moorland sustains important breeding colonies of great and arctic skuas.

Best time to visit

Sumburgh Head – May–end July. Loch of Spiggie – autumn, winter. Noss – only accessible May–August.

COUNTY DOWN ▶ 192, 193, 194

MURLOUGH

(NATIONAL TRUST)

764 acres of coastline beneath the Mourne Mountains comprising a fragile 5,000-year-old sand dune system with heathland and woodland surrounded by estuary and sea.

GETTING THERE

2 miles south-east of Dundrum, 2 miles north-east of Newcastle on the Belfast–Newcastle road (signposted).

FACILITIES

Visitor Centre (June to mid-September 10am–5pm), Guided Walks Wednesday 3pm mid-July to August and Sundays during September, car park (charge June–September).

Wheelchair access

No facilities.

Admission charge

Opening times

Daily.

SPECIES TO LOOK FOR

During summer the heathland holds important numbers of meadow pipit, stonechat and skylark as well as attracting nesting reed bunting, and whitethroat. In winter the mudflats of inner Dundrum Bay are home to dunlin, wigeon, redshank and shelduck while the outer bay draws large flocks of wintering sea duck, particularly common scoter which can number up to 4,000.

Best time to visit

January–February.

Shelduck

COUNTY DOWN

192, 193, 194 ◀

STRANGFORD LOUGH

The reserve embraces the entire foreshore of this muddy sea lough (an inlet of the Irish Sea) and several islands, totalling some 5,400 acres.

GETTING THERE

10 miles south-east of Belfast.

FACILITIES

National Trust Information Centre, shop, tea rooms at Strangford Lough Barn, Castle Ward, Strangford (Easter–August 1am–6pm; April–June, September, October weekends only; July, August daily), hides at Castle Espie Wildfowl & Wetlands Centre (see separate entry), Reagh Island, Mount Stewart Gas House, Anne's Point, Mount Stewart. Access is restricted to several of the important nesting islands April–end July.

Wheelchair access

Paths partially accessible, Reagh Island hide, toilets at Castle Ward.

Admission charge

Car park £3 per car.

Opening times

Daily.

SPECIES TO LOOK FOR

Most activity occurs in the northern mudflats. The lough holds internationally important numbers of Brent geese and during October–November two-thirds of the world population of light-bellied Brent geese. Large numbers of bar-tailed godwit, shelduck and knot are also present. During the summer the area is famous for its nesting terns, particularly sandwich and common terns. Other species include greylag geese, pintail, merganser, golden plover, greenshank and whooper swan.

Best time to visit

Summer for terns, winter for geese and waders.

CASTLE ESPIE WILDFOWL & WETLANDS CENTRE

(see also STRANGFORD LOUGH)

Flooded clay and limestone workings plus woodland on the shore of Strangford Lough.

GETTING THERE

North west shore of Strangford Lough, 3 miles south of Comber (13 miles south east Belfast), signposted from A22 Comber–Killleagh–Downpatrick road).

FACILITIES

Exhibition Area, hide, Woodland Trail, restaurant, shop, regular events and activities.

Wheelchair access

Main building, trail.

Admission charge

Adult £2.20, OAP/single parent/claimant £1.50, child £1.10.

Opening times

10.30am–5pm Monday–Saturday, 2–5pm Sunday, closed 24, 25 December.

SPECIES TO LOOK FOR

Large numbers of wild duck, geese and swan migrate here each winter from Arctic breeding grounds to augment such colourful residents as bufflehead (north American diving duck), king eider, Hawaiian goose and cinnamon teal.

Best time to visit

Winter waders December, January; November–April captive birds at their best; September, October large flocks of pale-bellied geese.

COUNTY ANTRIM ▶ 195, 196

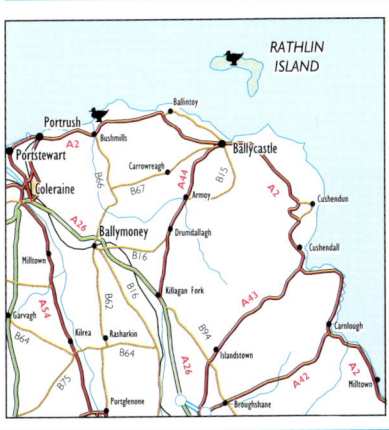

GIANT'S CAUSEWAY

(NATIONAL TRUST)

Coastal and cliff paths with rocky shores and unusual basalt and volcanic rock formations.

Fulmar

GETTING THERE

West of Ballycastle, off A2 on B146 causeway to Dunseverick road.

FACILITIES

National Trust Visitor Centre open year round 10am–7pm (July–Aug), earlier closing rest of year.

♿ Wheelchair access

Visitors Centre and tea rooms, partial access to site, wheelchair toilets.

Admission charge

(car parking charge).

Opening times

Daily.

SPECIES TO LOOK FOR

The cliffs hold important concentrations of nesting raptors including peregrine falcon, buzzard and kestrel plus rock pipit, rock dove, stonechat, twite and raven. This is also one of the last surviving nesting sites of the chough. Gannet, Manx shearwater, cormorant and shag are seen over the sea while guillemot, razorbill, black guillemot, kittiwake and fulmar fly offshore. In autumn and winter waders include turnstone and purple sandpiper.

Best time to visit

Late April–early June.

195, 196 ◀

COUNTY ANTRIM

RATHLIN ISLAND

(RSPB/NNR)

High chalk and basalt cliffs backed by heather moor, rough grassland, green pasture, small loughs and freshwater marshes.

Puffins

GETTING THERE

5 miles offshore across Rathlin Sound, reached by local boat service from Ballycastle (return trip £5).

FACILITIES

Contact the RSPB warden in advance (Telephone 02657 63935) for access to the West Light lighthouse platform (4 miles to the west of the harbour – transport available). Round-island boat trips in summer, details from RSPB N. Ireland office (Telephone 0232 491547), Interpretive Tours (Telephone 0267 63939/63920).

♿ Wheelchair access
No facilities.

Admission charge
(ferry charge – see above).

Opening times
Daily.

SPECIES TO LOOK FOR

Northern Ireland's finest seabird colony can be seen from the West Light platform, including large numbers of kittiwake, guillemot, razorbill, fulmar and puffin nesting on the cliffs and stacks. Around Church Bay in the breeding season look for black guillemot, ringed plover, oystercatcher and eider. Elsewhere on the island are peregrine, buzzard, wheatear, raven, stonechat and rock pipit while the marshes are breeding sites for lapwing, snipe, sedge warbler, reed bunting and black-headed gull.

Best time to visit
Late May to mid-July, especially June, for seabird breeding.

COUNTY LONDONDERRY ▶197, 198

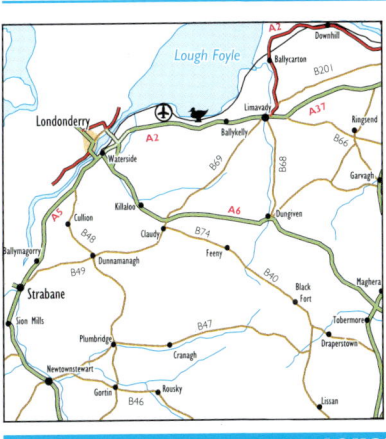

LOUGH FOYLE

(RSPB)

3,300 acres of wide mudflats with a fringe of saltmarsh, shingle and shell ridges bordered by arable farmland.

GETTING THERE

South-east foreshore of Lough Foyle, 7 miles east of Derry on A2 Londonderry–Limavady road.

FACILITIES

Good viewpoints at Longfield Point, Ballykelly and Faughanvale. (Take care when crossing unmanned level crossings.)

♿ Wheelchair access

No facilities.

Admission charge

Opening times

Daily.

SPECIES TO LOOK FOR

This is an outstanding site for wintering wildfowl – in autumn wigeon numbers can reach 26,000, and up to 1,000 Brent geese feed in the estuary; in winter up to 2,500 whooper swans and large numbers of Bewick's swans gather on the adjacent farmland. Mallard, teal, curlew, bar-tailed godwit, oystercatcher, dunlin, grey plover also winter here when snow buntings forage on the shore and unusual visitors include Slavonian grebe and three species of divers. Whimbrel, curlew sandpiper, little stint and spotted redshank are some of the passage migrants. Skuas, petrels and shearwaters often seek shelter in autumn.

Best time to visit

Autumn and winter.

Bar-tailed godwit

Top right *Wigeon*

95

COUNTY FERMANAGH

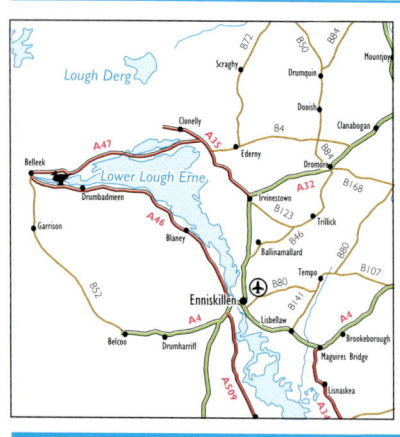

CASTLECALDWELL FOREST

(RSPB)

The reserve comprises 554 acres of conifer forest fringed by bays of the lough with willow and alder scrub and reedbeds. It also includes several low islands in the lough.

GETTING THERE

West side of Lower Lough Erne, 4 miles east of Belleek, on A47 Belleek–Pettigoe road.

FACILITIES

Information Centre (summer 9am–5pm daily, winter by appointment only), hide, toilets, car park. Boat trips may be arranged with the warden.

Wheelchair access
No facilities.

Admission charge

Opening times
Daily

SPECIES TO LOOK FOR

A small population of common scoters nest on the vegetated islands with mallard, tufted duck, red-breasted merganser and heron, while common and Sandwich terns use the barer islands. Sparrowhawk, long-eared owl, crossbill and siskin inhabit the forest and grebes the bay. Wigeon, goldeneye, teal, pochard, tufted duck and whooper swan can be seen in winter.

Best time to visit
Late May, June.

Great crested grebes

WHAT·TO·DO·AND·SEE

NORTH DEVON

WHAT TO DO AND SEE

i North Devon Library, Tuly Street, Barnstaple, Devon
☎ 0271 47177
i The Pill, The Quay, Bideford, Devon
☎ 0237 477676 summer only
i The Promenade, Ilfracombe, Devon
☎ 0271 863001

ADVENTURE

Shooting

North Devon Shooting School
Bickenbridge Farm, Ilfracombe
☎ 0271 863959

EQUESTRIAN

Riding and Pony Trekking

Comyn Farm Riding Stables
Comyn Farm, Ilfracombe
☎ 0271 865371

HEALTH

Leisure Centres

North Devon Leisure Centre
Seven Brethren Bank, Barnstaple
☎ 0271 73361

Woodside Adventure Centre
First Raleigh, Bideford
☎ 0237 476534

LOCAL FEATURES

Arts and Crafts

Burton Art Gallery
Victoria Park, Kingsley Road, Bideford
☎ 0237 476713

Historic Buildings

Appledore
Old wooden shipbuilding centre at mouth of River Torridge with Georgian houses and narrow streets.
2 miles north of Bideford

Chambercombe Manor
15th century house with famous 12th century cider press
Chambercombe, Ilfracombe
1 mile south-east of Ilfracombe
☎ 0271 862624

Museums

Bideford Museum
Local history and marine connections
Odun House, Odun Road, Appledore
☎ 0237 471455

Ilfracombe Museum
Wilder Road, Ilfracombe
☎ 0271 863541

NORTH DEVON

WHAT TO DO AND SEE

St. Anne's Museum
14th century chapel converted into local museum
Paternoster Row, Barnstaple
☎ 0271 78709

Theatre

Pavilion Theatre
Victoria Pavilion, The Promenade, Ilfracombe
☎ 0271 862228
P 🛆 🚌 ✕ ♿

Queens Hall Theatre
Boutport Street, Barnstaple
☎ 0271 43239
P 🛆 🚌 ✕ ♿

Festivals and Fairs

September
Barnstaple Fair and Carnival

OUTDOOR LEISURE/SPORT

Fishing

Mainly sea and river mouth fishing
The Kingfisher
22 Castle Street, Barnstaple
☎ 0271 44919

WATERSPORTS

Skern Lodge Outdoor Centre
Offers a wide range of water-based leisure activities
Watertown, Appledore
☎ 0237 475992

Sailing

Ilfracombe Yacht Club
The Quay, Ilfracombe
☎ 0271 863969

DEVON

WHAT TO DO AND SEE

i Tourist Office, 8 Sherborne Road, Newton Abbot, Devon
☎ 0626 67494

East Dart river

EQUESTRIAN

Riding and Pony Trekking

Elliott's Hill Riding Centre
Buckland-in-the-Moor
☎ 0364 53058

Smallacombe Farm Riding Stables
Ilsington
☎ 0364 661265

HEALTH

Leisure Centres

Dyron's Leisure Centre
Pool with fun slide, sauna, sunbeds, squash and tennis.
Highweek Road, Newton Abbot
☎ 0626 60426
Close to town centre

Trago Mills Shopping and Leisure Centre
Huge shopping complex; Edwardian penny arcade, miniature railway, cinema, adventuredome and coarse fishing lakes.
Stover, nr Newton Abbot
☎ 0626 821111
→A A38/382
P ✗ ♿

LOCAL FEATURES

Arts and Crafts

Dartington Cider Press Centre
Craft shops and visitor centre.
Shinners Bridge, Dartington
☎ 0803 864171
→A A384
P ♿

The Devon Guild of Craftsmen
Museum, demonstrations and changing craft exhibitions.
Riverside Mill, Bovey Tracey
☎ 0626 832223
→A A382
P ✗ ♿

Food and Drink

Whitestone Vineyard
Bovey Tracey, nr Moretonhampstead
☎ 0626 832280
→A old A382

Gardens

Plant World
4 acres of gardens, unique 'map of the world gardens', plant nursery and panoramic views.
St. Mary Church Road, Newton Abbot
☎ 0803 872939
→A A380
P

Historic Buildings

Bradley Manor
Mediaeval manor house and chapel set in woodland and meadows. National Trust.
Newton Abbot
☎ 0626 4513
→A A381

Buckfast Abbey
Founded nearly a thousand years ago, the abbey was rebuilt earlier this century by the present community. Today it is a living Benedictine monastery well-known for its beekeeping, stained glass and tonic wine.
Buckfastleigh
☎ 0364 42519
→A A38
P 🚻 🚌 ♿

Compton Castle
Fortified manor house. National Trust.
Marldon, nr Paignton
☎ 0803 872112
→A A381
P

Ugbrooke House and Park
Ancestral home of the Lords Clifford of Chudleigh; fine furniture and paintings; Capability Brown landscaped park.
Chudleigh
☎ 0626 852179
→A A38
P 🚌 ✗ ♿

Natural History

Buckfast Butterfly Farm and Otter Sanctuary
Tropical butterflies and moths; otter pools and underwater viewing.
Buckfast Steam and Leisure Park, Buckfastleigh
☎ 0364 42916
→A A38/A384
P 🚌 ✗ ♿

DEVON

WHAT TO DO AND SEE

Miniature Pony Centre
Collection of rare miniature ponies; adventure playground.
Wormhill Farm, nr Bovey Tracey
☎ 0647 432400
On the B3212 nr Moretonhampstead
P 🚌 ✗ ♿

Rare Breeds Farm
Farm trails, river walks and rare breeds of farm animals.
Parke, nr Bovey Tracey
☎ 0626 833909
Off the B3387
P ✗ ♿

Parks

River Dart Country Park
Adventure playgrounds, bathing lake, grass sledges, pony rides, nature trails and fly fishing.
Holne Park, Ashburton
☎ 0364 52511
Nr Ashburton
P ✗ ♿

Stover Country Park
14 acre lake with a wide variety of birds and wildlife.
Newton Abbot

Decoy Park
100 acres of woodland, a boating lake and playgrounds.
Newton Abbot

Railways

Dart Valley Light Railway
Buckfastleigh to Totnes steam trips; leisure park and museum.
The Station, Buckfastleigh
☎ 0364 42338
→A A38
P ✗

Gorse Blossom Miniature Railway
Small gauge passenger trains; picnic area, woodland walks and gardens.
Nr Bickington
☎ 0626 821361
→A old A38
P ♿

Zoos

Paignton Zoo
Totnes Road, Paignton
☎ 0803 527936
P ♿

OUTDOOR LEISURE

Birdwatching and Wildlife

Shaldon Wildlife Trust
Rare and endangered small mammals; exotic birds and reptiles; breeding centre.
Ness Drive, Shaldon
☎ 0626 872234
→A A379
♿ 🚌 ✗

Fishing

Trago Mills Nature Reserve
Fishing stretch for carp, rudd, roach, bream and tench.
Between Newton Abbot and Bovey Tracey

Decoy Lake
Stocked with tench, perch and rudd.

Rackerhayes Ponds
5 lakes stocked with bream, carp, tench, roach, rudd, perch, pike and eels. Available to day ticket holders.
Between Newton Abbot and Kingsteignton

Golf

Warren Golf Club ⛳18
Dawlish
☎ 0626 862255

Newton Abbot (Stover) Golf Club ⛳18
Newton Abbot
☎ 0626 52460

Walking

Becky Falls Estate
70 foot waterfall in lovely woodland, picnic areas and Nature Trails.
Manaton, nr Bovey Tracey
☎ 064722 259
On the B3344
P

Canonteign Falls and Water Park
The highest falls in southern England set in natural woodland in the Teign valley, lakeside picnic areas and barbecue centre.
Canonteign, nr Chudleigh
☎ 0647 52666
→A A38
P

Short Walks
i The Tourist Office can provide information about varied walks in the area.

DORSET

WHAT TO DO AND SEE

i Westover Road, Bournemouth, Dorset
☎ 0202 789789
i Hound Street, Sherborne, Dorset
☎ 0935 815341
i The White House, Shore Road, Swanage, Dorset
☎ 0929 422885

Littledown Centre
Aerobics, badminton, basketball, bowls, circuit-training, a fitness and health suite, five-a-side football, netball, racketball, squash, swimming, table tennis and tennis are available.
Chaseside, Bournemouth
☎ 0202 417600

LOCAL FEATURES

Aquariums

Natural World
Exotic fish, sharks and piranhas.
The Quay, Poole
☎ 0202 686712

Public Aquariums
Extensive displays of marine and freshwater animals.
Pier Approach, Bournemouth
☎ 0202 295393

Art Galleries

Russell-Cotes Art Gallery and Museum
Paintings, ceramics and oriental material in a witty building. The Bournemouth Art Gallery displays a fine collection of Victorian and Edwardian paintings.
Russell-Cotes Road, East Cliff, Bournemouth
☎ 0202 551009

Arts and Crafts

Walford Mill Craft Centre
Quality craft shops, exhibitions and a workshop area in an attractive riverside setting.
Stone Lane, Wimborne
☎ 0202 841400
Off the B3078, north of the town centre

Gardens

Compton Acres Gardens
Fabulous gardens with rare plants, a priceless collection of bronze and marble statuary and a famous Japanese garden.
Canford Cliffs Road, Poole
☎ 0202 700778

Cranborne Manor Gardens and Garden Centre
Superb collection of spring bulbs, a knot garden and an old fashioned rose collection.
Cranborne
☎ 07254 248
10 miles north of Wimborne Minster

Historic Buildings

Brympton d'Evercy
A magnificent family home with extensive gardens, a vineyard, Country Life Museum

EQUESTRIAN

Riding and Pony Trekking

Fir Tree Farm Riding Centre
Fir Tree Farm, Ogdens, Fordingbridge
☎ 0425 654744

The Glebe Riding Stables
Glebe Farm, Corfe Castle
☎ 0929 480280

HEALTH

Leisure Centres

Ferndown Sports and Recreation Centre
Badminton, basketball, circuit-training, a fitness centre, five-a-side, keep-fit, netball, racketball, a rock climbing wall, roller skating, squash, swimming, table tennis, trampolining and tennis are available.
Cherry Grove, Ferndown
☎ 0202 877468

DORSET

WHAT TO DO AND SEE

in the Priest House specialises in cider-making. I Zingari cricket club collection.
Yeovil
☎ 0935 862 528
Off the A30 or the A3088, just west of Yeovil, signposted
P ✗

Corfe Castle
Impressive and atmospheric ruins of a mediaeval royal fortress standing in the Purbeck Hills.
Corfe
☎ 0929 480921
Off the A351 Wareham to Swanage road, 5 miles north-west of Swanage

Kingston Lacey House and Park
A beautiful 17th century house built by Sir Ralph Banks with a fine private picture collection and a 250 acre park. National Trust.
Wimborne
☎ 0202 883402
On the B3082, 1 mile west of Wimborne
P 🛇 ✗ ♿ ♿

Sherborne Castle
A 16th century mansion built by Sir Walter Raleigh, the grounds around the lake were landscaped by Capability Brown.
Sherborne
☎ 0935 813182
1 mile east of Sherborne town centre

Smedmore House and Gardens
A 17th/18th century manor house with a fine collection of Dresden china, watercolours and dolls.
Kimmeridge
☎ 0929 480719
7 miles south of Wareham
P ♿

Museums

Christchurch Tricycle Museum
Victorian street scene and models.
Priory Car Park, Christchurch Quay
☎ 0202 479849
P ♿

Poole Museums
Three museums in the Old Town of Poole. The **Waterfront** is a maritime museum; **Guildhall** is a former Council Chamber and Court and **Scaplens Court** is a mediaeval merchant's house.
Poole Quay (Waterfront Museum), High Street (Scaplens Court), Market Street (Guildhall)
☎ 0202 675151

Natural History

Brownsea Island
A nature reserve with wading birds, migrants, red squirrels and Sika deer, it is the largest island in Poole Harbour.
Ferries from Poole harbour or Sandbanks
♿ ✗ ♿ ♿

Merley Bird Gardens
Exotic birds set in a beautiful historic walled garden.
Merley, nr Wimborne
☎ 0202 883790
P 🛇 ✗ ♿ ♿

Parks

Poole Park
100 acres of lakes and parkland on the edge of Poole Harbour with windsurfing, a mini-marina, crazy golf, putting, a zoo, a boating lake and a miniature railway.
☎ 0202 673322

OUTDOOR LEISURE/SPORTS

Fishing

Sea fishing

Sea Fishing Poole
Fisherman's Dock, The Quay, Poole
☎ 0202 679666

River fishing
The main rivers are the Avon, Stour, Frome and Piddle which are popular for salmon, trout and coarse fishing.
i Further information from the Tourist Information Centre.

WATERSPORTS

Sailing

Poole Bay, Poole and Christchurch Harbours offer sheltered areas for yachting. All types of watersports are available with sailing schools offering tuition and accompanied sailing or self-drive facilities.

Moonfleet Yachts
Cobbs Quay Marina, Hamworthy
☎ 0202 668410

Rockley Point School of Sailing
Rockley Sands, Hamworthy, Poole
☎ 0202 677272

Waterskiing

Ocean Bay Company
Also parascending, jet skiing.
2 Ulwell Road, Swanage
☎ 0929 422785

Windsurfing

Bournemouth Surfing Centre
127 Belle Vue Road, Southbourne
☎ 0202 433544

Bournemouth Windsurfing Centre
6 Falcon Drive, Bournemouth
☎ 0425 272509

SOMERSET

WHAT TO DO AND SEE

i Taunton Tourist Information Centre,
The Library, Corporation Street,
Somerset
☎ 0626 67494

ADVENTURE

Multi-activity Centres

Taunton Summer School
Over 50 summer courses in arts, sports and special interests, age range 7–70, full board available.
Taunton School, Staplegrove Road
☎ 0823 276543

AERIAL SPORTS

Ballooning

Taunton Hot Air Balloon Co. Ltd.
60 Bridge Street, Taunton
☎ 0823 333137

EQUESTRIAN

Riding and Pony Trekking

Curland Equestrian Enterprises
Crosses Farm Stud, Curland
☎ 0460 234234

HEALTH

Leisure Centres

Taunton Pools
Station Road, Taunton
☎ 0823 284108

LOCAL FEATURES

Arts and Crafts

Aller, The Pottery
Bryan and Julia Newman, The Pottery, Aller, Langport
☎ 0458 250244
On the A372, 2 miles north of Langport

E. J. Hill & Son Basketmakers
Unit 10–12, Wireworks Estate, Bristol Road, Bridgwater
☎ 0278 424003
On the A38 nr Bridgwater

Willow Craft Industry
P. H. Coates & Son, Meare Green Court, Stoke St. Gregory, nr Taunton
☎ 0823 490249
➤A A361/A378

Festivals and Fairs

October
Taunton's traditional Cider Barrel Race and Carnival Procession, third Saturday in October.

November
Bridgwater Carnival, the Thursday nearest 5th November

Food and Drink

Perry Brothers' Cider Mills
Museum, shop and traditional farmhouse cider.
Dowlish Wake, Ilminster
☎ 0460 52681
On the A303 and the A30, 2 miles from Ilminster

Sheppy's Cider
Three Bridges, Bradford on Tone, Taunton
☎ 0823 461233
On the A38 between Taunton and Wellington

Gardens

Hestercombe House Gardens
Designed by Sir Edwin Lutyens and Miss Gertrude Jekyll.
Cheddon Fitzpaine
☎ 0823 337222
➤A A361

Tintinhull House Garden
Modern formal garden with borders and ponds.
☎ 0935 822509
South of the A303, 5 miles north-east of Yeovil

Guided Tours

Guided Tours of Taunton
Louise Murrell, Spyspot, Staplehay, Taunton
☎ 0823 331527

Historic Buildings

Barrington Court
A model estate and farm buildings complex designed to support a large Tudor manor house. Estate trail and farm exhibition.
☎ 0460 40601
Off the A303, 5 miles north-east of Ilminster

SOMERSET

WHAT TO DO AND SEE

Brympton D'Evercy House
House, gardens and vineyard.
Brympton Estate Office, Yeovil
☎ 0935 862528
→A A30
P 🏠 ✕ ♿

Combe Sydenham Manor Hall
Elizabethan house with gardens, deer park, waymarked walks, trout ponds, fly fishing and children's play area.
Monksilver, nr Taunton
☎ 0984 56284
Off the B3188
P 🏠 🚌 ✕

Gaulden Manor
Tolland, Lydeard St. Lawrence
☎ 09847 213
Off the B3188
P 🏠 🚌 ✕

Lyte's Cary Manor and Gardens
Mediaeval manor house and chapel of local stone, with an excellent garden.
Charlton Mackrell, Somerton
☎ 04582 23297
On the A38, 4 miles north of Ilchester
P 🏠 🚌

Montacute House
16th century house with an H-shaped houseplan, surrounded by a formal garden and landscaped park.
☎ 0935 823289
South of the A3088, 4 miles west of Yeovil
P 🏠 🚌 ♿

Museums

Hornsbury Mill and Museum of Bric-a-Brac
Chard
☎ 04606 3317
P 🏠 ✕ ♿ ♿

Somerset County Museum
Taunton Castle
☎ 0823 275893
P 🏠 🚌

Somerset Cricket Museum
Priory Avenue, Taunton
☎ 0823 275893

Natural History

Widcombe Bird Gardens
Culmhead, Blagdon Hill
☎ 082342 268
Off the B3170
P 🏠 ✕ ♿

Parks

Exmoor National Park
600 miles of public footpaths in this area of wild moorland and deep wooded combes.
Exmoor House, Dulverton, Somerset
☎ 0398 23665

Railways

West Somerset Railway
Britain's longest preserved railway.
The Railway Station, Minehead
☎ 0643 704996
→A A39
P 🏠 ✕

Theatres

Brewhouse Theatre and Arts Centre
Coal Orchard, Taunton
☎ 0823 283244

OUTDOOR LEISURE

Cycling

Taunton Holiday Cycle Hire
Bridgwater Road, Bathpool, Taunton
☎ 0823 73016
On the A38 at Bathpool

Fishing

Detailed fishing information may be obtained from:
Area Fisheries and Recreation Officer
Wessex Rivers, King Square, Bridgwater
☎ 0278 457333

Golf

Vivary Park and Golf Course
Ideal for the serious golfer and beginner alike. Walks, playgrounds, tennis, putting, gardens and wildlife.
Vivary Park, Taunton
☎ 0823 333875

Skiing

Wellington Sports Centre
Corams Lane, Wellington
☎ 082347 3010

Tennis

Vivary Park
Book at Golf Course
☎ 0823 333875

Walking and Rambling

For information on walking in the Quantock Hills, telephone the Warden.
Fyne Court, Broomfield, Bridgwater
☎ 082345 526
P 🏠 ✕

WATERSPORTS

Boat Trips

Trips on the 'IWA Ruby' on the Bridgwater and Taunton Canal.
Mr & Mrs Rymell, Crewkerne
☎ 0460 72509

Windsurfing

Windsurfing Centre
13 Upper High Street, Taunton
☎ 0823 251729

AVON

WHAT TO DO AND SEE

i 8 Abbey Church Yard, Bath, Avon
☎ 0225 462831
i 14 Narrow Quay, Bristol, Avon
☎ 0272 260767

EQUESTRIAN

Riding

Mendip Riding Centre
Lyncombe Lodge, Churchill, nr Bristol
☎ 0934 852335

Midford Valley Riding Stables
Midford Road
☎ 0225 837613

Montpelier Riding Centre
Weston Farm Lane, Weston
☎ 0225 23665

LOCAL FEATURES

Art Galleries

Arnolfini Arts Centre
Modern art gallery with changing exhibitions and performances of contemporary music, dance, film and theatre.
16 Narrow Quay, Bristol
☎ 0272 299191
→A A36

Victoria Art Gallery
Collection includes European Old Masters and 18th–20th century British paintings.
Bridge Street, Bath
☎ 0225 461111

Festivals and Fairs

May/June
Badminton Horse Trials, 3–6 May
Bath International Festival of Music and the Arts, 25 May–10 June

Guided Tours

Car and Coach Tours
Private guided tours and open top bus tours are run at frequent intervals.
i Details from the Bath Tourist Information Centre.

Free guided Walking Tours
A detailed look at Bath's historic buildings, they leave from outside the Pump Room entrance in Abbey Church Yard. Mayor's Honorary Guides are all volunteers.

Ghost walks
Start at the Garrick's Head near the Theatre Royal.
☎ 0225 63618
☎ 0225 66541 for tickets

Historic Buildings

Bath Abbey
Late 15th century abbey built on the site of an earlier Saxon and Norman building. Magnificent example of the perpendicular style of English Gothic architecture.
☎ 0225 330289

Dyrham Park
Richly furnished mansion built in Bath stone set in beautiful parkland with views across the Bristol Channel. Fallow deer roam the park. National Trust.
☎ 027 582 2501
On the A46, 8 miles north of Bath

Museums

American Museum in Britain
18 period furnished rooms and galleries all illustrating American life between 17th and 19th centuries. Splendid views from the gardens.
Claverton Manor, Bath
☎ 0225 60503
Off the A36 Warminster road

Bath Postal Museum
History of the Post and its Bath connections – original letters from the 17th century, postcards, uniforms, working machinery. The building housed Bath's Post Office when the world's first postage stamp was used here on 2 May 1840.
Broad Street, Bath
☎ 0225 460333
→A A4/A36

City of Bristol Museum and Art Gallery
Displays include ancient history, Bristol ships, natural sciences, fine and applied arts, Egyptology, ethnography, and glass.
Queen's Road, Bristol
☎ 0272 223571

AVON

WHAT TO DO AND SEE

Roman Baths Museum
This Roman bathing establishment flourished between the 1st and the 5th centuries. The waters can be tasted in the 18th century Pump Room.
Bath
☎ 0225 462831

Theatres

Theatre Royal
One of Britain's oldest and most beautiful theatres; a varied all-year programme; backstage tours.
Sawclose, Bath
☎ 0225 448844 Box Office

Zoos

Longleat
The magnificent home of the Marquess of Bath and his famous lions.
Warminster, Wiltshire
☎ 0985 3551
➤A A362

OUTDOOR LEISURE/SPORTS

Cycling

Cycle path
Easy going, winding path along the Avon river valley using the flat, traffic-free route of a disused railway, it offers safe and peaceful cycling.

Fishing

Bath Trout Farm
Anglers' lake and fresh trout for sale.
Old Cleveland Baths, Hampton Row, Bathwick, Bath
☎ 0225 60714

Crudgington I.M. Ltd.
Tackle shop.
37 Broad Street, Bath
☎ 0225 466325

Skiing

Avon Ski Centre
All equipment provided.
Lyncombe Lodge, Churchill, nr Bristol
☎ 0934 852828

WATERSPORTS

Boat Hire

The Boathouse at Bath
Victorian boating station with wooden skiffs and punts for hire.
Forester Road, Bath
☎ 0225 466407
Less than a mile from the city centre

Boat Trips

Bristol and Bath Cruises
Passenger boat cruises of Bristol Docks or the River Avon.
☎ 0272 214307

HAMPSHIRE

WHAT TO DO AND SEE

i New Forest Museum and Visitor Centre, Lyndhurst, Hampshire
☎ 0703 282269

LOCAL FEATURES

Factory Visits

Eling Tide Mill
The only tide mill still producing wholemeal flour.
The Toll Bridge, Eling, Totton, nr Southampton
☎ 0703 869575

Falconry

New Forest Owl Sanctuary
Falconry displays, tours of aviaries, falconry lessons.
Crow Lane, Crow, Ringwood
☎ 0425 476487
Off the B3347

Food and Drink

Lymington Vineyard
Award winning wines produced here.
Wainsford Road, Pennington, Lymington
☎ 0590 672112
✕

EQUESTRIAN

Riding and Pony Trekking

Forest Park Riding Stable
Rhinefield Road, Brockenhurst
☎ 0590 23429

Wagon Rides

New Forest Wagons
Balmer Lawn Road, Brockenhurst
☎ 0590 23633

HEALTH

Leisure Centres

The Pyramids Resort Centre
Clarence Esplanade, Southsea, Portsmouth
☎ 0705 294444

Rapids of Romsey
Activity and leisure pools with fitness centre.
Southampton Road, Romsey
☎ 0794 830333

Beaulieu National Motor Museum

Gardens

Exbury Gardens
The de Rothschild family gardens; noted for rhododendrons, azaleas, camellias and magnolias.
Nr Southampton
☎ 0703 891203
3 miles from Beaulieu
P 🏠 ✕

HAMPSHIRE

WHAT TO DO AND SEE

Heritage

Rockbourne Roman Villa
Excavation of a large courtyard villa, over a 30-year period; a vast collection of interesting finds.
Rockbourne, nr Fordingbridge
☎ 07253 541

Historic Houses

Beaulieu
National Motor Museum, palace house and gardens, Abbey and exhibition; rides for the children on model cars.
Beaulieu
☎ 0590 612345
M3 and M27, easy access
P 🏠 ♿ ♿

Breamore House and Museums
Elizabethan Manor House in a tudor village.
Nr Fordingbridge
☎ 0725 22233
On the A338 between Salisbury and Bournemouth

Broadlands
Stately home of the late Lord Mountbatten; portraits, unique collections, riverside lawns and a Mountbatten exhibition.
Romsey
☎ 0794 516878
→A A31
P 🏠

Museums

New Forest Museum
Story of the New Forest, its traditions, wildlife and people.
High Street, Lyndhurst
☎ 0703 283914

The Sammy Miller Museum
Motor Cycle Museums; many unique cycles from 1900 onwards.
Gore Road, New Milton
☎ 0425 619696
🏠

Natural History

Dorset Heavy Horse Centre
Displays of horse-drawn farm machinery, working and show harness, pets corner; foals born every year.
Alderholt Road, nr Verwood
☎ 0202 824040
Off the B3081
P 🏠 ✕ ♿ ♿

Longdown Dairy Farm
A modern working farm that includes visitors.
Longdown, Ashurst, nr Southampton
☎ 0703 293326
→A A35
P 🏠 🚐 ♿ ♿

New Forest Butterfly Farm
Indoor tropical jungle, breeding butterflies and moths, insectarium with tarantulas, scorpions, praying mantis and other exotic creatures.
Longdown, Ashurst, nr Southampton
☎ 0703 292166
P 🏠 ♿ ♿

Parks

Paultons Park
Exotic wildlife; beautiful gardens; lake and working watermill; Kids Kingdom; minature railway; Land of Dinosaurs; Astroglide; Romany Village, museum and much more.
Ower, nr Romsey
☎ 0703 814442
A337/A31, 6 miles from Lyndhurst
P 🏠 ♿ ♿

Railways

Watercress Line
Steam locomotive rides.
Mid-Hants Railway, Alresford Station
☎ 0962 733810
Off the A31, 7 miles east of Winchester

OUTDOOR LEISURE/SPORTS

Cycling

The New Forest is ideal cycling country.
i Cycle routes and cycle hire information available from the Tourist Information Centre.

Fishing

There is excellent freshwater angling in the River Avon, a waterway renowned for its salmon and coarse fishing. Forest waters and ponds can be fished with the permission of the Forestry Commission. There is trout fishing at a lake close to Lyndhurst and sea fishing in the Solent.

Leominstead Trout Fishery
Emery Down, Lyndhurst
☎ 0703 282610

Sea Angling Trips
From Keyhaven
☎ 0590 642923

Walking

Many waymarked walks exist in the New Forest. Contact the Forestry Commission for details.
☎ 0703 283141

WATERSPORTS

Sailing

The Solent is a well known sailing area and both Lymington and Keyhaven are yachting harbours.

HAMPSHIRE/SUSSEX BORDERS

WHAT TO DO AND SEE

i St. Peter's Market, West Street, Chichester, West Sussex
☎ 0243 775888
i 1 Park Road South, Havant, Beachlands, Hampshire
☎ 0705 480024
i Sea Front, Hayling Island, Beachlands, Hampshire
☎ 0705 467111 summer only

AERIAL SPORTS

Ballooning

Golf Centres Balloons Ltd
Ballooning flights from a number of centres in the area.
Balloon Booking Clerk, Cray Valley Golf Club, Sandy Lane, St Paul's Cray, Orpington
☎ 0689 74388

Flying

Goodwood Flying School
Goodwood Airfield, nr. Chichester
☎ 0243 774656

Parachuting

Flying Tigers Skydiving Centre
Goodwood Airfield, nr Chichester
☎ 0243 780333

EQUESTRIAN

Riding and Pony Trekking

Escorted Rides
Lavant
☎ 0243 527035
☎ 0243 527431

HEALTH

Leisure Centres

Westgate
Wide range of activities: sports hall, swimming pool, creche, squash courts, bar and terrace, conditioning room, and a keep-fit programme.
Avenue de Chartres, Chichester
☎ 0243 785651

LOCAL FEATURES

Festivals and Fairs

June
Petworth Festival

July
Chichester Festivities

Food and Drink

Chilsdown Vineyard
13-acre vineyard and winery based in a unique Victorian station.
The Old Station House, Singleton, Chichester
☎ 0243 63398
➜A A286

Gardens

Apuldram Roses
Specialist rose nursery and mature rose garden.
Apuldram Lane, Dell Quay, Chichester
☎ 0243 785769

West Dean Gardens
35 acres of lawns, borders, specimen trees, old roses, a wild garden and pergola all set in a scenic downland valley.
West Dean, nr Chichester
☎ 0243 63303

Guided Tours

Mary Godby
Town walks, coach tours and visits, specialising in West Sussex.
Stable House, Amberley, Arundel
☎ 0798 831614

Heritage

Fishbourne Roman Palace and Museum
The remains of the north wing of a 1st century Roman palace.
Salthill Road, Fishbourne, Chichester
☎ 0243 785859
➜A A27

Historic Buildings

Chichester Cathedral
Beautiful cathedral in the heart of the city; the works of art range from Romanesque stone carvings to famous modern paitings, sculpture and tapestries.
The Royal Chantry, Cathedral Cloisters
☎ 0243 782595
➜A A27

Goodwood House
Treasure house of the Dukes of Richmond set in parkland with fine paintings including some Canalettos, fine furniture and Sevres porcelain.
☎ 0243 774107

HAMPSHIRE/SUSSEX BORDERS
WHAT TO DO AND SEE

Goodwood House

Pallant House
An authentically restored Queen Anne town house with an art gallery and garden.
9 North Pallant, Chichester
☎ 0243 774557

Stansted Park
A neo-Wren house with an ancient chapel, walled gardens and a theatre museum set in an enchanting forest with the longest beech avenue in the south of England. Cricket is played on summer Sundays.
Rowlands Castle
☎ 0705 412265
Off the B2148

Museums

Chichester District Museum
Displays of geology, archaeology, social history and special exhibitions.
29 Little London, Chichester
☎ 0243 784683

Tangmere Military Aviation Museum
Museum sited on an historic airfield.
Chichester
☎ 0243 775223

OUTDOOR LEISURE/SPORTS

Cycling
i The Tourist Information Centre publishes a useful leaflet entitled *Cycling Round West Sussex*.

Daughtry's (Cycle Hire)
Also supplies fishing tackle and information.
44 The Hornet, Chichester
☎ 0243 783858

Walking
i The Tourist Information Centres supply leaflets of walks in the area.

WATERSPORTS

Boat Hire

Chichester Harbour Water Tours
Peter Adams, 9 Cawley Road, Chichester
☎ 0243 786418

Canoeing

Chichester Canoe Club
Secretary, 7 Redmoor, Main Road, Birdham
☎ 0243 512144

Windsurfing

Hayling Windsurfing
Northney Marina, Hayling Island
☎ 0705 467334

Southern Leisure Centre
Windsurfing, water-skiing and equipment hire.
Vinnetrow Road, Chichester
☎ 0243 774678

Yacht Charter

Chichester Sailing Centre Inc
Cruising courses, holidays, dinghy sailing and windsurfing.
Chichester Marina
☎ 0243 512557

SUSSEX

WHAT TO DO AND SEE

Royal Pavilion

County: East Sussex
i Tourist Office, Marlborough House, 54 Old Steine, Brighton, East Sussex
☎ 0273 23755
i Tourist Office, King Alfred Leisure Centre, Kingsway, Hove, East Sussex
☎ 0273 720371

EQUESTRIAN

Riding and Pony Trekking

Brendon Riding School
Haresdean Farm, Pyecombe
☎ 07918 2158

Gatewood Farm
Robin Post Lane, Wilmington, Polegate
☎ 03212 3709

Three Greys Riding School
2 School Lane, Pyecombe
☎ 07918 3536

HEALTH

Leisure Centres

King Alfred Leisure Centre
Tropical leisure pool with beach, island and waterchute; sauna, sun beds, ten-pin bowling centre, table tennis, etc.
Kingsway, Hove
☎ 0273 734422

LOCAL FEATURES

Aquariums

Brighton Sea Life Centre
Dolphin shows, seals, sharks, marine, tropical and freshwater fish.
Marine Parade
☎ 0273 604234
→A A23/M23 (town centre)
✗

Festivals and Fairs

May
Brighton Festival

November
London–Brighton Veteran Car Rally

Food and Drink

Barkham Manor Vineyard
35 acre vineyard surrounding the manor house. Vinery gardens, Piltdown Manor memorial. Guided tours including tastings.
Piltdown, nr Uckfield
☎ 082572 2103
→A A272
P 🚌

Fun Parks

Pirates Deep
Indoor childrens adventure playground featuring ball crawls, slides, ropes, children's cocktail bar and video room.
Madeira Drive, Brighton
☎ 0273 674549
→A A23 (town centre)
✗

Gardens

Borde Hill Garden
Large garden and parkland.
Borde Hill, Haywards Heath
☎ 0444 450326
→A A272
P 🚌 ✗ ♿

Kidbrooke Park
Parkland laid out by Humphrey Repton.
Forest Row
☎ 034282 2275
B2110/A22
P ♿

SUSSEX

WHAT TO DO AND SEE

Sheffield Park Garden
Large 18th century garden laid out by Capability Brown, noted for its rare trees.
National Trust.
Danehill, nr Uckfield
☎ 0825 790655
P ✕ ♿

Historic Buildings

Alfriston Clergy House
Thatched, half-timbered 14th century building with an exhibition on Wealden house building and a cottage garden.
National Trust.
The Tye, Alfriston
☎ 0323 870001
Off the B2108

Firle Place
Tudor house with Georgian additions in downland park; notable for its art, ceramics and furniture.
Firle, nr Lewes
☎ 0273 858335
➜A A27
P 🚌 ✕

Glynde Place
16th century Sussex brick and flint house built around a courtyard; notable portrait collection.
Glynde, nr Lewes
☎ 079159 337
➜A A27
P 🚌 ✕ ♿

Lewes Castle
Shell keep of a Norman stronghold.
Lewes
☎ 0273 474379
➜A A277 (town centre)

Preston Manor
Georgian manor house with Edwardian interior and fine furnishings.
Preston Park, Brighton
☎ 0273 603005
➜A A23 (town centre)
P ✕ ♿

Royal Pavilion
Eastern style palace built by Holland and Nash; original and contemporary interiors; Chinese porcelain and a magnificent music room.
Old Steine, Brighton
☎ 0273 603005
➜A A23 (town centre)
🚌 ✕

Museums

Brighton Museum and Art Gallery
Fine collection of ceramics, art deco, art nouveau, archaeology and fine art.
Church Street, Brighton
☎ 0273 603005
➜A A23 (town centre)
✕

Hove Museum and Art Gallery
Paintings, pottery, porcelain and silver.
19 New Church Road, Hove
☎ 0273 779410
➜A A259 (town centre)
P ✕ 🚌 ✕ ♿

Natural History

Ashdown Forest Farm
Small farm with rare breeds of livestock and poultry; a spinning and weaving exhibition, thatching demonstrations, shearing and sheep dipping.
Wych Cross
☎ 082571 2040
➜A A22
P ✕

Bentley Wildfowl and Motor Museum
Private collection of over 1000 birds in parkland with lakes. Motor museum.
Bentley, nr Halland
☎ 082584 0573
➜A A26/A22
P 🚌 ✕ ♿

Railways

Lavender Line Steam Museum
Restored station buildings, vintage standard gauge steam engines.
Isfield Station, Isfield, nr Uckfield
☎ 082575 515
➜A A26
P 🚌 ✕

Bluebell Railway Living Museum
Five miles of standard gauge track with a large collection of steam locomotives. Victorian stations and a museum.
Sheffield Park Station, Sheffield Park, nr Uckfield
☎ 082572 2370
➜A A275
P 🚌 ✕ ♿

Theatres

Connaught Theatre
Union Place, Worthing ☎ 0903 35333

Theatre Royal
New Road, Brighton ☎ 0273 674357

Zoos

Drusilla's Zoo Park
New style zoo with generous enclosures. A farmyard, railway, adventure playground, butterfly house, pottery and gardens.
Alfriston
☎ 0323 870234
➜A A27
P 🚌 ✕ ♿

OUTDOOR LEISURE

Cycling

Harman Hire
31 Davigdor Road, Brighton
☎ 0273 26090

SUSSEX

WHAT TO DO AND SEE

Bicycle Hire
4 Temple Gardens, Brighton
☎ 0273 737979

Preston Cycling Track
Preston Park, Brighton

Fishing

The Brighton Angler
Aquarium Colonnade, 1 Madeira Drive
☎ 0273 671398

Jack Ball Fishing Tackle
171 Edward Street
☎ 0273 671083

The Tackle Box
Brighton Marina
☎ 0273 696477

Charter boats for sea fishing trips:

Blue Bird Speedboats
☎ 0323 765559
☎ 0323 29016

Brighton Marina Breakwaters
Brighton Marina
☎ 0273 693636

Golf

There are two municipal courses:

Hollingbury Park
Ditchling Road, Brighton
☎ 0273 500086

Waterhall Course
Devil's Dyke Road, Brighton
☎ 0273 508658

Private clubs include:

Brighton and Hove Golf Club
Dyke Road, Brighton
☎ 0273 556482

Dyke Golf Club
Dyke Road, Brighton
☎ 079156 296

East Brighton Golf Club
Roedean Road, Brighton
☎ 0273 604838

West Hove Golf Club
Oled Shoreham Road, Hove
☎ 0273 419738

Ice Skating

Sussex Ice Rink
Queen's Square, Brighton
☎ 0273 24677

Dry Slope Skiing

Stanley Deason Leisure Centre
Wilson Avenue, Brighton
☎ 0273 694281

Borowski Centre
New Road, Newhaven
☎ 0273 515402

Tennis

Numerous options exist for hire of courts.

Walking

Heaven Farm Country Tours and Museum
A prize-winning Nature Trail that crosses the Greenwich Meridian Line.
Furners Green, nr Uckfield
☎ 0825 790226
➔A A275

WATERSPORTS

Sailing

Brighton Marina
Brighton Marina has 1700 berths; bistros, bars, restaurants and speciality shopping. Yacht and fishing charter are available.
☎ 0273 693636
➔A A259

Dinghies and catamarans:

Sunsports
185 King's Road Arches, Brighton
☎ 0273 28584

Hove Lagoon
Kingsway, Hove
☎ 0273 430100

EAST SUSSEX

WHAT TO DO AND SEE

i De La Warr Pavilion, Marina, Bexhill-on-Sea, East Sussex
☎ 0424 212023

i 3 Cornfield Road, Eastbourne, East Sussex
☎ 0323 411400

EQUESTRIAN

Riding and Pony Trekking

Cophall Farm Stables
Eastbourne Road, Polegate
☎ 0323 483975

HEALTH

Leisure Centres

Eastbourne Sovereign Centre
Four fabulous pools, a giant water skelter, bubble pools, water fountains, children's adventure and soft play areas.
Royal Parade, Langney Point, Eastbourne
☎ 0323 412444

LOCAL FEATURES

Art Galleries

Towner Art Gallery
Permanent collection of 19th and 20th century British art and craft.
High Street, Old Town, Eastbourne
☎ 0323 411688

Food and Drink

Merrydown Vintage Cider Making
Horam Manor is the home of Merrydown who have been cider makers since Norman times.
Horam Road, Heathfield
☎ 04353 2254
Off the A267 north of Eastbourne

Gardens

Leonardslee Gardens
Extensive landscaped garden in a marvellous setting; wallabies and Sika deer inhabit the gardens.
Lower Beeding, nr Horsham
☎ 0403 891212
➤A A281/A279
P ✗

Sheffield Park Garden
Large 18th century garden designed by Capability Brown with lakes and rare trees. National Trust.
Danehill, nr Uckfield
☎ 0825 790655
P ✗ ♿

Historic Buildings

Bodiam Castle
Bodiam is a National Trust castle that was built in 1385 to block the Rother Valley from incursions by the French.
Bodiam
☎ 0580 830436
Off the A229
P ✗

Great Dixter House and Gardens
A fine timber-framed hall house built in 1460 and restored by Sir Edwin Lutyens with fine furniture and needlework; informal gardens with yew hedges and original farm buildings.
Northiam
☎ 0797 253160
➤A A28

Michelham Priory
Founded in 1229 for Augustinian Canons, the priory is surrounded by a moat and large gardens, it is approached through a magnificent gatehouse; a physic garden, working watermill, tudor barn, blacksmith and a rope museum.
Upper Dicker, Hailsham
☎ 0323 844224
Off the A22 and the A27
P

Museums

'How We Lived Then' Museum of Shops and Social History
Over 35,000 Victorian exhibits laid out in authentic shops.
Cornfield Terrace, Eastbourne
☎ 0323 37143

Local History Museum
The museum illustrates the history and development of the town from prehistory to the Edwardian era; it is on the lower floors of the Towner Art Gallery.
High Street, Old Town, Eastbourne
☎ 0323 411688

Wish Tower Invasion Museum
Housed in Martello Tower No 73, this museum concentrates on the defence of the south coast from Napoleonic times.
King Edward's Parade, Eastbourne
☎ 0323 410440

Natural History

Bentley Wildfowl and Motor Museum
Thousands of geese, ducks and swans; formal walled gardens, play areas for children, vintage cars and motorcycles.
Halland
☎ 0825 840573
Off the A22 and the A26, 7 miles north-east of Lewes, signposted
P

EAST SUSSEX

WHAT TO DO AND SEE

The Bluebell Railway

The Butterfly Centre
Tropical glasshouses with free flying butterflies.
Royal Parade, Eastbourne
☎ 0323 645522

Parks

Princes Park
Opposite the beach, a popular family park with a large boating lake, pedaloes and rowing boats for hire.
Royal Parade, Eastbourne

Railways

The Bluebell Railway
Steam and vintage trains operate between Sheffield Park and Horsted Keynes; a collection of 30 historic locomotives.
Off the A275 between Lewes and East Grinstead
☎ 082572 2370 timetable
☎ 082572 3777 enquiries

Kent and East Sussex Steam Railway
16 steam engines; rides.
Tenterden Town Station, Tenterden, Kent
☎ 05806 5155 enquiries

Zoos

Drusilla's Park
A notable small zoo; penguin bay, otter valley and owls world.
Off the A27 west of Eastbourne
☎ 0323 870234
P ✕

OUTDOOR LEISURE/SPORTS

Cycling

Cuckmere Carriage Co. Ltd.
Berwick
☎ 0323 870598

Fishing

Fishing is good in the Cuckmere River, Hampden Park, Lakelands Pond, Wallers Haven, Langney Haven and Pevensey Haven. Licences are available from local tackle shops.

Tony's Tackle Shop
211 Seaside, Eastbourne
☎ 0323 31388

Compleat Angler Shop
22 Pevensey Road, Eastbourne
☎ 0323 24740
☎ 0323 24700

Walking

i A guide to local walks is available from the Tourist Information Centres. It includes town walks and rambles on the South Downs Way.

WATERSPORTS

Boat Trips

Allchorn Brothers
Trips to Beachy Head Lighthouse and circular tours to Birling Gap and Seven Sisters.
Eastbourne
On the beach between the pier and the bandstand
☎ 0323 34701

EAST KENT

WHAT TO DO AND SEE

i Pierremont Hall, 67 High Street,
Broadstairs, Kent
☎ 0843 68399

i Fleur de Lis Heritage Centre,
13 Preston Street, Faversham, Kent
☎ 0795 534542

i Argyle Centre, Queen Street, Ramsgate,
Kent
☎ 0843 591086

i The Guildhall, Cattle Market
Sandwich, Kent
☎ 0304 613565 summer only

AERIAL SPORTS

Parascending

Seawise Leisure
Western Undercliff, Ramsgate
☎ 0843 294144

EQUESTRIAN

Riding and Pony Trekking

Manston Riding Stables
15 Alland Grange Lane, Manston,
Nr Ramsgate
☎ 0843 823622

Plum Pudding Equestrian Centre
Plum Pudding Island, Minnis Bay,
Birchington
☎ 0843 47142

HEALTH

Leisure Centres

Hartsdown Park Sports and Leisure Centre
Swimming pool, trampolining, volleyball,
tennis, table tennis, roller skating, netball,
keep fit, gymnastics, approach golf, football,
basketball, badminton and aerobics.
Margate
☎ 0843 226221

Tides
Tropical indoor seaside with wild water
slides, waves, poolside spa, sun-suite, health
and fitness studio.
Victoria Park, Park Avenue, Deal
☎ 0304 373399

LOCAL FEATURES

Festivals and Fairs

June
Broadstairs Dickens Festival

August
Broadstairs Folk Week

Historic Buildings

Canterbury Cathedral
Mother Church of the Anglican
Communion, founded in 597, it was the
scene of Becket's martyrdom.
☎ 0227 762862
Off the A2, Canterbury city centre

Dover Castle and Hellfire Corner
An imposing mediaeval fortress and
underground war tunnels
☎ 0304 201628
→A A258
P

117

EAST KENT

WHAT TO DO AND SEE

Museums

Dickens House Museum
Immortalised as Betsy Trotwood's house in *David Copperfield*; many of Dickens personal possessions are housed here.
2 Victoria Parade, Broadstairs
☎ 0843 62853
→A A255

Powell–Cotton Museum
Private collections from one man's lifetime travels through Asia and Africa housed in a beautiful Regency mansion set in parkland.
Quex Park, Birchington
☎ 0843 42168
→A B2048
P

Sarre Windmill
1820s wooden smock windmill, a traction engine in the yard drives a steam saw, milling machinery and a cider press. Bakery products are available.
Sarre
☎ 0843 47573
→A A28/A253
P

RAF Spitfire and Hurricane Memorial Building
A World War II Spitfire that saw active service and a Hurricane restored to top condition.
Manston
☎ 0843 823351

Natural History

Brambles English Wildlife
A large animal sanctuary set in natural woodlands; an adventure playground, farm animals and a nature trail.
Wealden Forest Park, Herne Common
☎ 0227 712379

Theme Parks

Dreamland White Knuckle Theme Park
The Marine Terrace, Margate
☎ 0843 227011

OUTDOOR LEISURE/SPORTS

Cycling

Ken's Bike Shop
26 Eaton Road, Margate
☎ 0843 221422

On Your Bike
20 Cutherbert Road, Westgate
☎ 0843 35577

Fishing

Coarse fishing
Freshwater fishing is popular in the River Stour, River Wansum, Stonar Lakes and in numerous dykes.

Sea fishing
The shoreline offers ample opportunity for the experienced and inexperienced angler; beaches, promenades, piers and rocks produce good catches. For bigger fish, charter boats are available from the harbour at Ramsgate.

Fisherman's Corner
Boat charter is available.
6 Kent Place, Ramsgate
☎ 0843 582174
☎ 0843 67655

Kingfisheries
Sea and freshwater bait and day tickets for Stonar Lake.
34 King Street, Margate
☎ 0843 223866

i A fishermans guide and tide tables are available from the Tourist Information Centres.

WATERSPORTS

Canoeing

Tidal Pool
Children's canoes are available for hire.
Main Sands, Margate

Thanet Canoe Club
Open to non-members.
Newgate Gap, Cliftonville
☎ 0843 225580

Jet Skiing

Water Sports International
Palm Bay, Cliftonville
☎ 0843 226079

Waterskiing and Windsurfing

Seawide Leisure
Waterskiing, windsurfing and wave riders.
Western Undercliff, Ramsgate and Main Sands, Margate
☎ 0843 294144

WEST KENT

WHAT TO DO AND SEE

i Monson House,
Monson Way,
Royal Tunbridge Wells
☎ 0892 515675

i Eastgate Cottage,
High Street,
Rochester
☎ 0634 843666

ADVENTURE

Multi-activity Centres

Bowles Outdoor Centre
Eridge Green,
Royal Tunbridge Wells
Multi-activity courses for up to one week, including adventure sports.
☎ 0892 665665

AERIAL SPORTS

Microlight Flying

Medway Microlight Club
Rochester
Contact Chris Draper.
☎ 0634 270780

EQUESTRIAN

Riding and Pony Trekking

Tollgate Stables
Monks Buildings, Northumberland Bottom,
Wrotham Road, Gravesend
Instruction in riding and jumping, livery and hacking, holiday courses.
☎ 0634 718521 (evenings)

HEALTH

Leisure Centres

Cascades Leisure Centre
Thong Lane,
Gravesend
☎ 0474 337471/2

The Swallows
Central Avenue,
Sittingbourne
Sports hall, squash courts, weights room, health suite, sauna, jacuzzi.
☎ 0795 420420

LOCAL FEATURES

Festivals and Fairs

May
Gravesham Riverside Fair

June
Rochester
Dickens Festival

July
Rochester
River Festival

August
Gravesend
Summer Regatta
Norman Rochester

December
Rochester
Dickensian Christmas

Food and Drink

Penshurst Place
Royal Tunbridge Wells
Originally a mediaeval manor house, developed over the centuries to a magnificent country house. Gardens, venture playground, toy museum.
☎ 0892 870307

Syndale Valley Vineyards
Newnham
White and red wines produced in a modern winery. Guided tours.
☎ 0795 89 711/693

Gardens

Camer Park
Gravesend
46 acres of landscaped gardens.

Cobham Hall
Gravesend
50 acres of grounds landscaped by Humphry Repton.

Owl House Gardens
Royal Tunbridge Wells; on the A21
Year-round floral displays, sunken water garden, woodlands.
☎ 0892 890230

Penshurst Place
North-west at Penshurst
Walled gardens and parkland with a Nature Trail.
☎ 0892 870307

Heritage

Bayham Abbey
Royal Tunbridge Wells
On the B2169
Remains of 13th century abbey beside the River Teise.
☎ 0892 890381

Eynsford Castle
Eynsford
11th century Norman castle ruins.
☎ English Heritage 0892 548166

119

WEST KENT

WHAT TO DO AND SEE

Historic Buildings

Hornes Palace Chapel
Appledore,
Royal Tunbridge Wells
Chapel erected in 1366 and consecrated in 1386.
☎ English Heritage 0892 548166
P 🚻 ♿ ✕ &

King Charles the Martyr
London Road,
Royal Turnbridge Wells
Fine plasterwork by Henry Doogood.
P 🚻 ♿ ✕ &

The Leather Bottle Inn
South-east at Cobham, Nr Gravesend
Timber-framed village pub which Dickens visited regularly.
P 🚻 ♿ ✕ &

Meopham Windmill
Meopham Green,
Gravesend
Early 19th century smock mill.
☎ 0474 813218
P 🚻 ♿ ✕ &

Milton Chantry
Fort Gardens,
Gravesend
14th century leper hospital chapel which became an inn during the 17th century.
☎ 0474 321520
P 🚻 ♿ ✕ &

New Tavern Fort
Fort Gardens
Gravesend
18th to 20th century fort, overlooking the Thames, with underground ammunition store and World War II exhibition.
Contact Tourist Information for details.
P 🚻 ♿ ✕ &

The Old Forge
Off the A226 at Chalk, Nr Gravesend
Weatherboarded and tiled building believed by many to be the original of Joe Gargery's forge in *Great Expectations*.
P 🚻 ♿ ✕ &

Musems

David Salomon's House
Broomhill Road, Southborough
19th century house containing memorabilia of the first Jewish Lord Mayor of London.
☎ 0892 515152
P 🚻 ♿ ✕ &

Dolphin Yard Sailing Barge Museum
Working barge dock.
☎ 0795 424132
P 🚻 ♿ ✕ &

Gravesham Museum
High Street
History and development of Gravesend over the last two centuries.
☎ 0474 323159
P 🚻 ♿ ✕ &

Old Court Hall Museum
High Street, Milton Regis
Timbered mid-15th century building with local history and archaeology.
☎ 0795 424341 Borough Council
P 🚻 ♿ ✕ &

The Dickens Centre
Eastgate House, High Street,
Rochester
16th century red-brick building with tableaux reconstructing scenes from Dickens' books, details of his life and other displays.
☎ 0634 844176
P 🚻 ♿ ✕ &

Tunbridge Wells Museum and Art Gallery
Local history, archaeology and woodwork, dolls and toys.
☎ 0892 526121 ext 3171 Borough Council
P 🚻 ♿ ✕ &

OUTDOOR LEISURE/SPORTS

Fishing

Coarse Fishing
Sittingbourne
For information and permits contact the National Rivers Authority.
☎ 0732 838858
☎ 0323 762691
☎ 0734 535000

Golf

Court Lodge Down
Neville Golf Club
Royal Tunbridge Wells
Day tickets available on site.
☎ 0892 527820

ESSEX

WHAT TO DO AND SEE

i County Hall
Market Road,
Chelmsford, Essex
☎ 0245 283400

ADVENTURE

Climbing

Terry Marsh Sports Centre
Eversley Park, Crest Avenue, Pitsea,
Basildon
☎ 0268 583076

AERIAL SPORTS

Microlight Flying

Micro-Air Flying Club
83a Mildmay Road,
Chelmsford
☎ 0245 490408

EQUESTRIAN

Riding

De Beauvoir Farm Livery Yard
Church Farm, Ramsden Heath
☎ 0268 710534/711302

Hill Farm
Pan Lane, East Hanningfield,
Chelmsford
Riding and jumping instruction.
☎ 0245 400115

Lillyputts Equestrian Centre
272 Wingletye Lane, Hornchurch,
Brentwood
Instruction in riding and jumping. BHS approved.
☎ 04024 53908

Park Lane Riding and Livery Stables
Park Lane, Ramsden Heath,
Billericay
☎ 0268 710145

Rayne Riding Centre
Fairy Hall Lane,
Braintree
General instruction, schooling for competition and livery.
☎ 0376 22231

Wethersfield Riding Stables
Hedingham Road, Wethersfield
☎ 0371 851089

HEALTH

Leisure Centres

Basildon Sports Centre
Nethermayne,
Basildon
☎ 0268 533166

Billericay Swimming Pool
Lake Meadow Recreation Ground
25-metre pool.
☎ 0277 657111

Brentwood Centre
Doddinghurst Road,
Brentwood
☎ 0277 229621

Gloucester Park Swimming Pool
Broadmane,
Basildon
33-metre pool, learner pool, fitness room.
☎ 0268 523588

The Markhams Chase Sports Centre
Markhams Chase, Lee Chapel North,
Basildon
☎ 0268 410126

Riverside Ice and Leisure Centre
Chelmsford
Sports hall, snooker hall, gym, leisure suite, pools, squash courts
and ice rink.
☎ 0245 492954

Wickford Swimming Pool
Market Avenue, Wickford,
Basildon
25-metre pool, solarium.
☎ 0268 765460

LOCAL FEATURES

Festivals and Fairs

May
Chelmsford Cathedral Festival
North Weald Fighter Meet at North Weald Airfield. Annual air
display of historic aircraft.
Brentwood
☎ 0737 764848

June
Chipping Ongar
Herb festival held at Greensted Church biannually.
☎ 0277 364694

Gardens

Hyde Hall Garden
On the A130 Chelmsford to Southend road
Garden and woodland.
☎ 0245 400256
P 🏠🚌✕ ♿

Saling Hall Garden
Great Saling, near Braintree
Water gardens and a walled garden dating from 1698; unusual trees.
P 🏠🚌✕ ♿

Heritage

Chelmsford Cathedral
Town centre
15th century perpendicular church, given cathedral status in 1914.
P 🏠🚌✕ ♿

ESSEX

WHAT TO DO AND SEE

Historic Buildings

All Saints Church
Brightlingsea
Perpendicular church with 94-foot tower.

Greensted Church
9th century church, the only surviving Saxon church with a nave wall built of logs.
☎ 0277 364694

Mountnessing Windmill
Mountnessing
Brentwood
19th century post mill in working order.
☎ 0277 215777

Museums

Barleylands Farm Museum
Wickford Road,
Billericay
Vintage farm machinery on a working farm.
☎ 0268 282090

Cater Museum
High Street,
Billericay
Victorian domestic settings and Fire Brigade history.
☎ 0277 622023

Heritage Centre
Town Hall, Market Square, Braintree
Town's development from Stone Age; engineering, textiles and photographs.
☎ 0376 552525 ext. 2332

National Motorboat Museum
Wat Tyler Country Park, Pitsea
Illustrated history of the motorboat over the last century.
☎ 0268 550077

Plotland Trail and Museum
Dunton,
Basildon
World War II lifestyles.
☎ 0268 419095

Natural History

Basildon Nature Trail
☎ 0268 419095

Norsey Wood Trail
Brentwood
Nature reserve.
☎ 0277 624553

Parks

Danbury Country Park
5 miles east of Chelmsford
39-acre country park with lakes, woodland, exotic shrubs and trees.
☎ 0245 412350

Marsh Farm Country Park
Chelmsford
Off the A130 at South Woodham Ferrers
Working farm centre (under cover), a nature reserve and an adventure playground.

Wat Tyler Country Park
Pitsea,
Basildon
Newly created, focus on conservation and natural history, two museums, craft workshops and marina.
☎ 0268 559833

Theatres

Towngate Theatre
Basildon
☎ 0268 532632

Zoos

Basildon Zoo
London Road, Vange
Animals and birds, children's zoo, café and picnic area.
☎ 0268 553985

OUTDOOR LEISURE/SPORTS

Caravanning and Camping

Kelvedon Hatch Camping and Caravanning Site
Just north of Bentley, on the A128 from Brentwood.
150 caravan and tent pitches (no singles).
☎ 0277 372153

Cycling

Routes designed by the Braintree District Council Community and Leisure Services Department, starting at Castle Hedingham youth hostel. For details contact Tourist Information.

Route 1
Castle Hedingham to Clare and the Belchamps

Route 2
Castle Hedingham to Halstead and the Colne Valley

Route 3
Castle Hedingham to Finchingfield

ESSEX

WHAT TO DO AND SEE

Fishing

Coarse Fishing
Fishing is free in many waters
For information and permits contact the National Rivers Authority.
☎ 0733 371811
☎ 0473 727712
☎ 0376 572091

Boreham
Contact the Chertsey Angling Club.
☎ 0932 564872

Cobblers Mead Lake
Corringham,
Basildon
☎ 0268 683946

South Weald Lakes
Weald Country Park, south-west of Brentwood

The Right Angle Tackle Shop
18 New Street,
Braintree
Tickets to fish on the rivers Blackwater and Pant.

Game Fishing
Hanningfield Reservoir is open to day ticket and season ticket holders. Details available from the Fishery Officer, Essex Water Company.
☎ 0268 710101

Golf

Basildon Golf Course
1 mile south of Basildon on the A176 at Kingswood
☎ 0268 533297

Chelmsford Golf Club
Widford Road, south of Chelmsford off the A12
☎ 0245 250555

Towerlands Golf Club
Panfield Road,
Braintree
☎ 0376 26802

Ice Skating

Riverside Ice and Leisure Centre
Victoria Road,
Chelmsford
☎ 0245 492954

Skiing

The Ski Centre
Brentwood Park, Warley Gap
☎ 0277 211994

Squash

Basildon Sports Centre
☎ 0268 533166

Brentwood Centre
☎ 0277 229621

Ongar Sports Centre
Chipping Ongar
☎ 0277 363969

Tennis

Clearview
Warley Hall Lane, Little Warley,
Brentwood
☎ 0277 811569

Walking

Backwarden Nature Reserve
Chelmsford
1½ mile Nature Trail through heath and woodland.
Contact the Essex Naturalists' Trust.

Crays Hill Circular Walk
Basildon
5-mile circular walk.
☎ 0268 419095

Hanningfield Reservoir
Chelmsford
Nature Trails and picnic area. The access does not permit coaches.
☎ 0268 710101

St Peter's Way
From Chipping Ongar to the Chapel of St. Peter's on the Wall at Bradwell.
☎ 0223 317404

WATERSPORTS

Sailing

Brightlingsea Sailing Club
Waterside
☎ 0206 303275

Colne Yacht Club
Brightlingsea
Yachting facilities available.
☎ 0206 303275

Waterskiing

Wat Tyler Water Ski Club
Wat Tyler Park, Pitsea,
Basildon
☎ 027 765 3479

Windsurfing

Brentwood Windsurfing
2 The Parade, Colchester Road
☎ 0268 711350

Harold Park
South Hanningfield Reservoir, Billericay
Tuition, board hire, shop and meals.
☎ 0708 856528

Stubbers Outdoor Pursuits Centre
Ockenden Road, Upminster, Brentwood
Tuition, residential courses, video coaching, showers, shop.
☎ 0402 224753

HERTFORDSHIRE

WHAT TO DO AND SEE

i County Library, Kings Road, Berkhamsted, Hertfordshire
☎ 0442 877638

EQUESTRIAN

Riding and Pony Trekking

Ashridge Farm Equestrian Centre
Ringshall, Little Gaddesden
☎ 0442 843443

Whippendell Riding School and Livery
Chipperfield Road, Kings Langley
☎ 0923 262396

HEALTH

Health Farms

Champneys
One of the oldest established health farms; set in a country estate.
Wigginton, Tring
☎ 042 873155

LOCAL FEATURES

Historic Buildings

Ashridge Estate
A 4000-acre estate which includes Ashridge Park, Aldury and Berkhamsted Commons, Pitstone Windmill, woodlands, heathlands and downlands rich in wildlife and fauna; there are superb views from Ivinghoe Beacon and the Bridgewater Monument.
Nr Berkhamsted
☎ 044 285227
Off the B4506, 3 miles north of the A41

Cliveden
On cliffs 200 feet above the Thames, it was once the home of Nancy, Lady Astor, now it is a hotel with gardens and woodlands, including a magnificent parterre, water garden and fine views.
Maidenhead, Berks
☎ 0628 605069
Off the B476, 2 miles north of Taplow

Hughenden Manor
Home of Benjamin Disraeli from 1847 until he died in 1881; many of his pictures and books are on display.
Nr High Wycombe
☎ 0494 32580
Off the A4128, north of High Wycombe

West Wycombe Park
Fine Palladian mansion built in the mid 18th century and set in a landscaped park which contains a swan-shaped lake and statuary.
Nr High Wycombe
☎ 0494 24411
South of the A40, nr West Wycombe

Museums

Zoological Museum
Nearly every kind of large mammal and countless different birds, reptiles, fish, insects plus a large selection of extinct animals are represented.
Akeman Street, Tring
☎ 044 282 4181
A41

Natural History

Chalfont Shire Horse Centre
Model farm, blacksmith shop, pets corner, vintage lorries and daily demonstrations.
Gorlands Lane, Chalfont St Giles
☎ 02407 2304
Off the M25, jct 17

Parks

Gadebridge Park
Over 300 acres of open parkland with nature trails, a paddling pool, bowls and golf.
Hemel Hempstead

Zoos

Whipsnade Wild Animal Park
Set in 600 acres of parkland, you can walk or drive around the wild animals at Whipsnade.
Dunstable
☎ 0582 872171
Off the M1, jct 9, signposted

OUTDOOR LEISURE/SPORTS

Birdwatching and Wildlife

Tring Reservoirs
A haven for bird and wildlife.
On the B489 north of Tring

Fishing

Coarse fishing
Excellent for trout, carp, tench, bream, roach, perch, pike and rudd.

National Rivers Authority
Public Relations Dept.
☎ 0734 593777

WATERSPORTS

Boat Hire

Bridgewater Boats
Castle Wharf, Berkhamsted
☎ 0442 863615

Cruises

Cruise into the Chilterns
Grebe Canal Cruises, Pitstone Wharf, Pitstone, nr Leighton Buzzard
☎ 0296 661920
☎ 0628 472500 evenings
Off the B488

GLOUCESTERSHIRE

WHAT TO DO AND SEE

i St. Michael's Tower, The Cross, Gloucester, Gloucestershire
☎ 0452 421188
i The Museum, 64 Barton Street, Tewkesbury, Gloucestershire
☎ 0684 295027

AERIAL SPORTS

Ballooning

Ballooning in the Cotswolds
36 Cheltenham Road, Rendcomb, nr Cirencester
☎ 028583 515

Jon Langley & Co.
Stroud
☎ 0453 825447

EQUESTRIAN

Riding and Pony Trekking

Badgworth Riding Centre
Cold Pool Lane, Up Hatherley, Cheltenham
☎ 0452 713818

HEALTH

Leisure Centres

Gloucester Leisure Centre
Bruton Way, Gloucester
☎ 0452 306498

LOCAL FEATURES

Art

Nature in Art
The International Centre for Wildlife Art is located in a Georgian mansion which houses a unique collection of wildlife painting; outside sculptures and a nature garden. Easels for hire.
Wallsworth Hall, Sandhurst, nr Gloucester
☎ 0452 731422
→A A38
P 🚌 ✕ ♿

Falconry

Birds of Prey Trust and Falconry Centre
Trained hawks, falcons, eagles and aviaries.
Newent
☎ 0531 820286
Off the B4215
P ✕

Gardens

Westbury Court Garden
Formal Dutch water garden.
Westbury-on-Severn
☎ 045276 461
Off the A48, 9 miles south-west of Gloucester
🚌 ♿ ♿

GLOUCESTERSHIRE

WHAT TO DO AND SEE

Historic Buildings

Berkeley Castle
A perfectly preserved castle over 800 years old; the scene of the murder of Edward II; ornamental gardens.
Berkeley, Gloucester
☎ 0453 810332
→A A38
P 🚐 ✗

Gloucester Docks
A collection of beautifully restored Victorian warehouses; attractions include the Waterways Museum, the Robert Opie Collection and an antique centre.
Southgate Street, Gloucester
→A A38

Sudeley Castle
The home and burial place of Katherine Parr, last wife of Henry VIII; art collection, craft centre, gardens, falconry displays, open-air theatre (late June) and adventure playground.
Winchcombe
☎ 0242 602308
On the A46, 6 miles north of Cheltenham
P ✗

Tewkesbury Abbey
Superb Norman abbey with 14th century vaulting and windows; a former Benedictine monastery, it has the tallest Norman towers in England and also the largest surviving Norman tower.
Church Street, Tewkesbury
☎ 0684 850959
→A A38
P 🚐 ♿

Museums

Cheltenham Museum and Art Gallery
Fine Dutch paintings, collections of ceramics and porcelain from China and the Far East, and a section devoted to Edward Wilson, who perished with Captain Scott on the ill-fated Antarctic Expedition of 1910.
Clarence Street, Cheltenham
☎ 0242 237431
→A A40
✗ ♿

Cotswold Countryside Collection
Collection of agricultural history housed in former house of correction.
Fosse Way, Northleach
☎ 0451 60715
Jct of the A40 and the Fosse Way, A429
P ✗ ♿

Natural History

Newent Butterfly and Natural World Centre
Tropical butterflies, snakes, insects and a pet animal zoo.
Birches Lane, Newent
☎ 0531 821800
Off the B4215

Zoos

Cotswold Farm Park
A collection of rare breeds of British farm animals; pets corner and picnic areas set high on the Cotswold Hills.
Guiting Power
☎ 0451 850307
Off the A46 north of Cheltenham
P 🚐 ✗ ♿

Cotswold Wildlife Park
200 acres of lawns and gardens, the animals range from the white rhino to reptiles; picnic areas and an adventure playground.
Burford outskirts
☎ 099382 3006

OUTDOOR LEISURE/SPORTS

Cycling

Crabtrees
50 Winchcombe Street, Cheltenham
☎ 0242 515291

Fishing

Coarse fishing
On the Gloucester and Sharpness Canal, the Rivers Severn and Avon; licenses and permits from Gloucester Angling Centre (see below).

Game fishing
On the Rivers Wye and Monnow and on stillwater lakes in the Cotswold Area. Salmon fishing on the Rivers Wye and Severn.

Allsports
126 Eastgate Street, Gloucester
☎ 0452 22756

Gloucester Angling Centre
45 Bristol Road, Gloucester
☎ 0452 20074

Skiing

Gloucester Ski Centre
2 slopes for beginners and accomplished enthusiasts.
Robinswood Hill, Gloucester
☎ 0452 414300
P ✗

WATERSPORTS

Boat Trips

Gloucester Docks
On the canal, from the quay by the Waterways Museum.

WEST MIDLANDS

WHAT TO DO AND SEE

i 2 City Arcade, Birmingham, West Midlands
☎ 021 643 2514
i Bayley Lane, Coventry, West Midlands
☎ 0203 832303
☎ 0564 794609

Sandwell Valley Riding Centre
Wigmore Farm, Wigmore Lane, West Bromwich
☎ 021 588 2103

Umberslade Riding School
Blunts Green Farm, Blunts Green, nr Henley-in-Arden
☎ 05642 4609

HEALTH

Health Clubs

Albany Hotel Club
Smallbrook Queensway, Birmingham
☎ 021 643 8171

LOCAL FEATURES

Art Galleries

Birmingham Museum and Art Gallery
A selection of British and European paintings and sculptures from the 14th to 20th century; noted Pre-Raphaelite collection.
Chamberlain Square, Birmingham
☎ 021 235 2834
City centre

Ikon Gallery
Regular exhibitions of contemporary art, sculpture and photography.
58–72 Bright Street, Birmingham
☎ 021 643 0708

Herbert Art Gallery and Museum
Frederick Poke Collection of English 18th century furniture and silver; Sutherland's sketches of Coventry tapestry and natural history section.
Jordan Well, Coventry
☎ 0203 832381

Coventry Cathedral

ADVENTURE

Multi-activity Centres

The Ackers Trust
Climbing and abseiling, mountain biking, canoeing and kayaking, skiing and development training on a large urban site.
Golden Hillock Road, Small Heath, Birmingham
☎ 021 771 4448

EQUESTRIAN

Riding and Pony Trekking

Bournevale Riding Stables
Little Hardwick Road, Streetley
☎ 021 353 7174

Arts and Crafts

Jewellery Quarter
Birmingham jewellery quarter and St. Paul's Square once housed many of Birmingham's silver and goldsmiths. It is now a conservation area with many workshops and jewellery retailers.

Festivals and Fairs

June
The Edgbaston Cup, Priory Tennis Club
The Ryder Cup, The Belfry Golf Club
Royal International Horse Show, National Exhibition Centre

August
Super Prix Road Race, Birmingham City Centre, August Bank Holiday

WEST MIDLANDS

WHAT TO DO AND SEE

Gardens

Birmingham Botanical Gardens and Glasshouses
15 acres of gardens in central Birmingham with glasshouses containing many rare plants; exotic birds and waterfowl, a children's adventure playground and bands play on Sunday afternoons in the summer.
Westbourne Road, Edgbaston, Birmingham
☎ 021 4541860

Guided Tours

Middle of England Guided Tours and Travel
Walking and coach tours in Birmingham and throughout the region.
14 Sandhurst House, Icknield Street, Kings Norton, Birmingham
☎ 021 459 9290

Historic Buildings

Aston Hall
A fine Jacobean house noted for its grand balustraded staircase and panelled Long Gallery.
Trinity Road, Aston, Birmingham
☎ 021 327 0062
2½ miles from the city centre

Blakesley Hall
A timber-framed yeoman's farmhouse built around 1575 and carefully refurbished.
Blakesley Hall, Yardley, Birmingham
☎ 021 783 2193
3 miles from the city centre

Coventry Cathedral
The new cathedral, designed by Sir Basil Spence and opened in 1962, stands alongside the 14th century ruins. The interior houses outstanding examples of the finest works of modern art.
City Centre, Coventry
☎ 0203 224323
P &

Sarehole Mill
An 18th century water-powered mill in working order, the setting for J. R. Tolkien's *The Hobbit*.
Cole Bank Road, Hall Green, Birmingham
☎ 021 777 6612

Museums

Birmingham Museum of Science & Industry
All aspects of science, engineering and industry, including transport; world's oldest working steam engine.
Newhall Street, Birmingham
☎ 021 236 1022

Birmingham Railway Museum
12 steam locomotives.
670 Warwick Road, Tyseley, Birmingham
☎ 021 707 4696

National Motorcycle Museum
British-built motorcycles spanning the period 1898 to 1980; over 600 cycles on display.
Coventry Road, Bickenhill, Birmingham
☎ 021 755 3311

Music, Dance and Drama

Birmingham International Arena
A major venue attracting star performers from the music world and accommodating audiences of 3000 to 12,000. National Exhibition Centre, Birmingham
☎ 021 780 4133

City of Birmingham Symphony Orchestra
City centre, Birmingham
☎ 021 236 1555

Infoteline
Telephone information service to help you book tickets.
☎ 0839 333999

OUTDOOR LEISURE/SPORTS

Ice Skating

Solihull Ice Rink
Hobs Moat Road, Solihull
☎ 021 742 5561

WATERSPORTS

The Birmingham area has a notable canal system, ideal for cruising in narrow boats, canal walks and fishing.

Boat Hire

Brummagem Boats
Holiday hire fleet of 25 narrow boats; passenger trips and a restaurant boat.
Sherborne Street Wharf, Sherborne Street, Birmingham
☎ 021 455 6163

STAFFORDSHIRE/DERBYSHIRE

WHAT TO DO AND SEE

i Glebe Street, Stoke-on-Trent, Staffordshire
☎ 0782 411222

Hang Gliding

Peak School of Hang Gliding
2-day taster courses available.
The Elms, Wetton, nr Ashbourne
☎ 0335 27257

EQUESTRIAN

Riding and Pony Trekking

Northfield Farm Riding and Trekking Centre
Northfield Farm Riding and Trekking Centre
Northfield Farm, Flash, nr Buxton
☎ 0298 22543
A53, 5 miles south of Buxton

HEALTH

Spas

Buxton Swimming Pool
Swim in Buxton's natural spa water; solarium, indoor bowls and more.
Pavilion Gardens
☎ 0298 26548

ADVENTURE

Caving and Rock Climbing

First Ascent
Courses in 'Cautious Caving' and 'Reassuring Rock Climbing'.
Far Cottage, Church Street, Longnor, nr Buxton
☎ 0298 83545

Multi-activity Centres

High Ash Farm Field Studies Centre
Longnor, nr Buxton
☎ 0298 25727

Moorside Activity Centre
Hollingsclough, Longnor, nr Buxton
☎ 0298 83406

White Hall
Residential centre for open country pursuits.
Long Hill, Buxton
☎ 0298 23260
Off the A5004, 3 miles north of Buxton

AERIAL SPORTS

Gliding

Derbyshire and Lancashire Gliding Club
Camphill, Great Hucklow, nr Tideswell, Buxton
☎ 0298 871270

LOCAL FEATURES

Arts and Crafts

Craft Centre
Old Stables Courtyard, Caudwell's Mill, Rowsley
☎ 0629 733185
Off the A6, nr Bakewell

Rooke's Pottery
Original terracotta pots in production.
Hartington, nr Buxton
☎ 0298 84650
Nr the village centre

Gardens

Pavilion Gardens
23 acres of gardens and woodland walks; a pavilion, erected in 1871 to a design by Milner; a beautiful conservatory, opera house, concert hall, children's play area, miniature railway, putting and restaurant.
☎ 0298 23114

Guided Tours

Blue Badge Guides
Qualified tourist guides offer Guided Walks around Buxton and Castleton as well as organising full Peak District tours.
i Further information is available from the Tourist Information Centre.
☎ 0298 25106

129

STAFFORDSHIRE/DERBYSHIRE

WHAT TO DO AND SEE

Historic Buildings

Chatsworth
The 'Palace of the Peak' with a fine collection of paintings, drawings and books; elaborate waterworks in the gardens.
Bakewell
☎ 0246 582204
On the A623, 4 miles east of Bakewell
P 🏛 ✗

Haddon Hall
A fine mediaeval House, seat of the Duke of Rutland, set in wooded hills overlooking the River Wye.
Bakewell
☎ 0629 812855
On the A6, 2 miles south of Bakewell
P 🏛 ✗

Hardwick Hall
Elizabethan home of Bess of Hardwick; notable needlework, tapestries and furniture.
Nr Chesterfield
☎ 0246 850430
On the M1, 2 miles south-east of jct 29
P 🏛 ✗

Museums

Buxton Micrarium
Special push-button projection microscopes to see the minutiae of the natural world.
The Crescent, Buxton
☎ 0298 78662
🏛 ♿

Buxton Museum and Art Gallery
'Wonders of the Peak' exhibition, displays of geology, discoveries from caves, prehistoric and Roman remains, monthly exhibitions of paintings, prints and photographs.
Terrace Road, Buxton
☎ 0298 24658
🏛

Glossop Heritage Centre
Authentic Victorian kitchen, changing exhibitions, art gallery showing local artists' work and a craft area.
Henry Street, Glossop
☎ 0457 869176
🏛

Natural History

Chestnut Centre Conservation Park, Otter Haven and Owl Sanctuary
Castleton Road, Chapel-en-le-Frith
☎ 0298 814099
Off the A625
🏛

OUTDOOR LEISURE/SPORTS

Cycling

Peak Cycle Hire
Cycling from seven centres located in and around the Peak National Park. Explore beautiful and varied countryside along disused railway lines and quiet country lanes; suitable for all ages.

Peak National Park
Parsley Hay Cycle Hire, Buxton
☎ 0298 84493

Fishing

Waters in the National Park fall mainly within the Severn Trent Water Authority, Abelson House, 2297 Coventry Road, Sheldon, Birmingham.

Chatsworth Estate
Fly fishing on stretches of the River Derwent and Wye. Permits from the Estate office.
Nr Bakewell
☎ 0246 582204

Errwood Reservoir
Leased to Errwood Fly Fishing Club, day tickets available.
Goyt Valley, nr Buxton
☎ 0663 732212

Lightwood Reservoir
Fly fishing only. Permits from water bailiff.
Buxton
☎ 0298 23710

Stanley Moor Reservoir
Fly fishing only, permits from Peak Pets.
Axe Edge, nr Buxton

Peak Pets
Fairfield Road, Buxton
☎ 0298 71370

Walking

First Ascent
Easy walking holidays.
Far Cottage, Church Street, Longnor
☎ 0298 83545

Wanderlust
Walking and sightseeing holidays in the Peak District.
4 Boswell Court, Ashbourne
☎ 0335 46594

BEDFORDSHIRE/CAMBRIDGESHIRE

WHAT TO DO AND SEE

i Wheeler Street, Cambridge, Cambridgeshire
☎ 0223 322640

EQUESTRIAN

The National Stud
Booking is essential for a tour of the stud.
☎ 0638 663464
Nr Newmarket July Race Course at the jct of the A1303 and the A1304

Riding
Sawston Riding School
Common Lane Farm, Common Lane, Sawston
☎ 0223 835198
6 miles south-east of Cambridge

LOCAL FEATURES

Gardens
The Swiss Garden
Romantic garden, 19th century, many original buildings and ironwork, adjacent to the Shuttleworth aircraft collection
Old Warden, nr Biggleswade
☎ 0234 63222
→A A1

Historic Buildings
Anglesey Abbey
A 13th century Augustinian Priory; a private house after 1591; 100 acres of world famous gardens; outstanding collection of European paintings, sculpture and objets d'art. National Trust. Lode Water Mill nearby is included in the price.
Lode
☎ 0223 811200
→A A1134

Cambridge Colleges
The colleges are private places where people live and work, but visitors are welcome to walk through the courts and visit the chapels and in some cases the halls and libraries.

Hinchingbrooke House
The ancestral home of the Cromwells and Earls of Sandwich.
Huntingdon
☎ 0480 51121
On the A604, ½ mile west of Huntingdon

Houghton Mill
The oldest remaining watermill on the Ouse, 17th century, a massive timbered structure with 19th century machinery. National Trust.
Mill House, Mill Street, Houghton
☎ 0480 301494
Off the A1132, 3 miles from Huntingdon

Wimpole Hall, Park and Home Farm
Imposing house, extravagant decoration, extensive gardens, walks, adventure woodland, home farm and restored Victorian stable block with working Suffolk Punches, children's corner. National Trust.
Arrington, nr Royston
☎ 0223 207257
Off the A603

Museums in Cambridge
Fitzwilliam Museum
Outstanding collection of paintings, antiquities, ceramics and armour.
Trumpington Street, Cambridge
☎ 0223 332900

BEDFORDSHIRE/CAMBRIDGESHIRE

WHAT TO DO AND SEE

Scott Polar Research Institute
Museum of polar life and exploration.
Lensfield Road, Cambridge
☎ 0223 337733

Sedgwick Museum
Extensive collection of geological specimens.
Downing Street, Cambridge
☎ 0223 333400

Museum of Zoology
Birds, insects, mammals and sea animals, stuffed and preserved.
Sidgwick Avenue, Cambridge
☎ 0223 336650

University Museum of Archaeology and Anthropology
Shrunken heads; totem poles; native dress; local finds.
Downing Street, Cambridge
☎ 0223 337733

Natural History
Wicken Fen
600 acres of wetland reserve, a remnant of the Great Fens, rich in plant, insect and bird life, nature trail, bird hides and exhibitions. National Trust.
Lode Lane, Wicken, Ely
☎ 0353 720274
A1123

Zoos
Linton Zoo
Beautiful gardens and wildlife in 10 acres of countryside.
Hadstock Road, Linton
☎ 0223 891308
Off the A604

Fishing
Information and licenses from:
Anglian Water
☎ 0223 61561

Grafham Water Reservoir
Trout fishing.
5 miles south-west of Huntingdon
☎ 0780 86 321

Thornton & Son
46 Burleigh Street, Cambridge
☎ 0223 358709

Skiing
Bassingbourn Ski Club
Hitchin
☎ 0462 34107

Walking
Devil's Dyke Walk
Early Saxon ditch embankment between Reach and Stetchworth built as a defensive fortification. Leaflet from Cambridgeshire Wildlife Trust.
☎ 0223 880788

Gog Magog Hills
Woods, grassland and iron-age fort at Wandlebury.
A1307

Icknield Way Long Distance Footpath
Route of the oldest road in Britain along the chalk spine of Southern England. Walkers guide is available from the Icknield Way Association.
☎ 0279 505602

Ouse Valley Long Distance Footpath
Bluntisham along the River Great Ouse to Eaton Socon. Leaflets produced by Huntingdonshire District Council.
☎ 0480 561561

Wicken Walks
2 interlinked waymarked walks through the Fenlands. Leaflet from Cambridgeshire County Council Rural Management Division.
☎ 0223 317404

OUTDOOR LEISURE/SPORTS

Birdwatching
Little Paxton
Gravel pit lakes, migratory birds and walks.
Diddington
A1

Cycling
Armada Cycles
47 Suez Road, Cambridge
☎ 0223 210421

I S Munro
Cambridge Street, Godmanchester
☎ 0480 452341

WATERSPORTS

Punting
Scudamore's
Granta Place, Cambridge
☎ 0223 359750

Windsurfing and Sailing
Grafham Water Reservoir
Grafham Water Sailing Club, West Perry, Huntingdon
☎ 0480 810478

Mepal Outdoor Centre
Sailing, playpark, canoeing, windsurfing.
Chatteris Road, Ely
☎ 0354 692251

SUFFOLK

WHAT TO DO AND SEE

i The Cinema, High Street, Aldeburgh, Suffolk
☎ 0728 453637 summer only
i Town Hall, Princes Street, Ipswich, Suffolk
☎ 0473 258070

AERIAL SPORTS

Parachuting

Ipswich Parachute Centre
Ipswich Airport, Nacton Road
☎ 0473 710044

EQUESTRIAN

Riding and Pony Trekking

Bentley Riding Centre
Bentley, Ipswich
☎ 0473 311715
→A A12

Newton Hall Equitation Centre
Swilland, nr Ipswich
☎ 0473 785616

HEALTH

Leisure Centres

Crown Pools
3-pool complex with a wave machine, waterfall, fountains, skydiver shute, sauna and solarium.
Town centre, Ipswich
☎ 0473 219231
✗

LOCAL FEATURES

Architecture

Leiston Abbey
14th century Abbey, remains include transepts of church and range of cloisters.
Nr Saxmundham
☎ 0728 455532

Art Galleries

Wolsey Art Gallery
Collection of works by Thomas Gainsborough and John Constable; fine art collection by Suffolk artists.
Christchurch Park

Arts and Crafts

Snape Maltings
On the River Alde, craft shop, garden, wholefood.
Snape, nr Saxmundham

Aldringham Craft Market
Pottery, wood, leather, glass, jewellery, sculpture and toys.
Nr Leiston

Festivals and Fairs

June
Aldeburgh Festival

August
Snape Maltings Proms

Gardens

Blakenham Woodland Garden
5-acre bluebell wood, many rare trees and shrubs.
Little Blakenham, Ipswich
☎ 0473 830344
4 miles north-west of Ipswich
P

Helmingham Hall Gardens
House; moat with drawbridges that are raised each night; large park with herds of deer and Highland cattle; gardens with renowned herbaceous borders.
Helmington, Stowmarket
☎ 0473 890363
Off the B1077
P

Historic Buildings

Framlingham Castle
Massive walls, 13 towers built by the second Earl of Norfolk.
Framlingham
☎ 072872 3330
Off the B1116
P

Orford Castle
Built by Henry II on the Suffolk coast in 1173, an important royal residence for over 100 years.
Orford
☎ 03944 50472
Off the B1084
P

Music, Dance and Drama

Snape Maltings
Old maltings now a world famous concert hall.
Snape
☎ 0728 452935
→A A12
P

Parks

Easton Farm Park
Victorian farm setting for many animals, rare breeds and Suffolk horses.
Easton, nr Wickham Market
☎ 0728 746475
→A A12
P

SUFFOLK

WHAT TO DO AND SEE

OUTDOOR LEISURE/SPORTS

Cycling

The Bicycle Doctor
18 Bartholomew Street, Ipswich
☎ 0473 259853

Fishing

Fishing on the Gipping and Orwell Rivers, and the Claydon and Barham Pits is controlled by:

Gipping Angling Preservation Society
19 Clover Close, Ipswich
☎ 0473 602828

Skiing

Suffolk Ski Slope
Bourne Hill
☎ 0473 602347

WATERSPORTS

Boat Trips

Orwell and Harwich Navigation Co Ltd
On the River Stour and Orwell
☎ 0255 502004

Lady Moira/Lady Florence
From Snape Maltings and Orford on the River Alde
☎ 0728 88303
☎ 0728 88305

Waldringfield Boat Yard
On the River Deben
☎ 0473 36260

Yacht Cruising

The Watersports Centre
A yacht cruising school; dinghy school; windsurfing, canoeing, adventure and instructional holidays or yacht and motor cruiser hire for continental holidays. Oysterworld, Wherry Quay Marina town
☎ 0473 230109

Sailing Holidays
Aboard the 90ft gaff ketch *Marjie*.
Ipswich
☎ 0379 898873

NORFOLK

WHAT TO DO AND SEE

i The Green, Hunstanton, Norfolk
☎ 0485 532610
i Station Approach, Sheringham, Norfolk
☎ 0623 824329 summer only

ADVENTURE

Climbing

University of East Anglia Sports Centre
University Plain, Norwich
☎ 0603 592399

Shooting

Ashill Clay Pigeon Club
Cutbush Farm, Ashill,
Thetford
☎ 0760 721771

Pentney Abbey SC Ground
King's Lynn
Off the A47 at Pentney Abbey
☎ 0760 337300

AERIAL SPORTS

Ballooning

Anglia Balloons
Peacock Lodge, Marlingfield, Norwich
Ballooning holidays.
☎ 0603 880819
☎ 0379 898079

Flying

Norwich School of Flying
Norwich Airport
☎ 0603 403107

Gliding

Norfolk Gliding Club
Tibenham Airfield, Long Stratton, Thetford
☎ 037 977 207
☎ 0359 31548

EQUESTRIAN

Riding

Grange Farm Riding School
Repps Road, Martham, Great Yarmouth
Instruction in riding and jumping.
☎ 0493 740245

Reeves Hall
10 miles from Diss off the A143 at Hepworth, Diss
Residential instructional holidays. BHS approved.
☎ 0359 50217

Runcton Hall Stud
Church Farm, North Runcton, King's Lynn
Instruction in riding and jumping.
☎ 0553 840676

Stanbrook Riding Centre
Paddock Farm, Lower Road, Holme Hale, Thetford
Instruction in riding and jumping. Small groups welcome. Breaking and schooling of ponies.
☎ 0760 22125

HEALTH

Leisure Centres

Diss Swimming Pool
Victoria Road
25-metre pool, learner pool; weight training and fitness room.
☎ 0379 652754

Great Yarmouth Marina Leisure Centre
Marine Parade
Pool with tropical beach, sports hall, table tennis, pool, snooker, squash, sauna and solarium, gym, indoor bowls, restaurants, bars and children's play area.
☎ 0493 851521

LOCAL FEATURES

Aquariums

Waveney Fish Farm
Park Road
Tropical and cold water aquarium. Water gardens, ornamental fish.
☎ 0379 642697

Art Galleries

Great Yarmouth Museums Exhibition Galleries
Centre Library
Paintings, arts and crafts, displays from local collections.
☎ 0493 858900

Norwich Gallery
Norfolk Institute of Art and Design, St. George Street
Exhibitions of contemporary art.
☎ 0603 610561

Sainsbury Centre for Visual Arts
University of East Anglia, Norwich
Art, sculpture and antiquities from around the world. Collection includes works by Francis Bacon and Henry Moore.
☎ 0603 56060

Arts and Crafts

The Art Gallery
The Guildhall, Thetford
Exhibitions of local artists.
☎ 0842 766599

The Dolls' House
7 Bagleys Court, Pottergate, Norwich
Handmade dolls' houses, kits and accessories.
☎ 0603 610807

NORFOLK

WHAT TO DO AND SEE

Taverham Craft Centre
Fir Covert Road, Taverham, Norwich
Purpose-built centre for many local crafts; manufacture and sales.
☎ 0603 860522

Festivals and Fairs
Easter
Craft and Art Fair at the King's Lynn Centre for the Arts

July
Festival of Music and the Arts at the King's Lynn Centre for the Arts
Norwich Union Carriage Driving Trials at Sandringham House, Sandringham
Sandringham Flower Show at Sandringham House, Sandringham

Gardens
Bressingham Gardens
2 miles west of Diss on the A1066
Famous gardens.
☎ 037 988 382

Cougham Hall Herb Garden
7 miles east of King's Lynn
☎ 0485 600250

Rainthorpe Hall Gardens
8 miles south of Norwich on the A140 at Tasburgh, Norwich
Large gardens with specialist trees.
☎ 0508 470191

Wellbank's Orchid World
West of King's Lynn on the A17 at Terrington St Clement

Heritage
Burgh Castle
Great Yarmouth
Remains of Roman fort overlooking River Waveney.

Castle Acre Priory
Cluniac priory founded by William de Warenne in 1090, remains clearly show the original dimensions, displays of mediaeval masonry can be seen in some rooms.

Castle Acre Village
North of Swaffham on the A1065
On the Roman Peddars Way, enclosed by earthworks of the castle of William the Conqueror's son-in-law, William de Warenne. 13th century bailey gate, fine priory.

Castle Rising
5 miles north-east of King's Lynn
Mid-12th century keep. Remains include gatehouse and bridge; English Heritage.
☎ 0553 631330

Cockley Cley Iceni Village
3 miles south-west of Swaffham
☎ 0760 721339

Norwich Castle
12th century Norman keep, now headquarters of the Norfolk Museums Service.
☎ 0603 621154

St. John's Cathedral
Norwich
Roman Catholic cathedral with 19th century Gothic style buildings. Tours of tower available.

Thetford Castle
Norman castle mound surrounded by Iron Age ramparts.

Thetford Warren Lodge
Ruins of 14th century two-storey hunting lodge built for the Prior of Thetford's gamekeeper.

Historic Buildings
Denver Windmill
South of town at Denver,
Downham Market
A six-storey mill built in 1835 with a granary, engine shed and display of old milling equipment. Tours by appointment.
☎ 0366 383374

Houghton Hall
14 miles east on the A148,
King's Lynn
Built for Prime Minister Sir Robert Walpole. 20,000 model soldiers.
☎ 0485 528569

Oxburgh Hall
8 miles south-west of Swaffham
15th century moated and fortified red-brick manor house.
☎ 0366 21 258

Sandringham House
King's Lynn
Royal residence, car and doll museums, gardens, woods, heath, Trail. Not open when Royal Family is in residence.
☎ 0553 772675

Thelnetham Windmill
Mill Road, Thelnetham, near Diss
Early 19th century towermill, recently restored and working.
☎ 0473 726996

NORFOLK

WHAT TO DO AND SEE

Trinity Hospital
5 miles north-east at Castle Rising, King's Lynn
17th century almshouses, chapel, dining hall and treasury.

Welle Manor Hall
On the A1101 at Upwell, Downham Market
Mediaeval fortified manor house and church. Curio museum includes Lafayette Collection of Victorian photographs.
☎ 0945 773333

Museums

Bressingham Steam Museum
2 miles west of Diss on the A1066
5-mile narrow gauge railway.
☎ 037 988 382

City of Norwich Aviation Museum
Old Norwich Road, Horsham, St. Faith, Norwich
☎ 0603 625309

Museum of Social History
27 King Street, King's Lynn
18th century house and brass rubbing centre.
☎ 0533 775004

Royal Norfolk Regiment Museum
1 mile north-east of the city centre off the B1140
Regimental history since 1685.

Station 146 Seeting Airfield Control Tower
Brooke, Norwich
Wartime control tower with exhibits and pictures from Second World War.
☎ 0508 50787

St. Peter Hungate Church Museum
Princes Street, Norwich
☎ 0603 667231

Swaffham Museum
Off London Street, Swaffham
Local history exhibits.
☎ 0760 721230

Tolhouse Museum
Tolhouse Street, Great Yarmouth
Mediaeval courthouse and jail.
☎ 0493 858900

Wolferton Station Museum
6 miles north-east on the A149
Edwardian Royal Travel.
☎ 0485 540674

Parks

Great Yarmouth Pleasure Beach
70 rides, sideshows and attractions, bar, food, exhibitions.
☎ 0493 844585

Merrivale Model
Marine Parade, Great Yarmouth
200 models in landscaped gardens.
☎ 0493 842097

The Venetian Waterways
North Drive, Great Yarmouth
Trips in launch through gardens, illuminated at night.
☎ 0493 853886

World of Wax
Regent Road, Great Yarmouth
Open all year round, weekends and holidays only during the winter months.
☎ 0493 842203

Railways

Bressingham Narrow Gauge Railway
Bressingham Steam Museum
☎ 037 988 382

Theatres

Royalty Theatre
Great Yarmouth
☎ 0493 842043

Theatre Royal
Norwich
☎ 0603 628205

Winter Garden Theatre
Great Yarmouth
☎ 0493 844945

Wildlife

Norfolk Wildlife Park
12 miles north-west of Norwich on the A1067 at Great Witchingham, Norwich
Largest collection of British and European wildlife in 40 acres of parkland.
☎ 0603 872274

Zoos

Banham Zoo and Monkey Sanctuary
6 miles north-west of Diss on the B1113
Extensive collection of wildlife and rare primates.
☎ 095 387 476

Great Yarmouth Butterflies and Tropical Gardens
Marine Parade
☎ 0493 842202

NORFOLK

WHAT TO DO AND SEE

OUTDOOR LEISURE/SPORTS

Cycling

Norfolk Cycling Holidays
Sandy Way, Ingoldisthorpe
Cycling holidays around the broads, brecklands and fens.
☎ 0485 560642

Fishing

Coarse Fishing
For information and permits contact the National Rivers Authority
☎ 0733 371811
☎ 0473 727712

Norfolk Broads and River Yare
Contact the Tourist Information Centre.
☎ 0603 666071

Sea Fishing
Contact the Tourist Information Centre.

Golf

Great Yarmouth and Caister Golf Club
½ mile north of Great Yarmouth on the A149
Natural links course by dunes and beach.
☎ 0493 728699

Kings's Lynn Golf Club
4 miles north-east of King's Lynn off the A148 at Castle Rising
Woodland course.
☎ 0553 631654

Norwich Golf Course
Long Lane, Bawburgh
☎ 0603 746390

Walking

Peddars Way
Swaffham
Peddars Way Association, 150 Armes Street, Norwich
97-mile footpath through woodland and along the coast. Official guide can be purchased from HMSO, or the East Anglia Tourist Board.
☎ 0473 822922

Santon Downham Forest Trail
Thetford
2-mile circular walk starting from the forest centre.

Wash Coast Path
King's Lynn
10-mile path between Sutton Bridge Lighthouse and West Lynn.

WATERSPORTS

Boat Hire

Harbour Cruisers
Riverside, Brundall, Norwich
Motor cruisers.
☎ 0603 712146

Horning Pleasurecraft Ltd
Ferry View Estate, Horning, Ludham
Self-drive holiday cruisers.
☎ 0692 630366

Johnson's Yacht Station
St. Olave's Bridge
Motor Launches and cruisers.
☎ 0493 488218

Pennant Holidays
Potter Heigham, Ludham
Hire cruisers, day trips.
☎ 0692 670711

Boat Trips

Norfolk Yacht Tours
Riverside, Martham, Great Yarmouth
Accompanied sailing trips through nature reserves for parties up to four per yacht. Optional sailing tuition.
☎ 0493 653597

Stalham Water Tours
28 St. Nicholas Way, Potter Heigham, Ludham
Broads cruises on luxury boat.
☎ 0692 670530

Sailing

Blakeney Sailing Club
Gorleston-on-Sea, Great Yarmouth
RYA affiliated.

Buckenham Sailing Club
Buckenham Ferry, Claxton
Norwich
☎ 0603 53317/660011 ext 303

Great Yarmouth and Gorleston Sailing Club
Pier Plain, Harbour entrance, Gorleston
RYA affiliated.
☎ 0603 612035/629992

Rollseby Broad Sailing Club
Great Yarmouth
☎ 0603 610217

Yare Sailing Club
River Yare
☎ 0508 8542
☎ 0603 619261

Water skiing

Pentney Water Sports Club
Pentney Pits
Contact the Secretary, Lyn York, for details.
☎ 0223 290391

Yacht Charter

Norfolk Wherry Albion
14 Mount Pleasant,
Norwich
☎ 0603 505815

Norfolk Yacht Tours
Great Yarmouth
☎ 0493 653597

CAMBRIDGESHIRE/LEICESTERSHIRE

WHAT TO DO AND SEE

i The Library, Princes Street, Huntingdon, Cambridgeshire
☎ 0480 425831

i Oakham Library, Catmos Street, Oakham, Leicestershire
☎ 0572 724329

EQUESTRIAN

Riding and Pony Trekking
Beaconsfield Equine Centre
London Street, Godmanchester
☎ 0480 830688

HEALTH

Leisure Centres
St Ivo Recreation Centre
Swimming pool, sports hall, squash courts, weight training, solarium and tennis courts.
Westwood Road, St. Ives
☎ 0480 64601

LOCAL FEATURES

Architecture
Peterborough Cathedral
Norman cathedral, 13th century painted nave ceiling; former grave of Mary Queen of Scots; grave of Katherine of Aragon.
Peterborough
☎ 0733 433342

Festivals and Fairs
March
Shire Horse Show, Peterborough

May
Truckfest, Peterborough
Cheese rolling, Stilton

June
Huntingdon Carnival

July
East of England Show, Peterborough

Guided Tours
East Anglian Tourist Guides Association
Guided tours around all the main centres.
Mrs Sheila Allen, 24 High Street, Brampton
☎ 0480 54087

Two Tours of Fenland
i Leaflet available from the Tourist Information Office.

Heritage
Flag Fen
Bronze age excavations.
Flag Fen Excavations, Fourth Drove, Fengate, Peterborough
☎ 0733 313414
Exit 7 from Peterborough ring road
P

Historic Buildings
Elton Hall
Elton, nr Peterborough
A605
☎ 08324 468
☎ 08324 223

Hinchingbrooke House
The ancestral home of the Cromwells and Earls of Sandwich.
Huntingdon
☎ 0480 451121
Brampton Road, ½ mile west of Huntingdon

Houghton Mill
Believed to be the oldest remaining watermill on the Ouse, a massive timbered structure built in the 17th century.
Mill House, Mill Street, Houghton
☎ 0480 301494
Off the A1132, 3 miles south-east of Huntingdon
P

Island Hall
Built in the 1740s this elegant house takes its name from the island that forms part of the pleasure gardens.
Godmanchester
☎ 0480 459676
In the centre of Godmanchester
P

Museums
Cromwell Museum
Formerly the Grammar School where both Oliver Cromwell and Samuel Pepys were educated, the museum relates specifically to Oliver Cromwell.
Grammar School Walk, Huntingdon
☎ 0480 425830
Town centre

Norris Museum
☎ 0480 65101

139

CAMBRIDGESHIRE/LEICESTERSHIRE

WHAT TO DO AND SEE

Ramsey Rural Museum
Items of local historical and agricultural interest displayed in a recently-restored barn.
Ramsey
☎ 0487 813223
☎ 0487 812016

Sacrewell Farm and Country Centre
Working water mill, bygones, farm, nature trail and gardens.
Sacrewell, Thornhaugh, Peterborough
☎ 0780 782222
Access off the A47

Natural History

Wood Green Animal Shelter
50 acre shelter with over 1000 animals.
Godmanchester
➔A A14
☎ 0480 830014

Parks

Hinchingbrooke Country Park
The park, once the grounds of Hinchingbrooke House, covers 156 acres of woodland, meadows, lakes and ponds and is open to the public for walking, picnics, riding and fishing.
Brampton Road, Huntingdon
☎ 0480 451568
➔A A141

Railways

Nene Valley Railway
A preserved steam railway running on 7½ miles of track between Wansford Station and Peterborough; over 25 steam and diesel locomotives.
Wansford Station, Stibbington, Peterborough
☎ 0780 782854
☎ 0780 782921 talking timetable

Zoos

Hamerton Wildlife Centre
Unique bird collection with rare species from around the world; lemurs, marmosets, meerkats, wallabies and a children's farm.
➔A A1/A604
☎ 08323 604

OUTDOOR LEISURE

Birdwatching and Wildlife

Little Paxton
Gravel pit lakes attracting migratory birds; walks.
Diddington
➔A A1

Cycling

Solec
Ermine Street, Huntingdon
☎ 0480 453492

Ferry Meadows
Ham Lane, Orton Waterville, Peterborough
☎ 0733 234418
➔A A605

Fishing

Grafham Water Reservoir
Trout fishing.
5 miles south-west of Huntingdon
☎ 0780 86 321

Hinchingbrooke Country Park
Brampton Road, Huntingdon
☎ 0480 451568

Tim's Tackle (Fishing permits)
88 High Street, Huntingdon
☎ 0480 450039

St. Ives Angling Centre
5 Crown Street, St. Ives
☎ 0480 301903

Stanjays
7 Old Court Road, Godmanchester
☎ 0480 453303

Information and licences from:

Anglian Water
☎ 0223 61561

National Rivers Authority
Bromholme Lane, Brampton
☎ 0480 414581

Golf

Ramsey Golf Club
Ramsey
☎ 0487 813573

Walking and Rambling

The Huntingdon Amble/Town Trails
i Leaflet from Tourist Office.

Ouse Valley Long Distance Footpath
Bluntisham to Eaton Socon.
Leaflets produced by Huntingdonshire District Council.
☎ 0480 561561

Little Paxton Area
i Leaflets from Tourist Information Office or Huntingdonshire District Council.

WATERSPORTS

Windsurfing and Sailing

Grafham Water Reservoir
Grafham Water Sailing Club, West Perry, Huntingdon
☎ 0480 810478

Mepal Outdoor Centre
Sailing, playpark, canoeing and windsurfing.
Chatteris Road, Ely
☎ 0354 692251

EAST LINCOLNSHIRE

WHAT TO DO AND SEE

i Embassy Centre, Grand Parade, Skegness, Lincolnshire
☎ 0754 4821
i Cottage Museum, Iddesleigh Road, Woodhall Spa, Lincolnshire
☎ 0520 58775

ADVENTURE

Multi-activity Centres

Tattershall Park Country Club
Waterskiing, windsurfing school, jet skiing, canoeing, rowing, pedalo, squash, snooker, gymnasium, saunas, solarium, horse riding, nature walks and lake swimming.
Tattershall
☎ 0526 43193
On the A153 Sleaford to Skegness road

AERIAL SPORTS

Flying

Ingoldmells
Skegness Aerodrome, Skegness
☎ 0754 2240

HEALTH

Leisure Centres

Seafront Complex
Indoor and outdoor pools with waterslides.
Grand Parade, Skegness
☎ 0754 610675

The Richmond Holiday Centre
Pool, sauna, sun beds and gymnasium.
Richmond Drive, Skegness
☎ 0754 69265

LOCAL FEATURES

Aquariums

Skegness Natureland Marine Zoo & Seal Sanctuary
Performing seals, sealions, penguins, aquarium, birds and butterfly house.
North Parade, Skegness
☎ 0754 4345

Arts and Crafts

Alford Craft Market
Demonstrations and street theatre.
→A A1104

Historic Buildings

Gunby Hall
Reynold's portraits. National Trust.
Nr Spilsby
☎ 0909 486411 NT regional office
→A A158
P 🏛 🚌 ♿

Sibsey Trader Mill
England's only remaining 6 sail, 6 storey tower mill.
Sibsey
☎ 0205 750036
Off the A16, 5 miles north of Boston
P 🏛

Tattershall Castle
Spectacular 15th century grandee's tower house, four great chambers with ancillary rooms, fine brick vaulting and Gothic fireplaces.
Tattershall
☎ 0526 42543
→A A153
🏛 ♿

Museums

Battle of Britain Memorial Flight
Spitfires, Hurricanes and Europe's only flying Lancaster bomber.
RAF Coningsby
☎ 0526 44041
→A A153
P 🚌 ♿ ♿ ✕

Woodhall Spa Cottage Museum
Fine collection of photographs and town history.
Iddesleigh Road, Woodhall Spa
☎ 0526 53775
🏛

Parks

Snipe Dales Country Park
200 acres, nature reserve, woods and marked pathways.
Lusby and Winceby, nr Spilsby
☎ 0522 552222 (Recreation Officer)
→A A1115

Bottons Pleasure Beach
Modern pleasure park with rides, arcades and bingo.
Skegness

Panda's Palace
Children's activity area.
Tower Esplanade, Skegness
☎ 0754 5494

Theatres

Embassy Centre
Concerts, cabarets; entertainment centre.
Grand Parade, Skegness
☎ 0754 68333

OUTDOOR LEISURE/SPORTS

Birdwatching and Wildlife

Gibraltar Point Nature Reserve
1500 acres of sandy dunes, saltmarsh, sandy and muddy shores, dune slacks and freshwater habitats for studying the flora and fauna of the east coast. Guided Walks.
☎ 0754 2677
→A A52
P 🚌 ♿ ♿

Tennis

North Shore Holiday Centre
Roman Drive, Skegness
☎ 0754 3815

WEST LINCOLNSHIRE

WHAT TO DO AND SEE

i 9 Castle Hill, Lincoln, Lincolnshire
☎ 0522 529828

EQUESTRIAN

Riding and Pony Trekking
Mawers Farm Riding Centre
Long Leys Road
☎ 0522 545547

HEALTH

Leisure Centres
Lincoln City Sports Centre
Swimming, sunbeds, roller skating, tennis, keep fit and squash.
☎ 0522 683946

LOCAL FEATURES

Archaeology
Roman Remains
From a military garrison established in Lincoln and dating from 48AD; an ingenious underground system of water supply and sanitation, a canal and road system.

Art Galleries
Usher Art Gallery
Paintings, ceramics, clocks and watches.
Lindum Road, Lincoln
☎ 0522 527980

Guided Tours
Guided Tours of Lincoln
Recreation and Leisure Department
City Hall, Beaumont Fee, Lincoln
☎ 0522 511511

Historic Buildings
Bishop's Palace and Vineyard
Largely derelict, but the remains are still impressive.
Minster Yard, Lincoln
☎ 0522 527468

Ellis Mill
Last surviving windmill in this area.
Mill Road, Lincoln
☎ 0522 541824
Off the B1398

Guildhall, Stonebow and Civic Insignia
15th century southern gateway to the city; collection of treasures and regalia.

WEST LINCOLNSHIRE

WHAT TO DO AND SEE

Lincoln Castle
The castle occupies a superb hill top position west of the Cathedral and holds summertime activities such as jousting, archery, vintage vehicle rally and historic reconstructions.
Castle Manager, Lincoln Castle
☎ 0522 511068
→A A15

Lincoln Cathedral
Lincoln's 900 year old Cathedral dominates the city, probably the most spectacular setting for any English Cathedral. William the Conqueror ordered it built in 1072.
☎ 0522 544544
→A A46

St. Mary's Guildhall
12th century building, the surface of the Roman Fosse Way is visible through a glass floor.
385 Lower High Street, Lincoln
☎ 0522 546422

Museums

City and County Museum
Natural history, prehistoric remains, Roman, Saxon and Viking finds.
Broadgate, Lincoln
☎ 0522 530401

Museum of Lincolnshire Life
Burton Road, Lincoln
☎ 0522 528448
→A A15

National Cycle Museum
Cycles dating from 1820.
Brayford Wharf, Lincoln
☎ 0522 545091
→A A57

The Incredibly Fantastic Old Toy Show
Toys from the 1850s to the present.
26 Westgate, Lincoln
☎ 0522 520534

Parks

Elsham Hall Country Park
Arboretum, butterfly garden, tropical bird garden, crafts, adventure playground, animal farm and gallery.
Barnetby
☎ 0652 688698
→A A15/M180

Hartsholme Country Park
100 acres of parkland.
Skellingthorpe Road, Lincoln
☎ 0522 686264
Off the B1180

Theatres

Theatre Royal
Clasketgate, Lincoln
☎ 0522 525555

The Ritz Theatre
High Street, Lincoln
☎ 0522 546313

Skegness Embassy Centre
Grand Parade, Lincoln
☎ 0754 68333

OUTDOOR LEISURE

Cycling

Arrow Cycles
2 Station Road, North Hykeham
☎ 0522 694564

F & J Cycles
Hungate, Lincoln
☎ 0522 545311

Fishing

Excellent local fishing on the River Witham and Fossdyke Canal and on nearby lakes and reservoirs.

Wheater Fieldsports
3–9 Tentecroft Street, Lincoln
☎ 0522 521219

Golf

Carholme Golf Club ⑱
Carholme Road, Lincoln
☎ 0522 523725

Southcliffe & Canwick Golf Club ⑱
Washingborough Road, Lincoln
☎ 0522 522166

Lincoln Golf Range ⑨
Washingborough Road, Lincoln
☎ 0522 522059

Walking and Rambling

The Viking Way, a picturesque national footpath, passes through much of Lincolnshire.
i The Tourist Board produces a series of excellent leaflets '*Lincolnshire Walks*' which give detailed maps and excellent descriptions of the area.

Ramblers Association
☎ 0522 689367

Lincolnshire Tourist Guides
Daily walks.
☎ 0522 595114

WATERSPORTS

Windsurfing

Ashby Park
West Ashby, Horncastle
☎ 0507 527 966

SOUTH HUMBERSIDE

WHAT TO DO AND SEE

i Central Library, Town Hall Square, Grimsby, Humberside
☎ 0472 240180
i Central Library, Carlton Street, Scunthorpe, South Humberside
☎ 0724 282301

ADVENTURE

Flying

Humber Flying Club
Humberside Airport, Grimsby Road, Kirmington
☎ 0652 680746

EQUESTRIAN

Riding

Chestnut Farm Riding School
Brigsley Road, Ashby-cum-Fenby, Grimsby
☎ 0472 825777

Normanby Park Riding School
Normanby Park, Normanby, Scunthorpe
☎ 0724 720783

HEALTH

Leisure Centre

Baysgarth Park Leisure Centre
Baysgarth Park, Brigg Road, Barton-on-Humber
☎ 0652 635979

LOCAL FEATURES

Heritage

Thornton Abbey
Ruins of ancient abbey including remains of magnificent fortified gatehouse.
Thornton Abbey Road, Illingholme, Grimsby
☎ 0469 540357

Historical Buildings

Normanby Hall
Splendid country mansion built in the 18th century for the Sheffield family. Located in the middle of Normanby Hall Park.
Normanby Hall Park, Normanby, Scunthorpe
4 miles north of Scunthorpe
☎ 0724 720588

St. Peters Church
Beck Hill, Barton-on-Humber
☎ 0652 632516

Industrial

Humber Bridge
Longest suspension bridge in the world, spanning the Humber Estuary from Barton-on-Humber to Hessle, near Hull.
P

SOUTH HUMBERSIDE

WHAT TO DO AND SEE

National Fishing Heritage Centre
The history of fishing including life on a typical Grimsby
trawler in the 1950s.
Alexandra Dock, Grimsby
☎ 0472 242000

Museums

Normanby Hall Museum
Rooms restored to their 18th century splendour
Normanby Hall Park, Normanby, Scunthorpe
☎ 0724 720215

Normanby Park Farming Museum
Farm implements and techniques from the 18th and 19th century.
Normanby Hall Park, Normanby, Scunthorpe
☎ 0724 720824

Scunthorpe Museum and Art Gallery
Local history and geology including Iron Age and Roman finds from the area.
Oswald Road, Scunthorpe
☎ 0724 843533

Parks

Elsham Hall Country Park
Large park with walks, fishing, animals, craft centre and art gallery.
Elsham, Brigg
☎ 0652 688698

Theatre

Caxton Theatre and Art Centre
128 Cleethorpes Road, Grimsby
☎ 0652 345167

WATERSPORTS

Sailing

Being on the south side of the Humber Estuary watersports are naturally popular in this area, particularly sailing. Major clubs include:

Grimsby and Cleethorpes Yacht Club
Flour Square, Grimsby
☎ 0652 356678

Humber Mouth Yacht Club
Humberston Fitties, Humberston, Grimsby
☎ 0652 812063

Humber Yacht Club
Club House, Waterside, Winteringham
☎ 0724 733458

North Lincolnshire Sailing CLub
Pasture Road North, Barrow Mere, Barton-on-Humber
☎ 0652 321514

Waterskiing

Humber Bridge Water Ski Club
West Marsh Lane, Barrow-on-Humber
☎ 0469 30018

HUMBERSIDE

WHAT TO DO AND SEE

i The Guildhall, Register Square, Beverley, Humberside
☎ 0482 867430

AERIAL SPORTS

Flying
Hull Aero Club
Full facilities for flying lessons and visiting aircraft.
Brough Airfield, Brough, nr Hull
☎ 0482 667985

Gliding
Wolds Gliding Club
A large gliding club with full facilities; 5-day courses available during the summer. One day membership with training flight.
The Airfield, Pocklington, York
☎ 0759 303579

EQUESTRIAN

Riding and Pony Trekking
Bleach Yard Stables
New Walk, Beverley
☎ 0482 882557

LOCAL FEATURES

Art Galleries
Ferens Art Gallery
Old Masters, marine paintings, 20th century and contemporary works.
Queen Victoria Square, Hull
☎ 0482 593912
➜A M62/A63 (city centre)

Arts and Crafts
Withernwick Forest Crafts
Resin casting of animals, birds, oriental and fantasy chess sets.
Main Street, Withernwick
☎ 0964 527858

Festivals and Fairs
May
Early Music Festival, Beverley

June
Victorian Hayride, Beverley

Fun Parks
Hornsea Pottery Leisure Park and Factory
Watch the complete manufacturing process from a gallery walk. Landscaped parkland attractions include butterfly world, adventure playground, mini bikes and a model village. A huge discount shopping area including discounted pottery.
Hornsea
☎ 0964 532161
On the B1242 on the outskirts of town
P ✕ ♿

Gardens
Burnby Hall Gardens
Extensive gardens with a fine display of water lilies, a rose garden, a selection of picnic areas and fishing spots.
The Balk, Pocklington
☎ 0759 302068
1 mile from the A1079
P 🚌 ✕ ♿

Historic Buildings
Beverley Minster
The present building dates from 1220 and is one of the finest Gothic churches of cathedral size in Europe.
☎ 0482 868540
➜A A1079
🚌

Burton Constable Hall
Magnificent Elizabethan house set in grounds landscaped by Capability Brown.
Sproatley
☎ 0964 562400
On the B1238 east of Beverley
P 🚌 ✕ ♿

Skidby Windmill
One of the best remaining working windmills in Britain.
Skidby, Cottingham
☎ 0482 882255
➜A A164
P 🚌 ✕

Skipsea Castle
Norman motte and bailey castle.
West of Skipsea village

Museums
Beverley Art Gallery and Museum
Champney Road, Beverley
☎ 0482 882255
➜A A164 (town centre)
P

HUMBERSIDE

WHAT TO DO AND SEE

Museum of Army Transport
Acres of road, rail, sea and air exhibits excitingly displayed.
Flemingate, Beverley
☎ 0482 860445

Streetlife – Hull Museum of Transport
Horse-drawn vehicles, motor vehicles 1890–1910, rare trams.
High Street, Hull
☎ 0482 593902
→A A63 (city centre)

Town Docks Museum
Whaling, fishing and trawling exhibits.
Queen Victoria Square, Hull
☎ 0482 593902
→A A63 (city centre)

Natural History

Cruckley Animal Farm
Working farm with modern and rare breeds of animals; hatchery; waterfowl lake and daily milking demonstration.
Foston-on-the-Wolds, nr Great Driffield
☎ 0262 488337
Off the B1249

Northern Shire Horse Centre
Shire horses, harness, museum, forge, country trail, horse-drawn vehicles; rare and unusual breeds.
Flower Hill Farm, North Newbald
☎ 0430 827270
→A A1034

Parks

Humber Bridge Country Park
Woodland, meadows, play area, picnic areas. Guided walks start from the restored mill on Hessle foreshore. Trails for the blind.
☎ 0482 641989
Vi. Hull on the A63 (across Humber Bridge)

Theatres

New Theatre
Kingston Square, Hull
☎ 0482 226655

OUTDOOR LEISURE

Cycling

Star Bikes
204 Willerby Road, Hull
☎ 0482 564673

Fishing

Beverley Beck
A small canalised stream running from the Forester's Arms to the River Hull; small-sized road, perch, gudgeon, skimmers, pike and eels.

Lakeminster Park Lakes
There are 2 ponds. Day permits allow fishing for carp, tench, roach and bream.
Woodmansey Road
South of Beverley off the Beverley–Hull road

Golf

Beverley Golf Club 18
Westwood
☎ 0482 867190

Ice Skating

Humberside Ice Arena
An Olympic sized arena.
Kingston Street, Hull
☎ 0482 25252
A63 next to Hull Marina

Tennis

Hodgson's Recreation Ground
Courts to hire.

Walking

The Minster Way
51 mile route linking York and Beverley Minsters.

The Wolds Way
80 mile path along the Yorkshire Wolds from the Humber to Filey.
i The Tourist Information Centre can provide details of these routes.

Bishop Burton College of Agriculture
Themed Nature Trails.
Bishop Burton
☎ 0964 550481

County Leisure and Tourism Rangers
i The Tourist Information Centre can provide details of dates and meeting points.

WATERSPORTS

Barton Clay Pits
All year round recreation; watersports (sailing and waterskiing for club members), fishing and bird watching, walking with a programme of Guided Walks.
Barton-upon-Humber
☎ 0652 33283
→A A1077/A15

147

NORTH YORKSHIRE

WHAT TO DO AND SEE

i De Grey Rooms, Exhibition Square, York
☎ 0904 621756

AERIAL SPORTS

Gliding
York Gliding Centre
Rufforth Airfield, York
☎ 0904 83694
On the B1224 York to Wetherby road, 5 miles west of York

EQUESTRIAN

Riding and Pony Trekking
Moor House Riding Centre
Sutton Road, Wigginton
☎ 0904 769029

Naburn Grange Riding Centre
Naburn, nr York
☎ 090487 283
Off the A19, 4 miles south-west of York

Tenthorne Farm
Knapton, nr York
☎ 0904 798130
3 miles from York

LOCAL FEATURES

Art Galleries
York City Art Gallery
European and British painting spanning seven centuries.
Exhibition Square
☎ 0904 623839

Festivals and Fairs
May
Early Music Festival, York

Guided Tours
Qualified guides take free daily walking tours starting from the Exhibition Square throughout the year.

Yorktour
Sightseeing tours both of the city and surrounding area (Whitby and Castle Howard, Fountains Abbey, Yorkshire Dales and Herriot Country) book through the Tourist Information Centre, hotels and guest houses. All coaches non-smoking. Private guides also available.
8 Tower Street
☎ 0904 641737

Historic Buildings
Beningbrough Hall
Fine Baroque house with collection of paintings on loan from the National Portrait Gallery; Victorian kitchen; adventure playground. National Trust.
Shipton-by-Beningbrough
☎ 0904 470666
Off the A19 York to Thirsk road, 8 miles north-west of York

Castle Howard
Thousands of acres of parkland with a plant centre, rose gardens and nature walks.
☎ 065384 333
Off the A64, 15 miles north-east of York

Fairfax House
Fine town house with 18th century furniture and clock collection.
Castlegate
☎ 0904 655543
City centre

Harewood House
Leeds
20 miles west of York

Newby Hall
Nr Ripon
20 miles north-east of York

Ripley Castle
Ripley
24 miles west of York

NORTH YORKSHIRE

WHAT TO DO AND SEE

Sutton Park
Attractive Georgian house with Chippendale, Sheraton and French furniture; Capability Brown gardens; woodland walks.
Sutton-on-the-Forest
☎ 0347 810249
On the B1363, 8 miles north of York

York Minster
The largest mediaeval cathedral in northern Europe.

Museums

Jorvik Viking Centre
Visitors sit in 'time cars' and are whisked back 1000 years in history to witness sight, sound and smell reconstructions of the city of Jorvik (Viking name for York); displays of archaeological artefacts.
Coppergate
☎ 0904 643211

National Railway Museum
Display covering 150 years of British railway history.
Leeman Road
☎ 0904 621261
P

Rail Riders World
Model railway recreates the modern British rail scene over an area of 2000 sq ft.
York Station
☎ 0904 630169
City centre

Yorkshire Museum
Displays of Roman, Anglo Saxon, Viking and mediaeval treasures of Britain; wildlife gardens.
Museum Gardens
☎ 0904 629745

York Castle Museum
Popular museum of everyday life; exhibition of children's games and toys.
Kirkgate
☎ 0904 653611

Theatres

York Theatre Royal
Georgian theatre, opened in 1740 offers a varied programme.
☎ 0904 623568

York Cycleworks
14–16 Lawrence Street
☎ 0904 626664

Auto Discount Cycling Tours
Touring holidays organised.
Ings Vie, Shipton Road
☎ 0904 630692

Fishing

Local fishing tackle shops can provide information on fishing in the Ouse and other rivers.

Golf

Fulford (York) Golf Club 18
Visitors welcome by prior arrangement.
Heslington Lane
☎ 0904 413579

Heworth Golf Club 9
Visitors welcome except Sun mornings.
Muncastergate, Malton Road
☎ 0904 422389

Pike Hills Golf Club 18
No visitors at weekends.
Tadcaster Road, Copmanthorpe
☎ 0904 708756

Walking

40 miles of dramatic upland scenery stretches across to the Yorkshire coast, for information on North York Moors contact:

National Park Visitor Centre
Town Hall, Market Place, Helmsley
☎ 0439 70173

WATERSPORTS

Boat Hire and Trips

Castle Line Cruises
Skeldergate Bridge
☎ 0836 739357

Hills Boatyard
Lendal Bridge
☎ 0904 623752

White Rose Line
King's Staith
☎ 0904 628324

OUTDOOR LEISURE

Cycling

Cycle Scene
2 Ratcliffe Street, Burton Stone Lane
☎ 0904 653286

149

LANCASHIRE

WHAT TO DO AND SEE

i Wyre Borough Council, The Esplanade, Fleetwood, Lancashire
☎ 03917 71141 summer only
i The Guildhall, Lancaster Road, Preston, Lancashire
☎ 0772 53731
i 112 Lord Street, Southport, Merseyside
☎ 0704 33133

Gardens

Botanic Gardens and Museum
Gardens, aviary, childrens playground and boating lake; museum display of Victoriana.
Churchtown, Southport
☎ 0704 27547
Off the B5244

EQUESTRIAN

Riding and Pony Trekking

Crookland's Riding Establishment
Goosnargh Lane, nr Preston
☎ 0772 863017

HEALTH

Leisure Centres

West View Leisure Centre
2 large sports halls, fitness room, swimming pools, squash courts, climbing wall and creche facilities.
Ribbleton, Preston
☎ 0772 796788

LOCAL FEATURES

Art Galleries

Atkinson Art Gallery
19th and 20th century paintings, watercolours, prints and drawings; modern sculpture.
Lord Street, Southport
☎ 0704 33133
→A A565

Grundy Art Gallery
Lively monthly exhibition programme of modern artists.
Queen Street, Blackpool
☎ 0253 75170

Haworth Art Gallery
Fine Edwardian building in 13 acres; permanent Tiffany glass collection, English and European watercolours; brass rubbing centre; picnic areas and concerts in grounds.
Haworth Park, Manchester Road, Accrington
☎ 0254 33782

Harris Museum and Art Gallery
Magnificent neo-classical building in Greek revival style with an extensive collection of fine art and exhibitions.
Market Square, Preston
☎ 0772 58248
Town centre

Historic Buildings

Astley Hall
Elizabethan half-timbered Hall with a fine collection of furniture, paintings and pottery.
Astley Park, Chorley
☎ 02572 62166

Hoghton Tower
16th century hilltop mansion, with banqueting hall, state apartments, historic documents and dolls houses.
Nr Preston
☎ 025485 2986
→A A675

Meols Hall
Ancestral home of the Fleetwood Hesketh family with some very fine paintings, silver and china. Game and Country Fayre held in May.
Churchtown, Southport
☎ 0704 28171
→A A565/A570

Rufford Old Hall
Late mediaeval half-timbered hall with an ornate hammer-beam roof and screen; fine collections of 17th century oak furniture, 16th century arms, armour and tapestries.
Rufford, nr Ormskirk
☎ 0704 821254
On the A59, 7 miles north of Ormskirk

Samlesbury Hall
14th century manor house. Sales of antiques and collectors items, crafts and other exhibitions are held here.
Preston
☎ 025481 2229
☎ 025481 2010
→A A677

Museums

Ribchester Museum of Roman Antiquities
Independent museum and remains of the fort of Bremetennacum.
Riverside, Ribchester
☎ 0254 878261

150

LANCASHIRE

WHAT TO DO AND SEE

Parks

Beacon Fell Country Park
304 acres of open countryside with recreational facilities and guided walks.
Nr Skelmersdale
☎ 0995 61693
On the A6, 8 miles north of Preston

Railways

Steamport Railway Museum
15 steam and 6 diesel locomotives.
Derby Road, Southport
☎ 0704 30693
A565

Zoos

Blackpool Zoo Park
Modern zoo set in landscaped gardens.
East Park Drive, Blackpool
☎ 0253 65027

Southport Zoo
Includes a breeding group of chimpanzees.
Princes Park, Southport
☎ 0704 38102

OUTDOOR LEISURE/SPORTS

Cycling

Lancashire cycleway provides an extensive tour of the Lancashire countryside via 2 fully waymarked circular routes.
i Further information is available from Tourist Information Centres.

Walking

Rossendale Way
A 45-mile circular route which explores Rossendale's hills, valleys and towns.
i 8 leaflets are available from the Tourist Information Centres with maps and historical snippets.

Ribble Way
A 40-mile public footpath following the course of the River Ribble.
i Further information is available from Tourist Information Centres.

WATERSPORTS

Watersports are available in the major seaside resorts along the coast, including Blackpool, Fleetwood and Morecambe.

151

CUMBRIA

WHAT TO DO AND SEE

i Glebe Road, Bowness-on-Windermere, Cumbria
☎ 05394 42895 (summer only)
i Coronation Hall, County Square, Ulverston, Cumbria
☎ 0229 57120

ADVENTURE

Multi-activity Centres

Bigland Hall Sporting Estates
Fishing, riding, trekking, clay pigeon shooting and archery.
Novices welcome.
Backbarrow, nr Ulverston
☎ 05395 31728

Summitreks
Outdoor activity courses and instruction including canoeing, windsurfing, mountain biking, abseiling/rock climbing and guided mountain walks. Weekend or weekly basis.
14 Yewdale Road, Coniston
☎ 05394 41212

YMCA National Centre
Outdoor adventure and activity skills training and nature discovery holidays geared to the needs of families, youngsters, teenagers and the over 50s.
Lakeside, Ulverston
☎ 05395 31758

EQUESTRIAN

Riding and Pony Trekking

Bigland Hall
Blackbarrow, Newby Bridge
☎ 05395 31728

Claife and Grizedale Riding Centre
Sawrey Knott's Estate, Hawkshead
☎ 05394 42105

LOCAL FEATURES

Falconry

Leighton Hall
Eagles fly (May–Sept) daily except Sat and Mon at 3.30pm at this beautifully sited country house. There are 1- and 4-day courses in handling birds available.
Carnforth
☎ 0524 734474
Off the M6 at exit 35, signposted

Gardens

Graythwaite Hall Gardens
Garden laid out in the 1880s; rhododendrons, azaleas and flowering shrubs.
Newby Bridge
☎ 05395 31248
→A A590

Historic Buildings

Dove Cottage
William Wordsworth's home during his most creative years.
Grasmere
☎ 05394 35544
Off the A591, just south of Grasmere village

Holker Hall
Former home of the Dukes of Devonshire, known for its fine wood carvings and impressive gardens. Craft and Countryside Museum and the Lakeland Motor Museum are also situated here; adventure playground; events throughout the year.
Cark-in-Cartmel
Flookburgh
☎ 05395 58328
On the B5278 from Newby Bridge via the A590

CUMBRIA

WHAT TO DO AND SEE

Rydal Mount
Wordsworth's home at the time of his death in 1850 still owned by descendants of his family; magnificent views.
Ambleside
☎ 05394 33002
Off the A591, approx 1 mile from Ambleside and Grasmere

Sizergh Castle
In parts dating from the 14th century, fine collection of Elizabethan carvings and panelling, furniture and portraits; 18th century gardens. National Trust.
Nr Kendal
☎ 05395 60070
3 miles south of Kendal, north-west of the A6/A591 interchange
P 🚌 ✕

Museums

Museum of Lakeland Life and Industry
Reconstructions of workshops and farmhouse rooms; agricultural exhibits; Arthur Ransome and Postman Pat rooms; Lake District Art Gallery and Museum all housed in a Georgian town house by the riverside.
Abbot Hall, Kendal
☎ 0539 722464
Nr Kendal Parish Church, M6 exit 36
P 🏛 🚌

Parks

Fell Foot Country Park
18-acre lakeside park offering bathing, fishing, adventure playground, rowing boat hire and boat launching facilities. National Trust. Park open all year 10am–dusk. Shop and boat hire Easter–end Oct.
Newby Bridge
☎ 05395 31273
At the extreme south end of Windermere, on the east shore
P 🏛 ✕

Lake District National Park Visitor Centre
Exhibitions, "Living Lakeland", slide shows, films, shop, gardens, lakeshore walk and drystone walling area.
Brockhole, Windermere
☎ 05394 46601
➜A A591
P ✕ ♿

Railways

Lakeside and Haverthwaite Railway
Steam locomotive trips from Haverthwaite station through lake and river scenery of the Leven Valley. Connections are made at Lakeside with Windermere Cruises for Bowness and Ambleside.
Nr Newby Bridge
☎ 05395 31594
On the A590 to Haverthwaite

OUTDOOR LEISURE/SPORTS

Birdwatching

South Walney Nature Reserve
Europe's largest gullery and big Eider colony with 4 hides.
Walney Island, Barrow-in-Furness
☎ 0229 41066
➜A A590
🚌

Cycling

Cumbria Cycle Way
Circular 280-mile (450km) waymarked route following quiet roads. Route available from Tourist Information Centres.

Lowick Mountain Bikes
Guided tours, itineraries and cycles for hire.
Red Lion Inn, Lowick, nr Ulverston
☎ 0229 85366

Fishing

Bosuns Locker
8-hour sea angling trips from Roa Island into Morecambe Bay on board *MFV Isla*. Passenger trips daily Easter–Oct 12 noon–6pm to Piel Island with its 12th century castle and South Walney Nature Reserve. Also available for private charter.
Roa Island, Barrow-in-Furness
☎ 0229 22520

Walking

Grizedale Forest Visitor Centre
Marked forest trails, picnic areas, cycle trails and fishing areas.
Grizedale, Ambleside
☎ 0229 860373

Guided Walks
Throughout the area during the season (Easter–Oct) accompanied by experts.
i Enquire at the Kendal Tourist Information Centre.

WATERSPORTS

Sailing

Lake Windermere Facilities
Permanent and holiday moorings, launching, recovery, boat registration, pump-out, winter storage and water supply.
Ferry Nab, Bowness-on-Windermere
☎ 05394 42753

DURHAM AND CLEVELAND

WHAT TO DO AND SEE

i 43 Galgate, Barnard Castle, County Durham
☎ 0833 690909
i Civic Centre, Victoria Road, Hartlepool, Cleveland
☎ 0429 869706

ADVENTURE

Multi-activity Centres

Hudeway Centre
For families, groups and individuals: canoeing, windsurfing, abseiling, riding, caving and orienteering.
Hudegate Farm East, Middleton-in-Teesdale, Barnard Castle
☎ 0833 40012

EQUESTRIAN

Riding and Pony Trekking

High Pennine Rides
Self-guided riding holidays for adults along a choice of routes.
Brook Villa, The Green, Lanchester, Durham
☎ 0207 521911

Hoppyland Trekking Centre
Pony trekking in Hamsterley Forest for novice and experienced riders.
Hoppyland Farm, Hamsterley, Bishop Auckland
☎ 0388 88617
☎ 0388 767419

LOCAL FEATURES

Art Galleries

Darlington Art Gallery
Exhibitions, loans and local artists.
Crown Street, Darlington
☎ 0325 462034
Town centre

Gardens

Durham College of Agriculture and Horticulture
Gardens used as training grounds for students so providing a fine display of gardening styles. Gardening questions answered at a gardening clinic.
Durham
☎ 091 3861351
On the A177, 1 mile south-east of Durham city centre

Durham University Botanic Gardens
Set in mature woodland with exotic trees from America and the Himalayas; display house with tropical plants and cacti.
Hollingside Lane
☎ 091 3742671
➔ A1050

Egglestone Hall Gardens
Informally laid out garden with winding paths and streams; many rare plants together with organically grown vegetables.
Eggleston village
☎ 0833 50378
South of Egglestone village

Heritage

Binchester Roman Fort
The house of the fort commander includes the best example of a Roman military bath-suite in Britain.
Bishop Auckland
☎ 0388 663089
1 mile north of Bishop Auckland

Historic Buildings

Auckland Castle
Principal country residence of the Bishops of Durham since Norman times; magnificent chapel built from the ruins of the 12th century Banqueting Hall in 1665. Public access to Bishop's Park.
Bishop Auckland
☎ 091 3864411 ext 2698

Barnard Castle
Imposing Norman stronghold overlooking the River Tees, extensively renovated. Bowes Museum has an art collection of national importance.
☎ 0833 38212

DURHAM AND CLEVELAND

WHAT TO DO AND SEE

Bowes Castle
Massive 12th century stone keep overlooking the valley of the River Greta on the site of a Roman Fort that commanded the approach to Stainmore Pass over the Pennines.
On the A67, 4 miles west of Barnard Castle

Durham Castle
Norman castle of the Prince Bishops of Durham founded in 1072; Norman chapel, Great Hall and extensive kitchens.
Durham city
☎ 091 374 3800

Egglestone Abbey
Ruined 12th century abbey with a picturesque setting above the River Tees; a fine mediaeval pack-horse bridge nearby.
Nr the A67, 1 mile south-east of Barnard Castle

Raby Castle
One of the largest 14th century castles in Britain with fine pictures and furniture and a collection of horse-drawn carriages and fire engines.
Staindrop, Darlington
☎ 0833 60202
1 mile north of Staindrop on the Barnard Castle/Bishop Auckland road

Rokeby Park
Palladian style country house with a unique collection of 18th century needlework pictures, period furniture and a print room.
Barnard Castle
☎ 0833 37334
On the A66 between the A1(M) and Bowes

Museums

Beamish – North of England Open Air Museum
One of the top tourist attractions of the region; vivid reconstruction of Northern life in the early 1900's with tramway, shops, pub and railway station.
☎ 0207 231811
Chester-le-Street
→A A1(M) 4 miles west of Chester-le-Street

Parks

Hardwick Hall Country Park
18th century landscaped park with lake.
Sedgefield
→A A177

Railways

Darlington Railway Centre and Museum
Historic engines "Locomotion" and "Derwent" are displayed.
North Road Station, Darlington
☎ 0325 460532
On the A167 north of the town centre

OUTDOOR LEISURE/SPORTS

Fishing

Northumbrian Water own 11 reservoirs operated as fisheries.
Recreation Dept, Northumbrian Water, Abbey Road, Pity Me, Durham City
☎ 091 384 4222

Walking

The Durham Dales offer a wide range of walks, from the long-distance Pennine Way to walks suitable for families. Information from the County Environment Department's Guided Walk Programme.
☎ 091 386 4411

155

TYNE AND WEAR

WHAT TO DO AND SEE

i Central Station, Newcastle, Tyne & Wear
☎ 091 230 0030
i City Information Service, Newcastle
☎ 091 261 0691 ext 231
i Unit 3, Crowtree Road, Sunderland, Tyne & Wear
☎ 091 565 0960

EQUESTRIAN

Riding
Lincoln Riding Centre
High Pit Farm, East Cramlington
☎ 0632 815376

HEALTH

Leisure Centres
There are 25 leisure centres in Newcastle, all with extensive facilities from roller skating to pop mobility.
Contact the City Information Service (see above).

LOCAL FEATURES

Archaeology
Arbeia Roman Fort
Remains of gateways, fort walls and defences; site museum and excavations.
Baring Street, South Shields
☎ 091 456 1369
➜A A183

Architecture
The Bridges over the River Tyne
Newcastle's skyline includes the Tyne Bridge which has the largest arch span of any bridge in Britain, at 531 feet and the High Level Bridge designed by Robert Stephenson.

Art Galleries
Bede Gallery
Small museum of Jarrow history and monthly exhibitions.
Springwell Park, Butcherbridge Road, Jarrow
☎ 091 489 1807
➜A A194

Hatton Gallery
Collection of 15th century paintings and drawings and exhibitions of contemporary art.
The University, Newcastle
☎ 091 222 6000
➜A A6127

Laing Art Gallery
British paintings and watercolours from the 17th century to the present. Works by John Martin; textiles, ceramics, silver and glass.
Higham Place, Newcastle
☎ 091 232 7734

Shipley Art Gallery
Victorian and Old Master paintings; traditional and contemporary crafts and temporary exhibitions.
Prince Consort Road, Gateshead
☎ 091 477 1495
➜A A6127

Heritage
The Roman Wall
The Roman Wall and the adjacent Military Road (B6318) run east-west parallel to but several miles north of the Tyne gap. Further details from the City Information Service (see above).

Historic Buildings
Aydon Castle
Built as a manor house at the end of the 13th century, converted to a farmhouse in the 17th century; captured by the Scots and English in turn.
On the B6321 or the A68, north-east of Corbridge
☎ 0434 632450

Castle Keep
Norman Keep with panoramic views of the city from the roof.
St. Nicholas Street, Newcastle
☎ 091 232 7938
➜A A6125

Gibside Chapel
The Bowes family mausoleum, designed by James Paine. National Trust.
Burnopfield
☎ 0207 542255
Off the B6314

Prudhoe Castle
Overlooking the River Tyne, Prudhoe Castle commanded the principal north-south route through Northumberland. Home of the Dukes of Northumberland.
Prudhoe
Off the A695
☎ 0661 33459

Washington Old Hall
17th century manor house, home of George Washington's direct ancestors.
Washington
☎ 091 4166879
➜A A1

156

TYNE AND WEAR

WHAT TO DO AND SEE

Museums

Hancock Museum
Zoo room, bird room, geology gallery and small side galleries.
Great North Road, Newcastle
☎ 091 232 2359
➜A Off the A1 to the A6125
P

John George Joicey Museum
Almshouses from 17th century with period rooms and military collections.
City Road, Newcastle
☎ 091 232 4562
➜A A6127
P 🚌 ✗ ♿

Military Vehicle Museum
World War II vehicles and others.
The Pavilion, Exhibition Park, Great North Road, Jesmond
☎ 091 281 7222
➜A A6127
P 🚌 ✗ ♿

Museum of Science and Engineering
Blandford House, West Blandford Street, Newcastle
☎ 091 232 6789
➜A A6115
✗ ♿ ♿

Natural History

St. Mary's Lighthouse
Lighthouse and bird watching centre.
Trinity Road, Whitley Bay
☎ 091 252 0853
➜A A193
P 🚌 ♿ ♿

Railways

Bowes Railway
Standard gauge rope-hauled railway; 3 steam locos.
Springwell Village, Gateshead
☎ 091 416 1847
➜A A1
P 🚌 ✗ ♿ ♿

Stephenson Museum
Railway engines and rolling stock.
Middle Engine Lane, North Shields
☎ 091 262 2627
➜A A1
P 🏛

Tanfield Railway
Oldest existing railway in the world, opened 1725; steam-hauled passenger trains, vintage carriages, vintage workshop.
Marley Hill, Sunniside, Gateshead
P 🚌 ✗ ♿

OUTDOOR LEISURE/SPORTS

Birdwatching and Wildlife

The Leas and Marsden Rock
Spectacular coastline famous for kittiwakes, cormorants etc; Guided Walks, National Trust.
South Shields
☎ 067074 691
➜A A1300

Cycling

Glenbar Hire
217 Jesmond Road, Newcastle
☎ 091 281 5376

Walking

Derwent Walk Country Park
Disused railway walk served by 2 visitor centres.
Rowlands Gill, Gateshead
➜A A694
P 🚌 ♿ ♿

The Heritage Way
Long distance footpath of some 68 miles (110 km) around Tyne & Wear. Numerous access points.
Mr J. C. Barford, Civic Centre, Regent Street, Gateshead
☎ 091 477 1011

157

NORTHUMBERLAND

WHAT TO DO AND SEE

i Belford Craft Gallery, 2-3 Market Place, Belford, Northumberland
☎ 0668 213888 summer only

camping and bivouacs, orienteering, riding, mountain biking, fitness-training and bird watching.
Windy Gyle Outdoor Centre, West Street, Belford
☎ 0668 213289

EQUESTRIAN

Riding and Pony Trekking

Bridgend Riding Stables
Bridge End Farm Cottage
Brewery Road, Wooler
☎ 0668 319

Slate Hall Riding Centre
174 Main Street, Seahouses
☎ 0665 720320

HEALTH

Leisure Centres

Alnwick Swimming Pool
Alnwick
☎ 0665 602933

LOCAL FEATURES

Arts and Crafts

Belford Craft Gallery
Local crafts, paintings, books, maps and cards for sale.
2–3 Market Place, Belford
☎ 0668 213888

Bondgate Gallery
Contemporary works by regional artists and craftsmen.
22 Narrowgate, Alnwick
☎ 0665 510771

The Brent Gallery
Watercolours of wildlife, farm life and Northumbrian landscapes by David Binns, ceramics by Stephen Binns.
Fenham Le Moor, nr Belford
☎ 0668 533

Festivals and Fairs

June
Alnwick Fair
July
Belford Carnival Week

Historic Buildings

Bamburgh Castle
Restored mediaeval castle with collections of Central Asian armour, arms of 16th and 17th century, china and tapestries; includes Armstrong Museum.
Bamburgh
☎ 06684 208
From the A1 take the B1342 and the B1340

ADVENTURE

Mountaineering and Rock Climbing

Bearsports
Wide range of adventure sports on offer including hill walking, rock climbing and abseiling.
Windy Gyle Outdoor Centre, West Street, Belford
☎ 0668 213289

Multi-activity Centres

Bearsports
Windsurfing, sailing, abseiling, hill walking, kayaking, canoeing, surf-skiing, rafting,

NORTHUMBERLAND

WHAT TO DO AND SEE

Chillingham Castle
Mediaeval castle with Tudor additions and Georgian refinements set in magnificent grounds with views of the Cheviots; woodland walks, lake and formal topiary gardens.
Chillingham, Alnwick
☎ 06685 359
Off the A1 and the A697

Dunstanburgh Castle
14th century ruins in a dramatic coastal position. Reached by footpath from Craster.
Craster
☎ 0665 576231
On the B1339

Lindisfarne Castle
Tiny fort built in about 1550 and converted to a private house by Lutyens. National Trust.
Holy Island
☎ 0289 89244
→A A1
Island not accessible during high tide.

Lindisfarne Priory
Ruins of a monastery dated 1090, the cradle of Christianity in the North. English Heritage.
Holy Island
☎ 0289 89200
→A A1
Island not accessible during high tide.

Preston Tower
14th century peel tower with displays of local history.
Chathill
☎ 066 589 227
→A A1

Museums

Grace Darling Museum
In honour of the heroine who rescued survivors from the wreck of the *Forfarshire*.
Bamburgh
☎ 0665 720037
On the B1340

Heatherslaw Mill
Restored working 19th century water-driven corn mill on the River Till.
Ford Forge, Cornhill-on-Tweed
☎ 089082 338
On the B6354

Natural History

Chillingham Wild Cattle Association Ltd
The purest surviving members of the wild white cattle which formerly roamed the forests of Northern Britain.
Estate House, Chillingham, Alnwick
☎ 06685 250
→A A697

Farne Islands
Home for the largest British colonies of grey seals. National Trust.
Warden/Naturalist, The Sheiling, 8 St Aidan's, Seahouses
☎ 0665 720651
National Trust Shop, 16 Main Street, Seahouses
☎ 0665 721099

Trips to the Farne Islands
On *MFV Glad Tidings*; landings and commentary.
Billy Shiel, 4 Southfield Avenue, Seahouses
☎ 0665 720308

OUTDOOR LEISURE/SPORTS

Cycling

Game Fair
12 Marygate, Berwick-on-Tweed
☎ 0289 305119

Furnevels
Touring and adult bikes.
Bamburgh
☎ 06684 513
☎ 06684 574

Fishing

Excellent fishing on offer in Northumbria and the Borders. Further details from the Tourist Information Centre.

Shellacres
Salmon and sea trout fishing on the River Till.
Further details from: Edwin Thompson & Co, 44-48 Hide Hill, Berwick-on-Tweed
☎ 0289 304432

For permits and further information:
Northumbrian Water
Abbey Road, Pity Me, County Durham
☎ 091 383 2222

Walking

Northumberland Wildlife Trust
Guided and themed walks.
Hancock Museum, Barras Bridge, Newcastle-upon-Tyne
☎ 091 232 0038

WEST GLAMORGAN

WHAT TO DO AND SEE

i Aberdulais Basin, Aberdulais
☎ 0639 633531 (summer only)
i Beefeater Restaurant, Sunnycroft Road, Baglan
☎ 0639 823049 (summer only)
i Singleton Street, Swansea
  ☎ 0792 468321
i Pont Nedd Fechan, Nr Glynneath
☎ 0639 721795 (open all year, weekends only October–March)

EQUESTRIAN

Horse Riding

Clyne Farm Riding School
Tuition from novice to experienced.
Clyne Farm, Mayals, Swansea
☎ 0792 403333

Forgemill Riding Academy
Cilonnen, Three Crosses, Gower
☎ 0792 873760

LOCAL FEATURES

Arts and Crafts

Glynn Vivian Art Gallery
Painting and local crafts and china.
Alexandra Street, Swansea
☎ 0792 651738

Gardens

Clyne Valley Country Park
Famous for azaleas and rhododendrons
South of Swansea going towards Mumbles.
Black Pill, Gower
☎ 0792 401737

Margam Abbey and Country Park
Spacious grounds, nature reserve, boating lake, adventure playground, elegant orangery and maze, medieval religious ruins.
Nr Port Talbot
☎ 0639 871131/881635

Afan Argoed Country Park & Welsh Miners' Museum
Countryside centre, forest walks, picturesque riverside. The Museum depicts the life and times of a South Wales miner.
Cynonville
☎ 0639 850564

Historic Buildings

Neath Abbey
Ruins of 12th century monastery.
Neath, 5 miles north-east of Swansea
☎ 0792 812387

Museums

Maritime and Industrial Museum
This museum tells the story of Swansea's long association with the sea.
Maritime Quarter, Swansea
☎ 0792 650351

Swansea Museum
Wales's first museum with a broad range of exhibits in beautiful surroundings.
Victoria Road, Swansea
☎ 0792 653763

Cefn Coed Colliery Museum
Colliery machinery, mining exhibitions.
Crynant
☎ 0639 750556

Natural History

Aberdulais Falls
National Trust
Waterfalls in colourful gorge; remains of tinplate works powered by the falls.
➜ Off A465 just north-east of Neath
☎ 0639 636674

Penscynor Wildlife Park
Wide range of animals and birds in parkland setting.
➜ Off the A465 close to the Aberdulais Falls, Nr Neath
☎ 0639 642189

Plantasia
Huge hothouse containing thousands of plants from around the world.
Parc Tawe, North Dock, Swansea
☎ 0792 474555

Theatres

Dylan Thomas Theatre
Gloucester Place, Swansea
☎ 0792 473238

Grand Theatre
Singleton Street, Swansea
☎ 0792 473742

OUTDOOR LEISURE

Fishing

Coarse river fishing and sea fishing.
Capstan House
Beaufort Court, Beaufort Road, Swansea
☎ 0792 310311

Linnard Sports
25 High Street, Swansea
☎ 0792 655631

Skiing

Swansea Ski Centre
Morfa Statium, Upper Bank, Landore, Swansea
☎ 0792 476578

WATERSPORTS

Boat Hire

Inshore Workboat Hire
Old Customs House, West Pier, Maritime Quarter, Swansea
☎ 0792 642608

Swansea Harbour Boatmen
Kings Dock, Swansea
☎ 0792 653787

DYFED (SOUTH)

WHAT TO DO AND SEE

i Old Bridge, Haverfordwest (summer only)
☎ 0437 763110
i The Croft, Tenby
☎ 0834 2402
i Kingsmoor Common, Kilgetty
☎ 0834 813672 (summer only)
i Milford Haven
☎ 0646 690866 (summer only)

EQUESTRIAN

Riding

Haysford Stud Farm
Specialising in instruction of nervous riders.
Haycastle Road, Haverfordwest
☎ 0437 710512

Mainport Training
All forms of riding instruction.
The Mainport Centre, Ferry Lane, Pembroke
☎ 0646 684315

LOCAL FEATURES

Arts and Crafts

Graham Sutherland Gallery
A unique collection of Sutherland's works.
Picton Castle, The Rhos, nr Haverfordwest
☎ 0437 751326
P 🏛 ♿ × ♿ ♿

Gardens

Manor House Wildlife and Leisure Park
Parkland with floral displays and varied collection of animals and birds.
St. Florence
☎ 0646 651201
P 🏛 × ♿ ♿

Picton Castle Grounds
Natural woodlands surrounding country home owned by the same family for around 600 years.
Picton Castle, The Rhos, nr Haverfordwest
☎ 0437 751326
P 🏛 × ♿

Caldy Island
1½-mile long island with sea-birds and seals. Conducted tours of Caldy Island Monastery by Cistercian monks who produce perfume.
Off Tenby

Oakwood Park
Adventure and leisure park with many attractions including go-karts, roller coaster, gold rush town and boating lake.
Canaston Bridge, nr Narberth
☎ 0834 891376/891373

Historic Buildings

Pembroke Castle
13th century castle dominating the town.
Castle Terrace, Pembroke
☎ 0646 684585/681510
P 🏛 ♿ × ♿ ♿

Tudor Merchant's House
National Trust
Preserved house showing how the rich merchants lived in medieval times.
Quay Hill, Tenby
☎ 0834 2279
🏛

Museums

Castle Museum and Art Gallery
Haverfordwest's history presented in the old Gaol alongside the ruins of the Castle.
Haverfordwest.
☎ 0437 763708
P 🏛

Motormania
Over 60 exhibits covering the history of transport.
Keeston Hill, Haverfordwest
➔ A487 3 miles from Haverfordwest
☎ 0437 710175
P 🏛 × ♿

Museum of the Home
Dedicated to showing the minutia of everyday home life over the last 300 years.
Westgate Hill, Pembroke
☎ 0646 681200

Tenby Museum
Tenby's maritime and natural history plus excellent picture gallery.
Castle Hill, Tenby
☎ 0834 2809
🏛

Natural History

Sea Historic Gallery
Aquarium and geological display.
Westgate Hill, Pembroke
☎ 0646 682919
🏛

Silent World Aquarium
A collection of the area's water creatures.
Mayfield Drive, Narberth Road, Tenby
☎ 0834 4498
🏛 ♿ ♿

OUTDOOR LEISURE

Cycling

The Skate and Bike Centre
South Parade, Tenby
☎ 0834 5134

Fishing

Excellent fishing, particularly sea fishing.

County Sports
3 Old Bridge Street, Haverfordwest
☎ 0437 763740

Penfro Fishing Tackle
31 Meyrick Street, Pembroke Dock
☎ 0646 682756

The Tackle Box
Willings Passage, Main Street, Pembroke
☎ 0646 621744

DYFED (NORTH)

WHAT TO DO AND SEE

i Terrace Road, Aberystwyth
☎ 0970 612125
i Church Street, New Quay
☎ 0545 2605 (summer only)
i The Quay, Aberaeron
☎ 0545 570602
i High Street, The Promenade, Borth
☎ 0970 871174 (summer only)

EQUESTRIAN

Riding and Pony Trekking

Moelfryn Riding Centre
Bethania, nr Aberystwyth
☎ 09746 228

HEALTH

Leisure Centre

Borth Health Club
A five-station multi-gym, exercise bicycles, jogging machine, weights, sunbed, sauna, swimming pool, and jacuzzi.
Cliff Haven Hotel
☎ 0970 871 659

LOCAL FEATURES

Arts and Crafts

Aberystwyth Arts Centre
The main venue for the visual arts and crafts in Mid Wales with live performances of music and theatre and a spectacular summer season.
☎ 0970 623232

Tregaron Pottery
Hand thrown and decorated stoneware pottery.
Castell Flemish, Tregaron
☎ 097421 639
→A A485

Museums

Ceredigion Museum
The story of Cardigan told in a restored Edwardian Theatre.
Terrace Road, Aberystwyth
☎ 0970 617911

Camera Obscura
A re-creation of a Victorian amusement on the summit of Constitution Hill, access by the Cliff Railway.
Aberystwyth

National Library of Wales
The main centre for research into the history, literature and life of Wales; it holds collections of valuable manuscripts and books.
Penglais Road, Aberystwyth
☎ 0970 623816

Railways

Cliff Railway
A conveyance for gentlefolk since 1896, it offers a sedate journey to the summit of Constitution Hill.
Cliff Railway House, Cliff Terrace, Aberystwyth
☎ 0970 617642
From the north end of the promenade

Vale of Rheidol Railway
It runs from Aberystwyth 12 miles to Devil's Bridge; explore the Rheidol Fall, climb Jacob's ladder and view the Devil's Punchbowl.
☎ 0685 4854 for the timetable.

OUTDOOR LEISURE

Fishing

This is a major fishing area.
i Pamphlets on freshwater angling with lists of clubs and associations and lists of boat operators for sea angling trips are available at Tourist Information Centres.
☎ 0970 612125

Walking

i Walk packs with maps and detailed guidance on the Rheidol Valley and the Teifi Valley are available at Tourist Information Centres and shops.

WATER SPORTS

Canoeing

Canoe excursions up the River Teifi depart daily from the foot of Cilgerran Castle.
☎ 0239 613966

Sand Yachting

Borth Sand Yachting Club
Geth Evans, Geth's Boatshop, Borth
☎ 0970 871427

Surfing

Peter Hunt Watersports
High Street, Borth
☎ 0970 81617

162

GWYNEDD

WHAT TO DO AND SEE

i Conwy Castle Visitor Centre, Conwy, Gwynedd
☎ 0492 592248
i Marine Square Salt Island Approach, Holyhead, Gwynedd
☎ 0407 762622
i Chapel Street, Llandudno, Gwynedd
☎ 0492 876413
i Station Site, Llanfair P.G.
☎ 0248 713177
i Theatr Gwynedd, Deiniol Road, Bangor
☎ 0248 352786 (summer only)
i Oriel Pendeitsch, Castle Street, Caernarfon
☎ 0286 672232

EQUESTRIAN

Riding and Pony Trekking

Bodysgallen Riding Holiday Centre
Bodysgallen Farm, Llandudno
☎ 0492 83537

Pinewood Riding Stables
Sychnant Pass Road, Conwy
☎ 0492 592256

Rhiwiau Riding Centre
Llanfairfechan, Gwynedd
☎ 0248 680094

ADVENTURE

Mountaineering and Rock Climbing

Franco Ferrero
High quality courses for small groups including canoeing, mountain walking and rock climbing.
3 Tan-y-Bwlch, Mynydd Llandegai, Bethesda
☎ 0248 602287

National Centre for Mountain Activities
Centre operated by the Sports Council to provide mountain activities for beginners and experts.
Plas-y-Brenin, Capel Curig
☎ 06904 214

Shooting

Plas Newydd Shoot
Driven or rough shooting on Anglesey's famous estate.
c/o Liverpool Arms Hotel, Menai Bridge, Isle of Anglesey
☎ 0248 713335

LOCAL FEATURES

Aquariums

Anglesey Sea Zoo
Huge and varied collection of sea life around the island displayed in natural environments.
The Oyster Hatchery, Brynsiencyn, Anglesey
☎ 0248 430411/430412
→A A5
♿

Arts and Crafts

Piggery Pottery
Large lakeside pottery. Throw or paint your own pot.
Llanberis
☎ 0286 872529

James Pringle
Huge selection of quality woollen and craft products.
Llanfair P.G., Gwynedd
☎ 0248 717171

163

GWYNEDD

WHAT TO DO AND SEE

Gardens

Bodnant Garden
National Trust
A fine garden with magnificent rhododendrons, camellias, magnolias and conifers.
Tal-y-Cafn
☎ 0492 650460
Off the A470, 8 miles south of Llandudno

Historic Buildings

Beaumaris Castle
Perfectly planned medieval fortress, the last – and largest – castle in North Wales built by Edward I.
Beaumaris
☎ 0248 810361

Beaumaris Courthouse
Unique survival of an old courtroom.
Beaumaris
☎ 0248 810367

Beaumaris Gaol
Grim reminder of the harshness of prison life in Victorian times.
Beaumaris
☎ 0248 810921/750262 ext 269.

Conwy Castle
An impressive fortress built by Edward I 700 years ago.
Conwy

Penrhyn Castle
A majestic mock Norman castle in wooded parkland overlooking the Menai Strait; lavishly decorated inside with a collection of dolls and steam engine museum. National Trust.
Bangor
☎ 0248 353084
On the A5122, 3 miles east of Bangor

Plas Newydd
The 18th century house of James Wyatt, it occupies an unspoilt position adjacent to the Menai Strait. National Trust.
Isle of Anglesey
☎ 0248 714795
On the A4080, south of Llanfairpwll

Museums

Museum of Childhood
A nostalgic collection. Enchants young and old alike.
Beaumaris
☎ 0248 810448

Time Tunnel
Audio-visual experience. Also tells the story of emigration to America.
Beaumaris
☎ 0248 810072

Childhood Revisited
Dolls, model railway and motorcycles.
Bodhyfryd Road, Llandudno
☎ 0492 870424

Great Orme Mines
See how copper was mined in ancient times. Underground visit, audio-visual display. No parking at mine. Access by free shuttle bus or Great Orme Tramway.
Llandudno
☎ 0492 870477

Natural History

Conwy Butterfly House
Butterflies flying free.
Bodlondeb Gardens, Conwy
☎ 0492 593149
Close to the quay and the town centre

Pili Palas
Enchanting 'butterfly palace' with tropical jungle and hundreds of exotic butterflies from all over the world. Reptile house, insectarium, pet's corner, bird house, adventure playground, picnic area.
Menai Bridge
☎ 0248 712474
On north-western outskirts of town

Parks

Great Orme Country Park
Massive limestone headland that rises 679 feet to dominate Llandudno; guided walks and field trips.
Country Park Warden
☎ 0492 874151

Cabin Lift
Float from Happy Valley Station to the Great Orme summit by cable car.
Happy Valley, Llandudno, Gwynedd
☎ 0492 877205

GWYNEDD

WHAT TO DO AND SEE

Padarn Country Park
Ride on the quaint little Llanberis Lake Railway along the shores of Llyn Padarn or stop awhile and view Snowdon; visit the Welsh Slate Museum, deserted village and old slate quarry or explore the nature trails and woodland walks.
Llanberis
→A A4086

OUTDOOR LEISURE

Fishing

Starida
Sea angler skipper of great experience will arrange sea fishing trips of any duration or cruises to Puffin Island aboard the *Starida* which is based in Beaumaris.
☎ 0248 810251

Skiing

Ski Llandudno
The longest artifical ski slope in England and Wales. At the end of the promenade, through Happy Valley.
Llandudno
☎ 0492 874707

The Rhiw Goch Ski Centre
Skiing tuition and facilities.
Trawsfynydd Log Cabin Holiday Village, Bronaber, Trawsfynydd
☎ 076687 578

WATERSPORTS

Canoeing

Conwy Canoe Tours
Explore the Conwy Estuary by Canadian canoe, no experience necessary.
36 Bryn Castell, Conwy
☎ 0492 596457

Diving

Anglesey Sea and Surf Centre
A new coastal centre offering courses in canoeing, sailing and diving.
Porthdafarch, Trearddur Bay, Anglesey
☎ 0407 2525

Sailing

Aqua Sports
Andy Coghill, 17 Sea View Terrace, Aberdovey
☎ 0654 767754

Plas Menai National Watersports Centre
Yacht cruising and dinghy sailing.
Caernarfon
☎ 0248 670964

Smugglers Cove Sailing School
Cruiser and dinghy sailing.
Frongoch, Aberdovey
☎ 0654 767842

Talyllyn Watersports
Tywyn
☎ 0654 710065

Windsurfing

Surfwind Rhosneigr
Beach Road, Rhosneigr, Anglesey
☎ 0407 720391

POWYS

WHAT TO DO AND SEE

i Vicarage Gardens Car Park, Welshpool
☎ 0938 552043
i Owain Glyndwr Centre, Machynlleth
☎ 0654 702401
i Council Offices, High Street, Llanfyllin
☎ 069184 8868 (summer only)
i Central Car Park, Newtown
☎ 0686 625580 (summer only)

HEALTH

Leisure Centre

Armoury Leisure Centre
Brook Street, Welshpool
☎ 0938 554143

LOCAL FEATURES

Arts and Crafts

Oriel 31 Art Gallery
High Street, Welshpool
☎ 0938 552990
P

Gardens

Powis Castle Gardens
Parkland with formal gardens which were created in the 17th century. National Trust Immediately south-west of Welshpool town centre
☎ 0938 554336
P

Historic Houses

Montgomery Castle
A ruined shell but still impressive.
Montgomery, on the A490 10 miles south of Welshpool

Powis Castle
One of the most magnificent mansions in the country with fine displays of furniture and paintings.
A one mile walk through Powis Castle Gardens from Welshpool town centre.
☎ 0938 554336
P

Welshpool Railway Station
Well worth a look, an ornate 19th century structure.
P

Museums

Clive of India Museum
Museum within Powis Castle dedicated to relics of Clive of India.
Powis Castle
☎ 0938 554336
P

Powysland Museum and Montgomery Canal Centre
Local history and industrial archeology.
Canal Wharf, off Severn Street, Welshpool
☎ 0938 554656
P

Natural History

Llanfyllin Bird and Butterfly World
Species from all over the world contained in 50 aviaries.
Domgay, Bachin Road, Llanfyllin
Off the A490 10 miles north-west of Welshpool
☎ 069 184 751
P

Moors Collection
Farm animals and rare breeds.
On the A438 Oswestry road, 1 mile north of Welshpool
☎ 0938 553395
P

Railway

Welshpool and Llanfair Light Railway
One of the 'Great Little Trains of Wales' running 8 miles and linking Welshpool in the Severn valley to Llanfair.
Caereinion in the Banwyn valley
☎ 0938 810441
P

OUTDOOR LEISURE

Cycling

G.M. Brooks
9 Severn Street, Welshpool
☎ 0938 553582

Fishing

Local fishing is available including on the Severn, for information on accessibility of waters and for tackle go to:

Brians Angling Supplies
North Road, Llanymynech
On the A438 10 miles north of Welshpool
☎ 0691 830027

CLWYD

WHAT TO DO AND SEE

i Town Hall, Wellington Street, Rhyl
☎ 0745 355068
i Craft Centre, Ruthin
☎ 08242 3992
i Town Hall, Castle Street, Llangollen
☎ 0978 860828
i Lambpit Street, Wrexham
☎ 0978 357845

ADVENTURE

Karting

Deeside Indoor Karting Centre
Race and leisure karts. Expert tuition, race suits, huge indoor circuit and chidren's track.
Engineers Park, Sandycroft, Deeside, Clwyd
☎ 0244 531652
➜A55
✗

HEALTH

Leisure Centre

Eirias Park
Leisure park and sports complex within park-like surrounds.
Colwyn Bay
☎ 0492 533223/4 (Leisure Centre)
☎ 0492 518111 (Dinosaur World)

LOCAL FEATURES

Arts and Crafts

Llangollen Craft Centre
Range of individual craft workshops in converted malthouse.
Llangollen
☎ 0978 861887

Tri Thy Craft and Needlework Centre
Colony of craft workshops.
Coed Talon, nr Mold
☎ 0352 771359
Off A5104, Chester to Corwen road, signposted
✗

Gardens

Tŷ Mawr Country Park
In Dee valley. Riverside walks, animals, picnic areas, ranger service.
Cae Gwilym Road, Cefn-mawr
☎ 0978 822780

Historic Buildings

Castell Dinas Brân
Dominates the Dee valley and the town.
Llangollen

Chirk Castle
Mansion which developed from border fortress. Magnificent entrance gates.
Chirk
☎ 0691 777701

Erddig Hall
A magnificent country house with a fascinating 'upstairs-downstairs' portrayal of life. National Trust.
Southern outskirts of Wrexham
☎ 0978 355314

Plas Newydd
Attractive home of the 'Ladies of Llangollen'. Contains a fine collection of medieval oak carvings
Llangollen
☎ 0978 861514

St. Asaph Cathedral
Britain's smallest medieval cathedral
St. Asaph

Museums

Canal Museum
Inland waterway displays
Llangollen
☎ 0978 860702

Motor Museum
Displays vehicles over 25 years old.
Llangollen
☎ 0978 860324
1 mile west on A542

Theatres

Theatr Clwyd
Mold
☎ 0352 55114
12 miles from Chester

Zoos

Welsh Mountain Zoo
Outstanding zoo in outstanding location.
Llanrwst Road, Colwyn Bay, Clwyd
☎ 0492 532938

OUTDOOR LEISURE

Fishing

Coarse fishing/salmon and migratory trout on the Dee and Clwyd rivers and their tributaries. Licences available from:

Welsh Water Authority
Shire Hall, Mold
☎ 0352 700176

Ice Skating

Deeside Leisure Centre
Queensferry
☎ 0244 812311

Walking

Llyn Brenig Visitor Centre
A fascinating introduction to the lake and its surroundings.
Located near the dam, Llyn Brenig
☎ 049082 463

DUMFRIES & GALLOWAY

WHAT TO DO AND SEE

i Tourist Information Centre,
Whitesands, Dumfries
☎ 0387 53862

LOCAL FEATURES

Festival and Fairs

May
KM152 Cycle Rally, 22–25 May
Arts Festival, 22–31 May
South of Scotland Sports Fair, 23–24 May

June
Lockerbie Gala & Riding of the Marches,
6–13 June
Guid Nychburris Festival, 14–20 June

July
Annan Riding of the Marches, 4 July
Drumlanrig Horse Driving Trials, 10–12 July

August
Dumfries & Lockerbie Agricultural Show
1 August

September
Burns Festival, 18–27 September

November
St. Andrew's Day Fireworks, 27 November (prov)

Gardens

Arbigland Garden
Formal, woodland and water gardens leading down to a sandy bay.
Kirkbean
☎ 0387 88 283

Threave Garden
National Trust for Scotland teaching garden featuring walled garden and greenhouse, formal garden, rose garden, heather garden and more. Visitor centre and tea-room.
1 mile west of Castle Douglas.
☎ 0556 2575

Heritage

Burnswark Hill
Native hill-top earthwork from 6th century BC whose flat top can be seen for miles. Flanked by two Roman seige camps, splendid view from top.
Near Ecclefechan.

Hadrian's Wall
Built by the Romans between AD122 and AD128 to mark the northern boundary of the Roman Empire in Britain. The wall was originally 15ft high and 40ft thick with forts and mile castles dotted along its length to keep out the marauding Picts. Abandoned in the 4th century, the wall is still well preserved particularly at Banks (south of the minor road east of Banks village) and Birdoswald (2 miles west of Greenhead on a minor road off the B6318).

Ruthwell Cross
Magnificent Anglian stone cross of 7th century bearing runic and Latin inscriptions.
Ruthwell Church off B724

Historic Buildings

Caerlaverock Castle
Dating from late 13th century this moated ruin is Britain's only triangular Castle. Remarkable twin-towered gatehouse.
Off B725 8 miles south-east of Dumfries.
☎ 0387 77 244

Comlongon Castle
A complete 15th century tower house with semi-restored Great Hall, vaulted basement, dungeons.
In Clarencefield 8 miles west of Annan.
☎ 0387 87 283

Corn Mill
Renovated 18th century water-powered mill in full working order.
New Abbey
☎ 0387 85 260

Drumlanrig Castle & Country Park
17th century Castle, Dumfriesshire home of Duke of Buccleuch & Queensberry, with renowned art collection. Country park with cycles, walking trails, craft shops, tea-room, falconry.
Thornhill
☎ 0848 31682/30248

Lincluden Collegiate Church
Early 15th century remains of collegiate church.
Off A76 1½ miles north of Dumfries town centre.
☎ 0387 55176

Maxwelton House
Early 14th century house, birthplace of Annie Laurie. Museum, chapel, gardens, tea-room.
13 miles north-west of Dumfries nr Moniaive.
☎ 08482 384/385

Sweetheart Abbey
Splendid remains of late 13th century Cistercian Abbey founded by Devorgilla, Lady of Galloway, in memory of her husband John Balliol.
New Abbey

Threave Castle
14th century island stronghold of Archibald the Grim.
A75 3 miles west of Castle Douglas.

Museums

Aviation Museum
Run by volunteers on site of former RAF Airfield and housing all types of aviation artefacts – you can even sit in a jet fighter. Open weekends only.
Signposted off A701 2 miles north of Dumfries.
☎ 0387 65957 (pm); 710491 (work)

DUMFRIES & GALLOWAY

WHAT TO DO AND SEE

Burns House
18th century sandstone house where Robert Burns spent the last 3 years of his life and died in 1796. Many fascinating items connected to the poet.
Burns Street, Dumfries.
☎ 0387 55297

Dumfries Museum and Camera Obscura
Largest in South West Scotland and tracing the history of the region's people and landscape. From the table top screen in the Camera Obscura (situated in the early 19th century windmill tower) a panoramic view of Dumfries is possible on fine days.
The Observatory, Corbelly Hill, Dumfries.
☎ 0387 55374

Savings Banks Museum
Savings Banks began here in 1810. Follow their growth to modern TSB and a worldwide movement.
Ruthwell
☎ 0387 87 640

Robert Burns Heritage Centre
The 'Dumfries Years' of Robert Burns traced through exhibitions, displays and audio-visual theatre. Bookshop, cafe.
Mill Road, Dumfries.
☎ 0387 64808

Open Farms

Mossburn Animal Centre
Hold and learn about various animals at Mossburn. Come and see Romeo the celebrated Vietnamese pot-bellied pig and Joker the calf who shouldn't be.
Lochmaben
☎ 0387 811 288

OUTDOOR LEISURE

Cycling

Craigshiels Activities, Dumfries.
Mountain bike hire, trails and route advice. Based at Drumlanrig Castle, Thornhill during summer.
☎ 0387 61818

Mabie Forest
Mountain bike hire and waymarked trails through conifer and broadleaved woodland.
☎ 0387 86247

Falconry

Falconry Centre, Drumlanrig Castle, Thornhill.
Flying demonstrations of birds of prey. Mews in Castle stables and Falconry courses. Handling days during winter.
☎ 0848 31682

Farm Bikes

Farm Buggy Trails, Cumstone Farm, nr Lockerbie
Accompanied trails through countryside, 1–2½ hours, on 4-wheel farm bikes.
☎ 05767 225

Golf

Dumfries and County Golf Club
Edinburgh Road, Dumfries
No visitors on Saturdays.
☎ 0387 53585

Lockerbie Golf Club
☎ 05762 3363

Southerness Golf Club
Championship links course.
☎ 0387 88 677

Thornhill Golf Club
☎ 0848 30546

Horseshoe Holidays

Short breaks or longer holidays through the tranquil lanes and byways of rural Dumfries by horse-drawn gypsy caravans.
Fairgirth Smiddy, Ruthwell.
☎ 0387 87 648

Walking

Wilson Ogilvie (Dumfries Brigend Tourist Services)
Guided Robert Burns and Heritage Walks in Dumfries.
☎ 0387 64267

BORDERS

WHAT TO DO AND SEE

i Henderson Park, Coldstream,
Berwickshire
☎ 0890 2607
i Turret House, Roxburghshire
☎ 0573 234464

EQUESTRIAN

Riding and Pony Trekking

Easter Langlee Pony Trekking Centre
Easter Langlee Farm, Galashiels
☎ 0896 58234

HEALTH

Leisure Centres

Kelso Swimming Pool
Swimming and sunbeds.
Inch Road, Kelso
☎ 0573 24944

The Tweedsider Sports Centre
Squash courts, sauna, jacuzzi, sunbeds,
solarium, snooker, pool.
5 Vault Square, Kelso
☎ 0573 25777

LOCAL FEATURES

Architecture

Smailholm Tower
16th century tower-house with good views
of the Border Country.

Art Galleries

Ancrum Gallery
Paintings by leading Scottish artists,
monthly exhibitions.
Cross Keys Inn, Ancrum
☎ 08353 340
Off the A68, 3½ miles from Jedburgh

Arts and Crafts

Water Lily Weavers
Rugs, tapestries and hand woven items.
Homestead Craft Centre. The Hirsel,
Coldstream, Berwickshire
☎ 0890 2977
On the A697, west of Coldstream

Festivals and Fairs

February
Jedburgh Hand Ba'

June
Melrose Festival Week

July
Kelso Civic Week

August
Coldstream Civic Week

December
Masons Walk, Melrose, December 27

Gardens

Dundock Wood and the Hirsel Grounds
Museum and craft workshops, flowers
through the year.
The Hirsel, Coldstream, Berwickshire
☎ 0890 2834
On the A697, 3 miles west of Coldstream

Heritage

Kelso Abbey
A fragment of this 12th century abbey.
Town centre

Historic Buildings

Floors Castle
Home of the Duke and Duchess of
Roxburghe, the largest inhabited castle in
Scotland.
Kelso
☎ 0573 23333

Museums

Coldstream Museum
Market Square, Coldstream
☎ 0890 2630

Natural History

Yetholm Loch
A nature reserve of the Scottish Wildlife
Trust. A lowland loch with a rich fen and
many migratory birds. Permits from: M. E.
Braithwaite, Cockspurs, Lilliesleaf, Melrose

OUTDOOR LEISURE

Cycling

Coldstream Cycles
Tours and accommodation arranged.
The Lees Stables, Coldstream
☎ 0890 2709

Fishing

Salmon is the prime catch, but brown
trout, sea trout and coarse fishing are
popular. Local tackle shops will provide
information and permits.

Golf

Kelso Golf Club ⛳18
Berrymoss, Kelso
☎ 0573 23259

Walking

Countryside Ranger Service
Guided walks available.
Borders Regional Council
Regional Headquarters, Newtown
☎ 0835 23301

STRATHCLYDE

WHAT TO DO AND SEE

i Hamilton Tourist Information Services, Road Chef Services, M74 Northbound, by Hamilton, Lanarkshire
☎ 0698 285590

EQUESTRIAN

Riding and Pony Trekking

Dalzell Riding School
Manse Road, Dalzell Estate, Motherwell
☎ 0698 68771

Woodfoot Equestrian Centre
Millheugh, Larkhall
☎ 0698 881608

HEALTH

Leisure Centres

The Aquatec Centre, Motherwell
Major leisure, ice and pool complex featuring tyre ride and flume, wild water channel, ice tunnel and health suite.
☎ 0698 76464

LOCAL FEATURES

Gardens

Viewpark Gardens. Uddingston, Lanarkshire
Plant collections and demonstration gardens.
Uddingston
☎ 0698 818269

Heritage

Tinto Hill, nr Symington, Lamarkshire
Highest hill in the Clyde Valley nr Biggar, it is capped by one of the largest bronze-age cairns in the country; well-defined but steep path to the summit (2,320 feet); allow three hours for the climb.

Historic Buildings

Bothwell Castle, nr Uddingston, Lanarkshire
An imposing red sandstone castle on the banks of the River Clyde, once the home of the Black Douglases, regarded as the finest surviving 13th century castle in Scotland.
☎ 0698 816894

Chatelherault Country Park, Hamilton, Lanarkshire
Beautifully restored 18th century hunting lodge of the Dukes of Hamilton designed by William Adam; the surrounding park has nature walks, Cadzow Castle, an ancient breed of white cattle and an adventure playground.
Ferniegair, nr Hamilton
☎ 0698 426213

Craignethan Castle, Crossford, Lanarkshire
Built in the 15th century with later additions, this is an outstanding example of military fortification.
☎ 055586 364

Hallbar Tower
15th century fortified tower.
Braidwood, Carluke
→A B7056
i Contact 0555 73462

Hamilton Mausoleum, Hamilton, Lanarkshire
Huge, remarkable monument built in the 18th century as a chapel and crypt for the Dukes of Hamilton; famous for its 15 second echo, the longest echo of any building in Europe.
The Director, Strathclyde Country Park, 366 Hamilton Road, Motherwell
☎ 0698 66155
West of the M74
🚌 booking essential.

Museums

Cameronian Museum, Hamilton, Lanarkshire
Museum housed in the Duke of Hamilton's former riding school.
☎ 0698 285382

Hamilton District Museum, Lanarkshire
Local history museum with a transport section, housed in a 17th century coaching inn.
☎ 0698 283981

David Livingstone Centre, Blantyre
Birthplace of the famous missionary/explorer.
☎ 0698 823140

Natural History

New Lanark and Falls of Clyde
An industrial village established in 1785; the site of Robert Owen's radical social and educational experiments, now a World Heritage Site. Twenty minutes walk from the village are the spectacular Falls of Clyde.
☎ 0555 65876

171

STRATHCLYDE

WHAT TO DO AND SEE

Parks

Dalzell Country Park and Baronshaugh Reserve, nr Lanarkshire,
Pleasant woodland walks, secluded picnic spots, adjacent marsh meadow forms a RSPB reserve noted for its wildfowl and woodland birds.
☎ 0555 70941

Strathclyde Country Park, nr Hamilton, Lanarkshire
Watersports, nature trails, visitor centre, fun fair, play and picnic areas, camping and caravan site.
☎ 0698 66155

Lanark Moor Country Park and Loch, Lanark
Country park with playing fields, boating, fishing, picnic spots, putting and pitch and putt.
☎ 0555 61853

Theatres

Puppet Theatre, Biggar, Lanarkshire
Complete Victorian theatre in miniature; puppet plays, guided tours and exhibitions.
☎ 0899 20631
P 🚌 ✕

Zoos

Glasgow Zoo
Uddingston, Lanarkshire
☎ 041 771 1185

OUTDOOR LEISURE

Birdwatching and Wildlife

Strathclyde Country Park, nr Hamilton, Lanarkshire
Over 150 species of birds have been recorded in the park since it was opened. Countryside rangers provide Guided Walks.
☎ 0698 66155

Baronshaugh Nature Reserve, nr Motherwell, Lanarkshire
Owned by the RSPB and open all year. Excellent viewing of dabbling ducks and waders.
☎ 0555 70941

Chatelherault Country Park, nr Hamilton, Lanarkshire
☎ 0698 426213

Fishing

Strathclyde Country Park, nr Hamilton, Lanarkshire
Fishing on the River Clyde and on Strathclyde Loch.
Permits from The Director, Watersports Centre, 366 Hamilton Road, Motherwell
☎ 0698 66155

River Avon, Lanarkshire
Fishing for brown trout and grayling.
Avon Angling Club,
Mr Peter Brooks, 3 The Neuk, Stonehouse, Lanarkshire

Kype Reservoir, Lanarkshire
Fishing for brown trout and rainbow trout.
Kype Angling Club,
8 Townshead Street, Stonehouse, Lanarkshire
☎ 0698 791970

Newmill Trout Fisheries
Fishing for rainbow trout.
Newmill Trout and Deer Farm, nr Lanark
☎ 0555 870730

Golf

Lanark Golf Course ⓘ₁₈
The Moor, Lanark
☎ 0555 3219

Strathclyde Park Golf Course ⓘ₉
Mote Hill, Hamilton
☎ 0698 66155

Strathclyde Park Golf Range
Mote Hill, Hamilton
☎ 0698 66155

Leadhills Golf Club ⓘ₉
Leadhills, nr Biggar
☎ 065974 222

Ice Skating

Lanarkshire Ice Rink
Mote Hill, off Muir Street, Hamilton
☎ 0698 282448

WATERSPORTS

Strathclyde Country Park, nr Hamilton, Lanarkshire
Windsurfing, rowing, canoeing and waterskiing.
☎ 0698 66155

LOTHIAN

WHAT TO DO AND SEE

i Waverley Market, 3 Princes Street, Edinburgh
☎ 031 557 1700

EQUESTRIAN

Riding and Pony Trekking

Edinburgh and Lasswade Riding Centre
Mr J. N. Beck, Kevock Road, Lasswade, Midlothian
☎ 031 663 7676

Tower Farm Riding Stables
Mrs J. Forrest, 85 Liberton Drive, Edinburgh
☎ 031 664 3375

Weftmuir Riding Centre
Totley Wells Grange, nr South Queensferry, West Lothian

HEALTH

Leisure Centres

Ainslie Park Leisure Centre
International standard competition pool, flumes, spa pool, toddler's pool, fountain and water cannon as well as fitness room and indoor sports facilities.
92 Pilton Drive, Edinburgh
☎ 031 551 2400

Meadowbank Sports Centre
The main Commonwealth Games Stadium.
London Road, Edinburgh
☎ 031 661 5351

Royal Commonwealth Pool
Fitness centre, sauna, sunbeds, flumes and other sports facilities.
Dalkeith Road, Edinburgh
☎ 031 667 7211

LOCAL FEATURES

Art Galleries

City Art Centre
Displays from the city's art collection, temporary exhibitions of fine and applied arts, open space exhibitions by local arts groups. Re-opens mid-1992.
2 Market Street, Edinburgh
☎ 031 225 2424 ext 6650

National Gallery of Scotland
Works by many famous artists as well as the Scottish Masters and temporary exhibitions.
The Mound, Edinburgh
☎ 031 556 8921

National Portrait Gallery
Queen Street, Edinburgh
☎ 031 556 8921

Scottish National Gallery of Modern Art
Belford Road, Edinburgh
☎ 031 556 8921

Arts and Crafts

The Adam Pottery
Pottery studio producing hand-thrown stoneware.
76 Henderson Row, Stockbridge, Edinburgh
☎ 031 557 3978

Brass Rubbing Centre
Mediaeval brasses and Scottish stone carvings.
Trinity Apse, Chalmers Close, High Street, Edinburgh
☎ 031 556 4364

Factory Visits

Edinburgh Crystal Visitor's Centre
Guided factory tours available.
Penicuik, Midlothian
☎ 0968 75128
➜A A701

LOTHIAN

WHAT TO DO AND SEE

Festivals and Fairs

March
Folk Festival

April
Edinburgh International Science Festival

June
Royal Highland Show, Ingliston

August
Edinburgh International Festival
Fringe
Military Tattoo
Edinburgh International Film Festival
Jazz Festival

Food and Drink

Royal Mile Entertainments
Mediaeval entertainment and feasting.
PO Box 6, Dalkeith, Midlothian
☎ 031 663 3603

Scotch Whisky Heritage Centre
358 Castlehill, The Royal Mile, Edinburgh
☎ 031 220 0441

Gardens

Royal Botanic Garden
Inverleith Row, Edinburgh
☎ 031 552 7171

Guided Tours

Edinburgh Classic Tour
Bus tour run by Lothian Regional Transport
☎ 031 220 4111 for bookings

Guide Friday
City tours by double decker bus with guide. Tours start from the Waverley Bridge.
☎ 031 556 2244

In City Guides
City and country tours in a 4/6 seater.
☎ 031 332 0727

Off the Beaten Track
Personally conducted tours through Lowland Scotland.
Margaret Kinnear
☎ 031 667 4473

Robin's Walking Tours
Tours of the old town start at the fountain over Waverley Market, Princes Street.
Robin Sinton, 66 Willowbrae Road, Edinburgh
☎ 031 661 0125/557 3443

Cadies Tours
The Witchey, Castlehill, Edinburgh
☎ 031 225 6745

Heritage

Scotland's Clans Tartan Centre
Where to track down your clan and tartan. In the James Pringle Woollen Mill,
70/74 Bangor Road, Leith
☎ 031 553 5100
☎ 031 553 5161

Historic Buildings

Craigmillar Castle
Mediaeval ruined castle associated with Mary Queen of Scots.
Craigmillar, Edinburgh
☎ 031 661 4445
On the A68 Edinburgh–Dalkeith Road

Dalmeny House
Period mansion house and grounds with a notable art collection, French furniture, porcelain and tapestries.
South Queensferry, West Lothian
☎ 031 331 1888

Edinburgh Castle
A famous historic stronghold, and home of the Scottish National War Memorial, the Scottish Crown Jewels, the Scottish United Services and the Royal Scots Regimental Museums.
☎ 031 225 9846

Hopetoun House
Scotland's biggest Robert Adam mansion set in 100 acres of parkland, with sumptuous rooms and state apartments, paintings by Gainsborough, Raeburn and Canaletto, a walled garden centre, nature trail and deer park.
South Queensferry, West Lothian
☎ 031 331 2451

Lauriston Castle
Mansion house with a fine furniture collection and an outstanding display of "Blue John" ware.
2 Cramond Road South, Edinburgh
☎ 031 336 2060

Palace of Holyroodhouse
Official Scottish residence of H.M. The Queen; an outstanding picture gallery and state apartments.
Royal Mile, Edinburgh
☎ 031 556 1096

Museums

Huntly House
Canongate, Edinburgh
☎ 031 225 2424 ext 6689

John Knox House
High Street, Edinburgh
☎ 031 556 9579

Lady Stair's House
A museum dedicated to the great Scottish writers, Burns, Scott and Stevenson.
Lawnmarket, Edinburgh
☎ 031 225 2424 ext 6593

LOTHIAN

WHAT TO DO AND SEE

Museum of Childhood
Historic toys, dolls, hobby items and costumes.
42 High Street, Edinburgh
☎ 031 225 2424 ext 6645

Royal Museum of Scotland
Decorative art and science.
Chambers Street, Edinburgh
☎ 031 225 7534

Royal Museum of Scotland
Queen Street, Edinburgh
☎ 031 225 7534

Music, Dance and Drama

Usher Hall
Lothian Road, Edinburgh
☎ 031 228 1155

The Queen's Hall
Clerk Street, Edinburgh
☎ 031 668 3456

Natural History

Edinburgh Butterfly and Insect World
Melville Nurseries, Dalkeith
☎ 031 663 4932

Theatres

Kings Theatre
Leven Street, Edinburgh
☎ 031 229 1201

Royal Lyceum Theatre
Grindlay Street, Edinburgh
☎ 031 229 9697

The Playhouse Theatre
Greenside Place, Edinburgh
☎ 031 557 2590

The Churchill Theatre
Morningside Road, Edinburgh
☎ 031 447 7597

Zoos

The Scottish National Zoological Park
Corstorphine Road, Edinburgh
☎ 031 334 9171

OUTDOOR LEISURE

Birdwatching and Wildlife

Duddingston Loch
A bird sanctuary since 1923, the loch has many rare birds. Permission available from: The Scottish Wildlife Trust
☎ 031 226 4602

Cycling

i Cycle touring routes available from the Tourist Office.

Fishing

Fishing is good in the rivers, lochs, and reservoirs around Edinburgh. Local tackle shops will supply information and permits.

Golf

Braids Hill Golf Course
Braids Hill
☎ 031 447 6666

Carrick Knowe Golf Course
29 Glendwan Park
☎ 031 337 1096

Craigentinny Golf Course
Lochend
☎ 031 554 7501

Portobello Golf Course
Stanley Street
☎ 031 669 4361

Silverknowes Golf Course
Silverknowes Parkway
☎ 031 661 5351

Ice Skating

Murrayfield Ice Rink
Riversdale Crescent, Edinburgh
☎ 031 337 6933

Skiing

Hillend Ski Centre
Europe's largest artificial ski slope.
Biggar Road, Pentland Hills
☎ 031 445 4433

Walking and Rambling

Mercat Walking Tours
☎ 031 661 4541

Guided Walks
New Town
☎ 031 557 5222

Guided Walks around Holyrood Park
Scottish Wildlife Trust
☎ 031 226 4602

Union Canal Guided Walks
☎ 0324 612415

WATERSPORTS

Boat Trips

Maid of Forth
Regular sailings from South Queensferry.
☎ 031 331 4857

The Edinburgh Canal Centre
Boat trips, cruises and boat hire.
Bridge Inn, Ratho
☎ 031 333 1320

Dinghy Sailing

Port Edgar Sailing Centre, South Queensferry, West Lothian
Sailing, boat hire and courses available.
☎ 031 331 3330

FIFE/TAYSIDE

WHAT TO DO AND SEE

i South Street, Leven, Fife
☎ 0333 29464
i South Street, St Andrews, Fife
☎ 0334 72021

ADVENTURE

Multi-activity Centres

East Neuk Outdoors
Abseiling, archery, windsurfing, canoeing, climbing, coastal walks, cycling, birdwatching and historic tours.
Anstruther, Fife
☎ 0333 311929

EQUESTRIAN

Riding and Pony Trekking

Charleton Riding Centre
Colinsburgh, Fife
☎ 0333 34535
Off the A915 to Largoward, on the B941

Stravithie Riding Stables
Stravithie Estate, by St. Andrews, Fife
☎ 0334 81251
On the B9131, 4 miles south of St Andrews

HEALTH

Leisure Centres

Cupar Sports Centre
Swimming pool, steambath, sunbeds and fitness room.
Cupar, Fife
☎ 0334 54793

East Sands Leisure Complex
Leisure pool with giant water slide, jacuzzi, steam bath, sunbeds, squash, snooker, bar and restaurant.
St. Andrews, Fife
☎ 0334 76506

LOCAL FEATURES

Festivals and Fairs

February
St. Andrews Arts Festival

April
Golf Week, St Andrews

July
St. Andrews Highland Games

November
St. Andrew's Day Celebrations

Gardens

Botanic Garden
Won international acclaim for its design and range of plants.
St. Andrews, Fife

Historic Buildings

Balcaskie
Sir William Bruce transformed a mediaeval tower into one of the finest classical houses in Scotland; beautiful gardens with view of Bass Rock.
☎ 0333 730213
Nr Pittenweem, Fife
On the B942

Earlshall Castle and Gardens
Romantic castle home of the Baron and Baroness of Earlshall built in 1546. Collections of antique arms, furniture and Jacobite relics.
Leuchars, Fife
☎ 0334 839205
On the A919, 1 mile east of Leuchars

The Royal Palace of Falkland
Country residence in the 15th and 16th centuries for the Stuart kings and queens.
Falkland, Fife
☎ 033 757 397
A912

FIFE/TAYSIDE

WHAT TO DO AND SEE

Kellie Castle
Fascinating 16th century castle with a beautiful Victorian walled garden. National Trust for Scotland.
Nr Pittenweem, Fife
☎ 033 38 271
On the B9171, 3 miles north-west of Pittenweem

Hill of Tarvit Mansion
Edwardian mansion provides a wonderful setting for fine furniture, paintings, tapestries, porcelain and bronzes. National Trust for Scotland.
Nr Cupar, Fife
☎ 0334 53127
On the A916, approximately 2 miles south-west of Cupar

Museums

British Golf Museum
The story of golf from its origins to the present day.
Golf Place, St. Andrews
☎ 0334 78880
Opposite the Royal and Ancient Golf Club

Crail Museum
The history and fishing heritage of Crail and the surrounding area.
☎ 0334 50869
Marketgate, Crail, Fife

Museum of the St. Andrews Preservation Trust
17th century building in North Street; photographs, paintings, grocers' and chemists' shops.
☎ 0334 72152
12 North Street, St. Andrews

Scottish Fisheries Museum
Record of Scotland's fishing trade.
☎ 0333 50869
Anstruther, Fife

Natural History

The Scottish Deer Centre
Ranger guided tours; nature walk; adventureland; craft shop.
Cupar, Fife
☎ 033781 391
➤A A91

Parks

Cambo Country Park
Farm machinery display; pets corner, nature trails and walks. Farm building converted to provide a restaurant.
☎ 0333 50810
On the A917 Crail road, 7 miles from St Andrews, Fife

Craigtoun Country Park
Dutch village, boating lake, woodland walks, picnic areas, miniature railway, putting, bowling and trampolines.
☎ 0334 73666
2 miles from St. Andrews, Fife

OUTDOOR LEISURE/SPORTS

Fishing

Angling on Rivers and Lochs
Good trout fishing waters at Cameron Reservoir. Permits at hut near loch.
☎ 0334 76347
Approximately 4 miles south of St. Andrews, Fife

Clatto Loch
Fly fishing for brown trout.
Waterman's Cottage, Clatto Loch
☎ 0334 52595
Off the A916, 5 miles south of Cupar, Fife

River Eden and Ceres Burn
Brown trout and salmon. Permits from:
J. Wilson & Sons, 169 South Street, St Andrews
☎ 0334 72477

Sea Angling
Sea angling trips run from several coastal villages and towns for cod, plaice, saithe, mackerel and wrasse.

Walking

i Details of many delightful local walks are available from Tourist Information Centres.

Guided Walks
North-east Fife Ranger Service organises summer walks.
☎ 0334 73666

Historical Guided Walks
St. Andrews and the University.
Tickets from the Tourist Information Centre.

WATERSPORTS

Boat Trips

Anstruther Pleasure Trips
Boat trips to the Isle of May.
14 Dreelside, Anstruther
☎ 0333 310103

Diving

East Coast Divers
Facilities for sports divers including boat charter, compressed air and accommodation.
Anstruther
☎ 0333 310768

177

TAYSIDE

WHAT TO DO AND SEE

i High Street, Crieff, Perthshire
☎ 0764 2578
i 22 Atholl Road, Pitlochry, Perthshire
☎ 0796 47215
☎ 0796 47251

ADVENTURE

Multi-activity Centres

Croft-na-Caber Watersports and Activities Centre
Windsurfing, canoeing, sailing, waterskiing, parascending, rafting, jet bikes, climbing, shooting, fishing and cross-country skiing.
Kenmore, Loch Tay, Perthshire
☎ 0887 830236
☎ 0887 830588

Highland Adventure
Riding and multi-activity holidays.
Glenisla, by Alyth, Perthshire
☎ 057582 238

EQUESTRIAN

Riding and Pony Trekking

Tullochville Trekking Centre
Tullochville Farm, Coshieville, nr Aberfeldy, Perthshire
☎ 08873 559

Strathearn Stables
Crieff Hydro Hotel, Crieff, Perthshire
☎ 0764 2401 ext 431

HEALTH

Leisure Centres

Perth Leisure Pool
Advanced leisure pool with flumes, wild water, outdoor lagoon, bubble beds, a 25-metre training pool, health suite, fitness room and children's pool.
Glasgow Road, Perth
☎ 0738 30535

LOCAL FEATURES

Arts and Crafts

Crieff Visitor Centre
See Thistle Pottery and Perthshire Paperweights being made.
Muthill Road, Crieff, Perthshire
☎ 0764 4014

The Highland Horn and Deerskin Centre
Range of leather goods made from deerskin, leather and hornware for sale.
City Hall, Dunkeld, Perthshire
☎ 03502 569

Pitlochry Pottery
Workshop and showroom in 200 year old cottage.
East Haugh, Perthshire
☎ 0796 472790
2 miles south of Pitlochry

Stuart Crystal
Free tours of crystal factory.
Muthill Road, Crieff, Perthshire
☎ 0764 4004

Factory Visits

Edradour Distillery
Smallest distillery in Scotland.
By Moulin, Perthshire
☎ 0796 472095
2½ miles east of Pitlochry

Glenturret Distillery Ltd
Scotland's oldest distillery.
Crieff, Perthshire
☎ 0764 2424
Off the A85, 1 mile west of Crieff

Historic Buildings

Blair Castle
A white-turreted baronial castle, seat of the Duke of Atholl. Notable collections of furniture, pictures, embroidery, arms, porcelain and Jacobite relics; extensive grounds, nature trails, deerpark.
Blair Atholl, Perthshire
☎ 079 681 207
Off A9, 6 miles north-west of Pitlochry

Museums

Atholl Country Collection
Display of local life including folklore and trades of the past. Includes: Blacksmiths Smiddy, Post Office, Crofter's Stable and Living Room.
Old School, Blair Atholl, Perthshire
☎ 079 681 232

Scottish Tartans Museum
Exhibition illustrating the development of tartan and highland dress; research and technical centre.
Drummond Street, Comrie
☎ 0764 70779

Music, Dance and Drama

Pitlochry Festival Theatre
The famous 'Theatre in the Hills', magnificently situated on the River Tummel. Popular plays, concerts and fringe events.
☎ 0796 2680

TAYSIDE

WHAT TO DO AND SEE

Natural History

Glengoulandie Deer Park
Deer and wildlife park. Visitors are able to walk or drive around the park.
☎ 08873 261
On the B846, 8 miles north-west of Aberfeldy

Pitlochry Power Station, Fish Ladder and Dam
Hydroelectric station where migrating salmon may be seen through windows in the fish ladder.
☎ 0796 473152
P

OUTDOOR LEISURE/SPORTS

Birdwatching and Wildlife

Loch of the Lowes
Osprey nest and wildlife may be watched from hides.
Scottish Wildlife Trust
☎ 0350 72337
Off the A923, 2 miles north-east of Dunkeld

Fishing

Perthshire contains a wealth of salmon, sea trout and brown trout waters and an increasing number of rainbow trout fisheries. There is also excellent grayling, pike, perch and roach fishing. The fishing is dominated by the mighty River Tay, one of the principal salmon rivers in Europe.
i For detailed information see *Fishing in Perthshire*, a comprehensive leaflet available from the Tourist Information Centre. Tackle shops:

A. Boyd
Tackle Dealers, King Street, Crieff
☎ 0764 3871

Highland Gathering

Guns & Tackle, 8 West Monlin Road, Pitlochry
☎ 0796 473047

Ice Skating

Atholl Curling Rink
Open and hotel competitions; visitor viewing.
Pitlochry
☎ 0796 473337

Walking

Detailed leaflets are available from the Tourist Information Centre.

Falls of Bruar
3 miles west of Blair Atholl. Spectacular forest walk by 3 grand cascades celebrated by Robert Burns.

Garry-Tummel Walks, Pitlochry
Network of marked paths beside rivers and lochs, through forest and woodland. Linked to walks to Killiecrankie.

Glen Lednock Circular Walk
Woodland walk with waterfalls.
Starts at Comrie village.

WATERSPORTS

Sailing

Lochearn Sailing & Watersports Centre
Sailing, windsurfing, canoeing and waterskiing: instruction and hire.
South Shore Road, St. Fillans
☎ 0764 2292
☎ 076485 257

TAYSIDE

WHAT TO DO AND SEE

i The Library, High Street, Carnoustie, Angus
☎ 0241 52258 (summer only)
i 4 City Square, Dundee
☎ 0382 27723

ADVENTURE

Multi-activity Centres

Ancrum Outdoor Centre
Dry ski-slope.
10 Ancrum Road, Dundee
☎ 0382 644159

EQUESTRIAN

Riding and Pony Trekking

Camperdown Pony Trekking
Camperdown Park, Dundee
☎ 0382 623879

HEALTH

Leisure Centres

Dundee Swimming and Leisure Centre
Swimming pool, health suite, sauna, sunbed, steamroom, spa pool, keep-fit, pool tables and table tennis.
Earl Grey Place, Dundee
☎ 0382 203888

LOCAL FEATURES

Art Galleries

McManus Galleries
Fine Victorian Gothic building houses local history museum and art galleries with impressive collections of Victorian and Scottish paintings.
Albert Square, Dundee
☎ 0382 23141 ext 136

Seagate Gallery
Touring exhibitions of mainly modern art.
38–40 Seagate, Dundee
☎ 0382 26331

Arts and Crafts

Eduardo Alessandro Studios
Gifts, crafts, artwork and paintings by local artists and crafts people.
Gray Street, Broughty Ferry, Dundee
☎ 0382 737011

Peel Farm Craft Shop
Pottery, quilting, patchwork, dried flowers, basketwear and knitwear.
Lintrathen, by Kirriemuir, Angus
☎ 05756 205
Just off the B954

Riverstone Domestic Stoneware
Workshop viewing and shop.
Oathlaw Pottery, Oathlaw, by Forfar, Angus
☎ 0307 85272
→A A94

Factory Visits

Shaws Dundee Sweet Factory
See how original toffees, fudges and boilings are made.
Fulton Road, Wester Gourdie Industrial Estate, Dundee
☎ 0382 610369
→A A972

Festivals and Fairs

June
Dundee City Festival (until August)
July
Dundee Highland Games
August
Dundee Water Festival

TAYSIDE

WHAT TO DO AND SEE

Food and Drink

Cairn O'Mhor Winery
A unique range of country wines; tours of the winery.
East Inchmichael, Errol, Perth
☎ 0821 642214
☎ 0821 642781

Gardens

Branklyn Garden
Lovely 2-acre garden. National Trust for Scotland.
Dundee Road, Perth
☎ 0738 25535
On the A85, 1½ miles east of Perth

Historic Buildings

Glamis Castle
Childhood home of the Queen Mother, a romantic castle set in a magnificent park and framed by the Grampian Mountains.
Angus
☎ 030784 242
☎ 030784 243
☎ 030784 274

Scone Palace
Crowning place of the Kings of the Scots on the Stone of Scone, this historic place is set in magnificent parkland. Highland cattle; adventure playground; veteran agricultural machinery display.
Perth
☎ 0738 52300
On the A93 Braemar road

Museums

Broughty Castle Museum
Local history gallery which includes exhibits relating to Dundee's former whaling industry.
Broughty Ferry, Dundee
☎ 0382 76121

Parks

Camperdown Country Park
Wildlife park and adventure playground.
Dundee
☎ 0382 623555
→A A923

Clatto Country Park
Canoeing, sailing, windsurfing and a programme of activities.
Dundee
☎ 0382 89076
→A A923

Monikie Country Park
Sailing, canoeing and windsurfing.
Newbigging, Perthshire
☎ 082623 202
On the B962

OUTDOOR LEISURE/SPORTS

Cycling

Cycle hire from:

Boddens Mountain Equipment
Mountain Bikes.
104 Annfield Road, Dundee
☎ 0382 645310

Mac Cycles
143c Nethergate, Dundee
☎ 0382 201471

Nicholson's Cycling Centre
2 Forfar Road, Dundee
☎ 0382 461212

Fishing

Fishing in the Tay Estuary for salmon, sea trout and flounder.
i Leaflet on fishing in local lochs is available from the Tourist Information Centre.
Tackle shops:

John R Gow & Sons Ltd
12 Union Street, Dundee
☎ 0382 25427

Shotcast Ltd
8 Whitehall Crescent, Dundee
☎ 0382 25621

Walking

Tayside is a walkers' paradise with low-level woodland walks, coastal paths, glen walks and higher-level hill walks; *Walks in Tayside* is available from the Tourist Information Centre.

WATERSPORTS

Waterskiing

East Coast Watersports Ltd
Surf-skis, waterskiing, jet-skis and paragliding.
Esplanade, Broughty Ferry, Dundee
☎ 0382 79889

TAYSIDE

WHAT TO DO AND SEE

i Market Place, Arbroath, Angus
☎ 0241 72609

EQUESTRIAN

Riding and Pony Trekking

Glenmarkie Farm Riding Centre
Hacking and trekking through spectacular scenery.
Glenisla, Perthshire
☎ 057 582 341
3 miles north of Glenisla Post Office

HEALTH

Leisure Centres

Lochside Leisure Centre
Within the Forfar Country Park, this centre has sports halls, squash courts, a gym and drama studio. Also a cafeteria with views over Forfar Loch.
Forfar Country Park, Angus
☎ 0307 64201
Eastern shore of Forfar Loch

Montrose Swimming Pool
Pool with spring boards and family sessions with an inflatable chute.
The Mall, Montrose, Angus
☎ 0674 72026

LOCAL FEATURES

Architecture

Arbroath Abbey
Ruins of an abbey founded in 1178 by King William the Lion in memory of his friend Thomas à Becket. Eventual burial place of the King himself.
Arbroath, Angus

Pictish Stones
Aberlemno Sculptured Stones: cross slab in the churchyard and 3 other stones by the roadside.
On the B9134, 5 miles north-east of Forfar, Angus

Arts and Crafts

Peel Farm
Coffee and craft shop for home baking and local crafts.
Lintrathen Road
Just off the B954 Alyth to Glenisla road, Angus

Food and Drink

Forester's Seat Winery
View the whole wine-making process from the hand-squeezing of locally grown Angus fruit to the laying down of the year's vintage.
By Forfar, Angus
☎ 0307 81 304
On the A932 Forfar to Friockheim road
P ✕ ♿ ♿

Gardens

Damside Garden
History of herbs and herb gardening plus traditional styles of gardening including Celtic, Knot, Roman, Monastic and Elizabethan.
By Johnshaven, Montrose
☎ 0561 61498
Off the A92 and the A94
P 🚻 ♿ ♿

Historic Houses

Barrie's Birthplace
First home of novelist and playwright J. M. Barrie who wrote *Peter Pan*.
Kirriemuir, Angus

Edzell Castle and Gardens
Beautiful walled garden created by Sir David Lindsay in 1604. The 'Pleasance' is a formal garden whose walls are decorated with sculptured stone panels. Historic Scotland.
☎ 031 244 3101
On the B966, 6 miles north of Brechin, Angus

House of Dun
Palladian House designed by William Adam. Fine views across Montrose Basin and woodland walks through the estate.
☎ 067 481 264
On the A935, 4 miles west of Montrose, Angus

✕

Museums

Signal Tower Museum
The signalling station for Bell Rock lighthouse now houses displays of local history.
Arbroath, Angus
☎ 0241 75598

Natural History

Mains of Dun Farm
Farm and wildlife estate with marvellous trees, woods and birdlife. 4 mile long railway between Bridge of Dun and Brechin has occasional steam service on Sundays.
Nr Montrose on the A935, Angus
☎ 067 481 332
☎ 0674 76336 (Countryside ranger)

TAYSIDE

WHAT TO DO AND SEE

Parks

Crombie Country Park
Loch and surrounding woodlands; walks and rambles with a ranger; mini highland games; orienteering course; tree trails; angling.
Carmylie, Broughty Ferry, Dundee
☎ 02416 360
Off the B961
P ♿ ♿

Monikie Country Park
Lochs, woodlands and parkland with a host of activities. Sailboards for hire, dinghy sailing on Toppers, canoeing, rowing and angling.
☎ 082 623 202 (Ranger)
On the B962 approx 1 mile beyond Newbigging, Perthshire
P ♿

OUTDOOR LEISURE/SPORTS

Birdwatching and Wildlife

Montrose Basin Nature Reserve
This 2000-acre tidal basin is a local nature reserve with a full-time ranger-naturalist. Large flocks of waders, wildfowl and seabirds use the Basin as a sanctuary. Hides are provided by the Scottish Wildlife Trust.

St. Cyrus National Nature Reserve
Lava cliffs and sand dunes, saltmarsh and sand flats.
St. Cyrus, Kincardineshire
☎ 06748 3736

Fishing

Monikie Angling
Superb fishing on 2 ponds and at Crombie Loch is managed by Monikie Angling Club which has 18 boats.
Nr Newbigging, Perthshire
☎ 082 623 300 Club Bailiff

Walking

Tayside Hilltours
Guided walking holidays in the Tayside mountains to suit a wide range of abilities and interests.
26 North Loch Road, Forfar
☎ 0307 62045

GRAMPIAN

WHAT TO DO AND SEE

i 54 Broad Street, Peterhead,
Aberdeenshire
☎ 0779 71904 Easter–October

ADVENTURE

Shooting
Game International Ltd
Driven and rough game shooting, stalking and clay pigeon shooting.
The Firs, Mountblairy, Banff
☎ 0888 68618

EQUESTRIAN

Fourwinds Equestrian Centre
Lootingstone Croft, Rathen, Aberdeenshire
☎ 03465 2326

Kirkton Riding Centre
Crudie
☎ 08885 610
Just off the A98, 7 miles east of Macduff, Banffshire

HEALTH

Leisure Centres
Peterhead Swimming Pool
A modern indoor pool with a sauna and solarium.
Queen Street, Peterhead, Aberdeenshire
☎ 0779 71757

GRAMPIAN

WHAT TO DO AND SEE

LOCAL FEATURES

Art Galleries

Aberdeen Art Gallery
Impressionist, Victorian, Scottish and 20th century British painting, silver and glass collections.
Schoolhill, Aberdeen
☎ 0224 646333

Arbuthnot Museum and Art Gallery
Based on the collection of a local trader, Adam Arbuthnot, the museum depicts local history and boasts a fine coin collection.
St. Peter Street, Peterhead
☎ 0779 77778

Arts and Crafts

Portsoy Marble Workshop and Pottery
Marble polishing, pottery workshop and shop.
Shorehead, Portsoy, Banffshire
☎ 0261 42404

Scottish Sculpture Workshop and Sculpture Walk
Workshop and gallery open daily.
1 Main Street, Lumsden, by Huntly, Aberdeenshire
☎ 04646 372

Factory Visits

Ugie Fish House
The oldest building in Peterhead and the oldest working fish house in Scotland. It still oak-smokes wild salmon and trout in the traditional manner.
Golf Road, Peterhead
☎ 0779 76209

Falconry

North East Falconry Centre
The only falconry centre in Northern Scotland. The birds are on display and there are hour-long flying displays twice daily.
Bruntbrae Farm
☎ 0466 87328
4 miles south of Banff

Gardens

Hatton Garden Centre
Large centre that specialises in growing heathers; gift packs available.
Northfield, Hatton, Aberdeenshire
☎ 077984 490

Historic Buildings

Duff House
One of William Adam's finest buildings, built between 1725 and 1740. Now owned by Historic Scotland who are restoring it to its former glory.
Banff
☎ 0261 812825

Fyvie Castle
One of the most spectacular castles in Scotland it has long and chequered history during which many extensions and modifications have taken place. National Trust for Scotland.
Fyvie, Aberdeenshire
☎ 0651 891266

Slains Castle
One of the most famous ruins in Scotland; inspiration to Bram Stoker when he wrote *Dracula*. Today it is an extensive cliff-top ruin reached by foot from the Main Street car park at Cruden Bay, Aberdeenshire

Natural History

Bullers of Buchan
Sea chasm some 200 feet deep where the ocean rushes in through a natural archway open to the sky. Cliff scenery is spectacular and seabirds of many varieties may be seen. Rough footpath leads from the car park to the edge of the chasm.
Off the A975, 3 miles north of Cruden Bay

Rattray Head
A true wilderness lying north of Peterhead where 70 foot sand dunes create a lunar landscape. Nearby is an RSPB reserve at Loch of Strathbeg.

OUTDOOR LEISURE/SPORTS

Cycling

Robertson Sports, Cycle Hire
1–3 Kirk Street, Peterhead
☎ 0779 72584

Fishing

Trout, sea trout and salmon fishing on the River Ugie. There is a variety of fishing opportunities in and around Peterhead and Cruden Bay. For details contact the Tourist Information Centre.

Crimonmogate Fishery
6-acre lake well stocked with rainbow and brown trout; boat and jetty fishing. Permits issued on bank.
Lonmay, nr Fraserburgh
☎ 0346 32203

WATERSPORTS

Waterskiing

Dolphin Watersports
Waterski tuition, power bikes, speed boats and wave riders for hire. Wet suits and equipment supplied.
Port Erroll Harbour, Cruden Bay, Aberdeenshire
☎ 03302 3816

GRAMPIAN AND HIGHLAND

WHAT TO DO AND SEE

i Grampian Road, Aviemore,
Inverness-shire
☎ 0479 810363

ADVENTURE

Multi-activity Centres

Highland Ventures Ltd
Fishing, shooting and off-road driving.
The Log Cabin, Aviemore Centre
☎ 0479 810 833

Loch Insh Watersports
Canoeing, sailing, windsurfing, cycling, fishing and a dry ski-slope.
Hire and instruction.
Loch Insh, Kincraig, Inverness-shire
☎ 0540 651272

Shooting

Alvie Estate
Grouse, pheasant, duck, rabbit, roe and red deer in the appropriate seasons. All types of shooting can be arranged from rough shooting to stalking and clay pigeons.
Alvie Estate Office, Kincraig, Inverness-shire
☎ 0540 651255
☎ 0540 651249

AERIAL SPORTS

Gliding

Cairngorm Gliding Club
Fly at Blackmill Air Field; training and passenger flights available.
Feshie Bridge, Kincraig, Inverness-shire
☎ 0540 651317

EQUESTRIAN

Riding and Pony Trekking

Ballintean Riding Centre
Kincraig, Kingussie, Inverness-shire
☎ 0540 651352

Carrbridge Pony Trekking Centre
The Ellan, Station Road, Carrbridge,
Inverness-shire
☎ 047984 602

HEALTH

Leisure Centres

The Aviemore Centre, Inverness-shire
All-weather leisure centre with swimming pool, ice rink, theatre, cinema, sauna, solarium, restaurants, discos and amusements.
☎ 0479 810624

LOCAL FEATURES

Factory Tours

Dalwhinnie Highland Malt Whisky
Distillery tours.
Dalwhinnie, Inverness-shire
☎ 05282 208

The Malt Whisky Trail
Follow the signposted road tour which visits 8 malt whisky distilleries in the Grampian Highlands. Leaflet from the Tourist Information Centre.

GRAMPIAN AND HIGHLAND

WHAT TO DO AND SEE

Gardens

Speyside Heather Centre
Heather heritage centre with show garden displaying 200 varieties. Tea room with home baking.
Skye of Curr, Dulnain Bridge, Inverness-shire
☎ 047985 359
On the A95, 6 miles from Grantown

Musuems

Highland Folk Museum
Regional museum of country life.
Kingussie
☎ 0540 661307

Natural History

Cairngorm Reindeer Centre
Britain's only herd of reindeer.
Glenmore, Aviemore
☎ 047986 228

Highland Wildlife Park
Large drive-through reserve.
Kincraig, Inverness-shire
☎ 0540 651270
On the B9152 off the A9
P 🏠 ♿ ♿

Parks

Landmark Highland Heritage and Adventure Park
Pine forest nature centre, show and exhibitions, treetop trail, forest tower, adventure playground, steam powered sawmill and woodland maze.
Carrbridge, Inverness-shire
☎ 047984 613
Just off the A9 between Inverness and Aviemore
🏠

Rothiemurchus Estate
Forest and wildlife walks, farm tours and safaris, clay pigeon shooting school, fishing in well stocked lochs and birdwatching.
Rothiemurchus Visitor Centre, Aviemore
☎ 0479 810858
On the B970
P 🚌 ✕

Railways

Strathspey Railway Co. Ltd.
Steam railway between Aviemore and Boat of Garten. Special Osprey Tours.
Aviemore Speyside Station, Dalfaber Road, Aviemore
☎ 0479 810725

Theatres

Waltzing Waters
Aqua theatre with a 50-minute show.
Balavil Brae, Newtonmore
☎ 0540 673752

OUTDOOR LEISURE/SPORTS

Birdwatching

Loch Garten Ospreys
RSPB viewing hide and visitor centre. Open late April to late August.
Follow AA signs
☎ 0479 83694

Cycling

Inverdruie Mountain Bikes
Bikes with 18 gears, snow/mud bikes and road bikes; network of trails; maps and rucksacks provided.
Rothiemurchus Visitor Centre, Inverdruie
☎ 0479 810787

Sports Hire
Over 50 cycles for hire including mountain bikes and tandems.
Rear of Nethybridge Ski School
☎ 047982 333
☎ 047982 418

Fishing

Alvie Estate
Fishing on Rivers Spey, Feshie, Dulnain and Feithlinn. Boat fishing on Loch Insh and Loch Alvie. Ghillie assistance if required.
Estate Office, Kincraig, Inverness-shire
☎ 0540 651255
☎ 0540 651249

Grampian View
Fishing arranged on rivers or lochs. Ghillie available.
☎ 0540 651383

Osprey Fishing School
Fly fishing courses, fishing holidays and tackle hire.
Aviemore
☎ 0479 810132
☎ 0479 810911

Skiing

Cairngorm is the premier ski area in the country with a high standard of ski instruction.

Aviemore Ski School
Cairdsport, Aviemore Centre
☎ 0479 810310

Highland Guides
Nordic and cross-country skiing centre including guide service for wildlife, mountain climbing and historical tours.
Inverdruie, Aviemore
☎ 0479 810729

Walking

Ossian Guides
Professional trekking and tour guide.
Sanna, Newtonmore
☎ 0540 673402

EAST HIGHLANDS

WHAT TO DO AND SEE

i The Square, Dornoch, Sutherland
☎ 0862 810400

EQUESTRIAN

Riding and Pony Trekking

East Sutherland Riding Centre
Culmaily Farm, Golspie, Sutherland
☎ 04084 254

East Sutherland Riding Centre
Skelbo Farm
By Dornoch, Sutherland
☎ 0408 633045

Invershin Trekking Centre
The Bungalow, Invershin
☎ 054982 296

HEALTH

Leisure Centres

Sutherland Swimming Pool
Golspie, Sutherland
☎ 0408 633437

LOCAL FEATURES

Architecture

Croick Church
Parliamentary church built by Thomas Telford in 1827, associated with the Highland Clearances.
12 miles from Ardgay, Sutherland

Dornoch Cathedral, Sutherland
Fine examples of 13th century ecclesiastical architecture; former cathedral of the Bishops of Caithness.

Art Galleries

Dorothy Dick Gallery
Exhibitions of sculpture, paintings and prints.
47 The Village, Scourie, Sutherland
☎ 0971 2013

Arts and Crafts

Dornoch Craft Centre
Tartan manufacturers and craft retailers.
Old Town Jail, Dornoch, Sutherland
☎ 0862 810555

Sutherland Wool Mills
Manufacturers of tweeds, rugs, scarves, knitting and weaving yarns.
Brora
☎ 0408 21366

Factory Visits

Clynelish Highland Malt Whisky Distillery Tours.
Brora, Sutherland
☎ 0408 21444

Historic Buildings

Dunrobin Castle and Gardens
The most northerly of Scotland's great houses and one of the largest with 189 rooms. Opulent collection of furniture, paintings, objets d'art and family memorabilia.
Golspie, Sutherland
☎ 0408 633177
On the A9 just north of Golspie village

Museums

Timespan
Highland heritage centre with scenes recreated from the past; herb garden, salmon leap, shops.
Helmsdale, Sutherland
☎ 04312 327
→A A9

Natural History

Highland and Rare Breeds Farm
Traditional breeds of Scottish farm animals, pets corner.
Knockan, Elphin
☎ 085 486 204
Between Inverpolly Nature Reserve and Ledmore junction, Sutherland

OUTDOOR LEISURE/SPORTS

Cycling

Inverhouse Sports
Road and mountain bikes for hire. Round trip routes through stunning scenery.
Culrain, Ardgay, Sutherland
☎ 054982 213

Fishing

With over 2000 Lochs and lochans, Caithness and Sutherland is the foremost fishing area in the UK for freshwater recreational fishing; brown trout, salmon, sea trout and char.
  Coastal waters teem with cod, haddock, whiting, conger eel, plaice, skate, turbot, halibut and mackerel. Boats can be hired in Embo and Golspie.
i Further information from the Tourist Information Centre.

WEST HIGHLANDS

WHAT TO DO AND SEE

i Cameron Centre, Cameron Square, Fort William, Inverness-shire
☎ 0397 703781

ADVENTURE

The Fort William area is a haven for climbers wanting to tackle Ben Nevis and Glen Coe. The local tourist information centre will provide information on local routes and guides.

HEALTH

Leisure Centre

Lochaber Leisure Centre
Belford Road, Fort William
☎ 0397 704359

LOCAL FEATURES

Heritage

Commando Memorial
Imposing statue sculpted by Scott Sutherland to commemorate the Commandos who trained in the area during the Second World War
Off A82 near Spean Bridge 10 miles north-east of Fort William

Glenfinnian Monument
A statue of a Highlander atop a tower commemorates Bonnie Prince Charlie raising his standard at Glenfinnian in August 1745 and starting the Jacobite Rebellion. The Visitor Centre by the monument tells the complete story of the rebellion from Glenfinnian to Culloden.
Off A830 about 15 miles west of Fort William
☎ 039783 250

Historic buildings

Old Inverlochy Castle
Ruins of 13th century castle
Off A82 2 miles north-east of Fort William

Industry

Caledonian Canal
Built by Thomas Telford and completed in 1822 the canal follows The Great Glen and links the west and east coasts of the Highlands from Fort William to Inverness. There are three main canal sections linking together Loch Linnhe, Loch Lochy, Loch Ness and the Firth of Inverness. The scenery is spectacular and it is regarded as one of the most beautiful and breath-taking canals in the world.

Neptune's Staircase
The most complex of Thomas Telford's structures on the Caledonian Canal this series of 8 interlocking locks drops the height of the canal by about 80 feet in less than 2 miles
At Banavie, near the junction of the A830 and B8004 3 miles north of Fort William

Museums

Glencoe Folk Museum
The story of the Highlands, the Clans and the Jacobite Rebellion and the day-to-day life of people in the Highlands
On A82 in Glencoe village 14 miles south of Fort William

West Highland Museum
Relics of the Jacobite Rebellion
Cameron Square, Fort William
☎ 0397 2169

Natural History

Ben Nevis
Standing 4,406 feet high this is Britain's highest mountain and overshadows Fort William. It is about 4 miles from the town to the summit and there is a footpath from Achintee Farm but be warned, other approaches to the summit and particularly the north face need experienced mountaineering skills.
East of Fort William

Glen Coe
Wonderful mountain scenery and wildlife combined with the memory of the Massacre of 1692 and the accessibility of the main A82 travelling straight up the Glen make this probably the most famous of all Scottish Glens. There is a Visitor Centre with shop and food bar.
On A82 about 15 miles from Fort William
Visitor Centre
☎ 085 52 307

OUTDOOR LEISURE/SPORT

Outdoor leisure and sport around the Fort William area is centred around hill walking and mountaineering and, during the winter, skiing. The local Tourist Information Centre can give up-to-the-minute information on routes and weather conditions.

ORKNEY AND SHETLAND
WHAT TO DO AND SEE

The majority of birdwatchers visiting the Orkneys or the Shetlands will probably do so as part of a longer holiday and visit both groups of islands. The following information is a guide to some of the best attractions that can be seen but the islands are so rich, particularly in natural history and antiquities around 5,000 years old that it can only be an 'appetite-whetter'. The local tourist information centres will be able to provide you with much more detailed information.
i 6 Broad Street, Kirkwall, Orkney
☎ 0856 2856
i The Market Cross, Lerwick, Shetland
☎ 0595 3434

HEALTH

Leisure Centres

Clickimin Leisure Centre
Lochside, Lerwick, Shetland
☎ 0595 4555

Old School Centre
Firth, Mossbank, Sullom Voe, Orkney
☎ 0806 242095

ORKNEY AND SHETLAND

WHAT TO DO AND SEE

LOCAL FEATURES

Heritage

Jarlshof
This major archeological site shows the remains of three large settlements with evidence of occupancy from the Bronze Age onwards. The site also includes a medieval farmhouse and a 16th century country house.
On Sumburgh Head about 20 miles south of Lerwick, Shetland

Quoyness Chambered Tomb
A remarkable tomb with the main chamber having more than 12 feet of headroom, archeologists think that the tomb was probably built almost 5,000 years ago.
On the south coast of Sanday, Orkney

Skara Brae
A Stone Age village consisting of a number of houses linked by covered passages Skara Brae was probably built around 3,000 BC. Remarkably many of the contents including fireplaces and cupboards are preserved thanks to the entire site having been buried in sand for more than 4,500 years
On the west coast 19 miles from Kirkwall, Orkney

Art

Black Pig Gallery
Victoria Street, Kirkwall, Orkney
☎ 0856 4328

Pier Art Gallery
Victoria Street, Stromness, Orkney
☎ 0856 850 209

Historic Buildings

Earl Patrick's Palace
Built in the early 17th century alongside the much earlier Bishop's Palace, although it is now roofless this palace is regarded as the greatest example of Renaissance architecture in the whole of Scotland.
Kirkwall, Orkney

Bishop's Palace
Much of this palace dates from the 12th century although it was reconstructed in the 16th century when its fortifications were increased, mainly through the building of a massive round tower on the north-west side of the palace.
Kirkwall, Orkney

St. Magnus Cathedral
Jarl Rognvald founded this cathedral in 1137 and dedicated it to his uncle Jarl Magnus, both of their remains are entombed in the central pillars of the cathedral.
Kirkwall, Orkney

Industrial/Military

Scapa Flow
Scapa Flow is a large body of water almost enclosed by the islands of the Orkney group. This huge natural harbour was a major naval anchorage for the Royal Navy during the First and Second World Wars and the setting for the surrender, internment and scuppering of the German High Seas Fleet in 1919. These naval associations are explained at the Stromness Museum and the Orkney Wireless Museum. Scapa Flow is nowadays a centre for industrial activities related to North Sea oil.

Museums

Shetland Museum
The history of the Shetlands and the story of their inhabitants over the millenia.
Lower Hillhead, Lerwick, Shetland
☎ 0595 5052

Tankerness House Museum
The story of the last 5,000 years of life in the Orkneys, housed in a rich 16th century merchant's house.
Broad Street, Kirkwall, Orkney
☎ 0856 3191

Natural History

Old Man of Hoy
Just one example of the wealth of natural features which can be seen on Orkney and Shetland, but a spectacular one. The Old Man of Hoy is a narrow 450 feet tall sea stack standing alongside but isolated from the towering cliffs of north-west Hoy. Magnificent to look at, murder to climb even for the most experienced of climbers.
West coast of Hoy, Orkney

Theatre

Orkney Arts Theatre
Mill Street, Kirkwall, Orkney
☎ 0856 2047

WATERSPORTS

Being islands the sea and fishing are important factors of life in Orkney and Shetland. However, the seas can be very dangerous, particularly in winter and if you want to go sailing you are advised to discuss your needs with the local Tourist Information Centres who will be able to advise you or contact the:

Orkney Sailing Club
The Girnal, Harbour Street, Kirkwall, Orkney
☎ 0865 2331

COUNTY DOWN/BELFAST

WHAT TO DO AND SEE

i 59 North Street, Belfast, County Antrim
☎ 0232 246609
i Down Leisure Centre, Market Street, Downpatrick, County Down
☎ 0396 613426
i Arts Centre, Bank Parade, Newry, County Down
☎ 0693 66232

Maysfield Leisure Centre
Swimming pool, sauna, solarium, squash courts, gym.
East Bridge Street, Belfast
☎ 0232 241633

Tropicana
Pools, giant inflatables, water slides, springing animals, elephant slide and deck chair patios.
Newcastle Centre, Central Promenade
☎ 039 67 22222

ADVENTURE

Mountaineering and Rock Climbing

Mountain Centre
Situated in Tollymore Forest Park; training in canoeing, mountaineering and adventure activities.
Bryansford, Newcastle
☎ 039 67 22158

LOCAL FEATURES

Aquarium

Northern Ireland Aquarium
Featuring about 70 marine species found in Strangford Lough; models of seabed.
Rope Walk, Portaferry
☎ 024 77 28062

Archaeology

Nendrum Monastic Site
The remains of a pre-Norman monastery include 3 concentric enclosures and a ruined church round tower stump.
Mahee Island, Comber
Off the A22 and lough shore road

EQUESTRIAN

Riding and Pony Trekking

Castlewellan Riding Centre
Drumee Road, Castlewellan
☎ 039 67 71497

Easthope Equestrian Centre
71 Killynure Road West, Carryduff, Belfast
☎ 0232 813186

Lagan Valley Equestrian Centre
Longhurst, 172 Upper Malone Road, Belfast
☎ 0232 614853

Mourne Trail Riding Centre
96 Castlewellan Road, Newcastle
☎ 039 67 24351

Architecture

Inch Abbey
Ruins of Cistercian monastery on an island in Quoile marshes, reached by a causeway.
Off the A7, 1 mile north-west of Downpatrick

Art Galleries

Arts Council Gallery
Contemporary art.
16 Bedford Street, Belfast
☎ 0232 321402

Bell Gallery
Irish artists.
13 Adelaide Park, Belfast
☎ 0232 662998

Tom Caldwell Gallery
Living Irish artists.
40–42 Bradbury Place, Belfast
☎ 0232 323226

HEALTH

Leisure Centres

Down Leisure Centre
Swimming, sauna, squash courts, conditioning room, aerobics classes and keep-fit.
114 Market Street, Downpatrick
☎ 0396 613426
☎ 0396 613427

COUNTY DOWN/BELFAST

WHAT TO DO AND SEE

Gardens

Botanic Gardens, Palm House and Tropical Ravine
Coffee, banana and cotton plants grow in this splendid curvilinear glass and cast-iron conservatory.
Belfast Botanic Gardens, Belfast
☎ 0232 324902

Dixon Park
Magnificent rose display all summer; host to the City of Belfast International Rose Trials.
Upper Malone Road, Belfast
☎ 0232 320202
P

Rowallane Gardens
Magnificent rhododendrons and azaleas, rare trees, shrubs and plants. National Trust.
Saintfield, Ballynahinch
On the A7, 1 mile south of Saintfield
☎ 0238 510131

Guided Tours

Belfast City Tours
3½ hour tours including the shipyards, Stormont and Belfast Castle.
Buses leave Castle Place
☎ 0232 246485

Around the Province
Ulsterbus runs day and ½ day tours to the Glens of Antrim, Antrim Coast, Giant's Causeway, Fermanagh Lakeland, Lough Neagh, Tyrone, Mournes, Ards Peninsula and Armagh.
☎ 0232 320011

Historic Buildings

Annalong Corn Mill
Powered by a waterwheel, the mill overlooks the harbour.
Marine Park, Annalong
☎ 039 67 68736

Castle Ward
Unique 18th century house with facades in different styles set in a 700-acre country estate with woodland, lake and seashore. Victorian laundry; formal and landscaped gardens; corn and saw mills, wildfowl.
Strangford, County Down
☎ 039 686 204
On the A25, 1 mile west of Strangford village
P

Dundonald Old Mill
18th century cornmill with a huge waterwheel.
231 Belfast Road, Quarry Corner, Dundonald, Belfast
☎ 0232 480117

Dundrum Castle
Built by John de Courcy in about 1177, later occupied by the Magennises.
Access from centre of Dundrum village.

Malone House
Early 19th century house set in beautiful parkland.
Barnett Park, Upper Malone Road, Belfast
☎ 0232 681246

Mount Stewart House and Gardens
The boyhood home of Lord Castlereagh, a fascinating 18th century house with one of the greatest gardens in Europe. The Temple of the Winds overlooks Strangford Lough. National Trust.
Newtownards
☎ 024 774 387
On the A20, 5 miles south-east of Newtownards
P

Museums

Down County Museum
Stone Age artefacts and Bronze Age gold found locally are displayed in this former jail.
The Mall, Downpatrick
☎ 0396 615218

Newry Museum
History of the 'Gap of the North'; archaeological items, touring exhibitions.
Arts Centre, Bank Parade, Newry
☎ 0693 66232

Transport Museum
Over 200 years of Irish transport; locomotives, street trams and road vehicles.
Witham Street, Belfast
☎ 0232 451519

Ulster Museum and Art Gallery
Noted for its Irish antiquities and art collection.
Botanic Gardens, Belfast
☎ 0232 381251

Natural History

Butterfly House
Over 30 species of butterfly.
Seaforde Nursery, Seaforde
☎ 039 687 225
On the A24

Streamvale Open Dairy Farm
Watch the milking from a viewing gallery or bottle feed a lamb. Pet's corner, nature trail, donkey rides.

COUNTY DOWN/BELFAST

WHAT TO DO AND SEE

38 Ballyhanwood Road, nr Dundonald Ice Bowl, Belfast
☎ 0232 483244

Parks

Castlewellan Forest Park
The national arboretum, begun in 1740, is an outstanding feature. Tropical birds in the glasshouse; lake stocked with trout.
Off the A25 on Bannanstown Road
☎ 039 67 78664

Lagan Valley Regional Park
10 miles of towpath along the banks of the Lagan River.
Starts near Belfast Boat Club on Loughview Road, Stranmillis and ends upstream from Moore's Bridge, Hillsborough Road, Lisburn
☎ 0232 491922

Tollymore Forest Park
Stone follies and bridges, Himalayan cedars and a 100ft sequoia tree in the arboretum. Wildlife and forestry exhibits; pony trekking; fishing; walks in the foothills of the Mournes. (see Mountain Centre)
☎ 039 67 22428
Off the B180 on Tullybrannigan Road

Theatres

Grand Opera House
Varied programme from opera to pantomime.
Great Victoria Street, Belfast
☎ 0232 241919

Zoos

Belfast Zoo
In a picturesque mountain park overlooking the city. See the spectacled bear, the only one in the UK.
Antrim Road, Belfast
☎ 0232 776277
Off Antrim Road, 5 miles north of Belfast

OUTDOOR LEISURE/SPORTS

Cycling

i Cycling routes are available from the Tourist Information Centre, including a 51-mile route around the Ards Peninsula and a route from Belfast to the Mournes. Cycle hire from:

Bikeit
Mountain bikes.
4 Belmont Road, Belfast
☎ 0232 471141

McConvey Cycles
Mountain and touring bikes.
476 Ormeau Road, Belfast
and Unit 10, Pottinger's Entry, Belfast
☎ 0232 330322

Ross Cycles
44 Clarkhill Road, Castlewellan
☎ 039 67 78029

Fishing

The heart of Down is 'drumlin country', with over 100 small lakes where, in addition to a rod licence, you may only require the farmer's or local angling club's permission to fish. Game fishing in lakes and rivers is controlled by the Dept of Agriculture. Game fishing is good in Upper Bann River, Shimna River in Tollymore Forest Park, Castlewellan Lake, Ballykeel Lougherne, Spelga Dam and Fofanny Dam.
  Sea fishing is good in Strangford Lough and along the Mourne Coast.
  Good coarse fishing in the River Quoile and many lakes. Detailed fishing leaflets are available from the Tourist Information Centre.

Walking

Mourne Countryside Centre
Guided walks.
91 Central Promenade, Newcastle
☎ 039 67 24059

The Ulster Way
A challenging long distance walking route which encircles the province.
Walks include Lagan Valley walks, Belfast and Cave Hill, the North Antrim coast and the Mourne Trail.
i Route guides are available from the local Tourist Information Centres.
House of Sport, Upper Malone Road, Belfast
☎ 0232 381222

COUNTY LONDONDERRY/COUNTY ANTRIM

WHAT TO DO AND SEE

i Council Offices, Cloonavin,
Portstewart Road
Coleraine
☎ 0265 52181

i Council Offices, 7 Connell Street,
Limavady
☎ 050 47 22226

AERIAL SPORTS

Gliding

Magilligan Point Ulster Gliding Club
Ardnagle House
Seacoast Road
Limavady

Riding and Pony Trekking

Hill Farm Riding & Trekking Centre
47 Altikeeragh Road
Castlerock
☎ 0265 848629

City of Derry Riding Centre
189 Culmore Road
Londonderry
☎ 0504 351687

Streeve Riding School
25 Dowland Road
Limavady
☎ 050 47 62127

Timbertop Riding Centre
160a Curragh Road
Aghadowey
☎ 0265 868788

HEALTH

Leisure Centres

Coleraine Leisure Centre
Railway Road
☎ 0265 56432

Swimming

Water world
Harbour Road
Portrush
☎ 0265 822001

Castlerock Swimming Pool
Main Street
Castlerock
☎ 0265 848258

LOCAL FEATURES

Antiques

Dunluce Antiques
33 Ballytober Road
Bushmills
☎ 026 57 31140

Alexander Antiques
108 Dunluce Road
Portrush
☎ 0265 822783

Kennedy Wolfenden
Edgwater Hotel, 88 Strand Road
Portstewart ☎ 0265 832224

Factory Visits

Bushmills Distillery
2 Distillery Road
Bushmills
☎ 026 57 31521

Festivals & Fairs

April
Coleraine Folk Dancing Festival

May
Coleraine Music Festival
North West '200' Motor Cycle Road Race

June
Portstewart Music Festival
Coleraine Agricultural Show

July
Limavady Car Hill Climb
Portrush Open Amateur Golf
Championships

Gardens

Main Street Gardens
Portrush

The Crescent
Portstewart

Wilson Daffodil Garden
University of Ulster, Coleraine
☎ 0265 44141

Heritage

Downhill Castle
42 Mussanden Road
Castlerock
☎ 0265 848728

Mountsandel Fort
Mountsandel Road
Coleraine

Historic Houses

Hezlett House
Liffock
Castlerock
☎ 0265 848567

COUNTY LONDONDERRY/COUNTY ANTRIM

WHAT TO DO AND SEE

Natural History

The Giant's Causeway
2 miles north of Bushmills
38,000 stone columns, most of them hexagonal formed millions of years ago by the cooling of molton lava, or was it the work of giants? Exhibition centre and audio visual theatre.
☎ 026 57 31855

Portrush Countryside Centre
Bath Road
Portrush
☎ 0265 823600

Portrush Nature Reserve
Landsdown Crescent
Ammonite impressions

Parks

Springwell Forest
5 miles southwest on the A37.
Coleraine. No cars allowed.

Ramore Head
Portrush
Cliffside area with sporting facilities.

Flowerfield
Coleraine Road
Portstewart
P 🏠 🚐 ✕ ♿

Railways

Portrush Railway Station
Eglinton Road
Portrush flyer round trip from Belfast leaves Central Belfast Station.

Cinema

The Playhouse
Main Street
Portrush
☎ 0265 823917

OUTDOOR LEISURE

Cycling

Car and Home Supplies
8 Queen Street
Coleraine
☎ 0265 42354

Coleraine Motorcycles and Cycle Centre
8 Newmarket Street
Coleraine
☎ 0265 52655

Fishing

Detailed leaflet available from the Tourist Information Office.

River Bann
Pike, bream, salmon and sea trout. 10 mile stretch. 1 March–mid October.

Agivey River
12 mile stretch. Brown trout and salmon. 1 March – 30 September.

Fanghan River
Seatrout and salmon.
20 May – 20 October.

Sea Fishing

This area contains a wealth of variety with cod, bass, flounder, turbot, whiting, mackerel and sea trout. Local tackle shops will provide information and permits.
For detailed information and boat charter enquiries, ask at the Tourist Information Centre.

Golf

Benone Golf Club ⛳9
53 Benone Avenue
☎ 050 47 50555

Castlerock Golf CLub ⛳18 ⛳9
65 Circular Road
Castlerock
☎ 0265 848314

Royal Portrush Golf Club ⛳18 ⛳9
Bushmills Road
Portrush
☎ 0265 822311

Portstewart Golf Club ⛳18
117 Strand Road
Portstewart
☎ 0265 832015

Walking and Rambling

Downhill Forest
6 miles west of Coleraine. Waterfalls, fish pond, prehistoric mound, Dungannon Hill. Contact the Tourist Information Centre for further details of Skerry Trail – from Portballintrae to Castlerock via Coleraine.

WATERSPORTS

Coleraine Sailing Marina
64 Portstewart Road
Coleraine
☎ 0265 44768

Portrush Yacht Club
Harbour Road
Portrush

Yacht Cruising

Cygnet
Bann Cruises
2 Stone Row
Coleraine
☎ 0265 44744

COUNTY LONDONDERRY

WHAT TO DO AND SEE

i Foyle Street, Londonderry, County Londonderry
☎ 0504 267284

ADVENTURE

Rock Climbing
Roe Valley Country Park
Canoeing, rock climbing and fishing in this country park.
Off the B192, 2 miles south of Limavady
☎ 050 47 22074

AERIAL SPORTS

Parachuting and Parascending
Wild Geese Centre
Train and jump in one day. Fantastic display team.
116 Carrowreagh Road, Garvagh
☎ 026 65 58609

EQUESTRIAN

Riding and Pony Trekking
City of Derry Riding Centre
189 Culmore Road, Londonderry
☎ 0504 351687

Hill Farm Riding and Trekking Centre
47 Altikeeragh Road, Castlerock
☎ 0265 848629

HEALTH

Leisure Centres
Lisnagelvin Leisure Centre
Tropical heat, crystal clear water, foam-topped waves, sauna, solarium and fitness centre.
Londonderry
☎ 0504 47695

Water World
Twin 85-metre covered slides, aquarium, giant frog slide, water cannons, pirate ship, jacuzzis, whirlpool, playpool, giant toadstool umbrella shower: a large fun-filled water leisure complex.
The Harbour, Portrush, County Antrim
☎ 0265 822001

LOCAL FEATURES

Architecture
Banagher Old Church
An impressive ruin; the nave was built about 1100.
On the B74, 2 miles south-west of Dungiven

The Walls of Derry
These famous walls have withstood several sieges, the most celebrated lasted 105 days. Fine views from the top of the walls which encircle the old city.

COUNTY LONDONDERRY

WHAT TO DO AND SEE

Art Galleries

Gordon Gallery
Irish artists.
Ferryquay Street, Londonderry
☎ 0504 266261

Orchard Gallery
Centre for the visual arts.
Orchard Street, Londonderry
☎ 0504 269675

Arts and Crafts

Crafts Village
Shipquay Street, Londonderry
☎ 0504 268402

Festivals and Fairs

February
City of Derry Drama Festival
Londonderry Feis (runs into March)
Feis Cholmcille (Easter Week)

Oct/Nov
Foyle Film Festival

Gardens

Wilson Daffodil Garden
Rare collection of Irish-bred daffodils on the University campus.
☎ 0265 44141
On the A2 nr Coleraine Marina

Historic Buildings

Downhill Castle
Ruins of the home of the eccentric Earl–Bishop of Derry; the Mussenden Temple on the cliff top was built in 1783. 1-mile glen walk passes interesting architectural features. National Trust.
Mussenden Road, Castlerock
☎ 0265 848728
➔A A2

Hezlett House
17th century thatched cottage; the roof has an interesting cruck truss construction.
Liffock, Castlerock
☎ 0265 848567
On the A2 Coleraine to Downhill coast road

Springhill
A 17th century manor house with costume museum; family belongings have been preserved. National Trust.
Moneymore, Magherafelt
☎ 064 87 48210
On the B18, 1 mile from Moneymore
P ✕

St. Columb's Cathedral
Stained glass depicts heroic scenes from the great siege of 1688/9; locks and keys of the gates and some interesting relics.
Londonderry
☎ 0504 262746

Museums

Earhart Centre
Cottage exhibition on Amelia Earhart, first woman to fly the Atlantic solo; the famous aviator landed in a field here in 1932.
Ballyarnet Field, Londonderry
☎ 0504 353379
1½ miles from Foyle Bridge

Natural History

Portstewart Strand
Magnificent 2 mile strand and important dune system. National Trust.
West of Portstewart

Parks

Ness Country Park
Broadleaved woodland walks; path passes the point where the Burntollet River plunges 10 metres over Ulster's highest waterfall. Nature trails.
Off the A6, 7 miles south-east of Londonderry
☎ 050 47 22074

Railways

Foyle Valley Railway Centre
The railway history of Derry; ride on a 1934 diesel railcar on a mile of track.
Foyle Road, Londonderry
☎ 0504 265234
Nr Craigavon Bridge

OUTDOOR LEISURE/SPORTS

Fishing

Sea fishing from boats and the shore is excellent along the north coast.

Some of the best game fishing waters are in the North West; the Finn, the Derg, the Mourne, the Dennet and the Glenelly run into the Foyle. Rod licenses and advice from:
The Foyle Fisheries Commission
8 Victoria Road, Londonderry
☎ 0504 42100

Walking

The Sperrin Mountains offer some fine walking opportunities.

WATERSPORTS

Sailing

Prehen Boathouse
River water sports centre offering sailing, waterskiing, rowing and canoeing.
☎ 0504 43405

COUNTY FERMANAGH

WHAT TO DO AND SEE

i Lakeland Visitors Centre, Shore Road, Enniskillen, County Fermanagh
☎ 0365 323110

ADVENTURE

Caving

Marble Arch Caves
Marlbank Scenic Loop
Florancecourt
Enniskillen
☎ 036 582 8855

HEALTH

Swimming

Lakeland Forum
Broadmeadow, Enniskillen
☎ 0365 324121
Facilities includes squash, volleyball, archery, judo, bowls, football, badminton and tennis.

LOCAL FEATURES

Antiques

Crock o' Gold
14 Church Street
☎ 0365 323761

Architecture

Convent Chapel
Belmore Street
Enniskillen
(Byzantine Revival Style)

Methodist Church
Darling Street
Enniskillen
(Corinthian fronted edifice)

Presbyterian Church
Queen Elizabeth Road
Enniskillen
(English Gothic Style)

St. Macartin's Church of Ireland Cathedral
Darling Street
Enniskillen

St. Michael's Roman Catholic Church
Darling Street
Enniskillen
(French Gothic Revival Style)

Town Hall
High Street
Enniskillen
(Renaissance)

Factory Visits

Belleek China
Belleek
☎ 036 565 501

Festival and Fairs

April
Enniskillen Daffodil Spring Flower Show
May
Erne Boat Rally, Enniskillen
June
Lisbellow Festival, Enniskillen
Enniskillen Summer Regatta
Fiddlestone Festival, Belleek
August
Erne Vintage Car Rally
Enniskillen County Agricultural Show
Enniskillen Festival

Heritage

Enniskillen Castle
Off Henry Street
Enniskillen
☎ 0365 325000

Portora Castle
Portora Royal School Grounds
Enniskillen

Inishmacsaint Island
Early 6th century monastic site. North of Camagh Bay. 10 miles east on the A46.

Cole's Monument
Forthill Park
Forthill Street
Enniskillen

Historic Houses

Florence Court
National Trust property, 8 miles south-west of Enniskillen on the A4/A32 Swanlinbar Road.
☎ 036 582 249/788

Museums

Fermanagh County Museum and Royal Enniskillen Fusiliers Museum
Enniskillen Castle Keep
Off Henry Street
☎ 0365 325000

Parks

Forthill Park
Forthill Street
Enniskillen
☎ 0365 325050

COUNTY FERMANAGH

WHAT TO DO AND SEE

Florence Court Forest Park
200 year old yew trees
6 miles south-west on A4/A32
☎ 036 582 497

Theatres

Ordhowen – The Theatre by the Lakes
Dublin Road
Enniskillen
☎ 0365 325440

OUTDOOR LEISURE

Cycling

From Enniskillen there is a main road circling Lower Lough Erne covering a distance of 56 miles. Contact Tourist Information Centre for further details.

Fishing

For details contact local Tourist Information Centre. Permits available from the Lakeland Visitor Centre, Shore Road, Enniskillen and the Carlton Hotel, Belleek.

River Erne
Brown trout and salmon between 1 March – 30 September.

Lough Keenaghan
Brown trout and rainbow trout between 1 March–30 September.

Lough Melvin
Spring salmon, grilse, brown trout, perch and char 1 February–30 September.

Navar Forest Lakes
Brown and rainbow trout, and perch. 1 March–30 September.
For coarse fishing Lough Scolban is open all year round.

Golf

Enniskillen Golf Club
Castle Coole Grounds
☎ 0365 325250

WATERSPORTS

Enniskillen is an ideal centre for canoeing, diving, sailing, waterskiing and windsurfing.

Yacht Charter

There are many local charter businesses to choose from. With cruising available from Lakeland Marina. For further details contact the Lakeland Visitor Centre.
☎ 0365 323110

Erne Tours
Waterbus Kestrel for 63 passengers
13 Whitla Road
Lisburn
☎ 0346 664624 or 0365 322882

VISITING RSPB RESERVES

When visiting any bird reserve, remember these point:
- The birds' welfare must come first.
- Habitat must be protected.
- Disturbance to birds and their habitat must be kept to a minimum.
- Think carefully about whom you should tell when you find a rare bird.
- Do not harass rare migrants.
- Abide by the bird protection laws at all times.
- The rights of landowners should be respected.
- Respect the rights of other people in the countryside.
- Any records should be made available to the local bird recorder.

Enquiries

RSPB offices to which enquiries should be made:

Reserves Division, The Royal Society for the Protection of Birds, The Lodge, Sandy, Bedfordshire SG19 2DL
(☎ 0767 680551).

RSPB Scottish Headquarters, 17 Regent Terrace, Edinburgh EH7 5BN
(☎ 031 557 3136).

RSPB Wales Office, Bryn Aderyn, The Bank, Newtown, Powys SY16 2AB
(☎ 0686 626678).

RSPB Northern Ireland Office, Belvior Park Forest, Belfast BT8 4QT
(☎ 0232 491547)

RSPB North of England Office, 'E' Floor, Milburn House, Dean Street, Newcastle upon Tyne NE1 1LE (☎ 091 232 4148).

RSPB South-East England Office, 8 Church Street, Shoreham-by-Sea, West Sussex BN4 5DQ (☎ 0273 463642).

RSPB South-West England Office, 10 Richmond Road, Exeter EX4 4JA
(☎ 0392 432691).

RSPB Orkney Officer, Smyril, Stenness, Stromness KW16 3JX (☎ 0856 850176)

RSPB Shetland Officer, Seaview, Sandwick ZE2 9HP (☎ 095 05 506).

RSPB East Anglia Office, 97 Yarmouth Road, Thorpe St Andrew, Norwich NR7 0HF
(☎ 0603 700880).

RSPB East Midlands Office, The Lawn, Union Road, Lincoln LN1 3BU
(☎ 0522 535596).

RSPB Reserves Nature Conservation, Naturalists', Wildlife and other Trust Offices to which enquiries can be made:

AVON
Avon Wildlife Trust, The Old Police Station, 32 Jacob's Wells Road, Bristol. BS8 1DR
☎ 0272 268018/265490

BEDS & CAMBS
Bedfordshire & Cambridgeshire Wildlife Trust, Priory Country Park, Barkers Lane, Bedford. MK41 9SH

☎ 0234 364213
5, Fulbourn Manor, Fulbourn, Cambs CB1 5BN
☎ 0223 880785

BERKS, BUCKS & OXON
Berkshire, Buckinghamshire & Oxon Naturalists' Trust (BBONT), 3 Church Cowley Road, Rose Hill, Oxford. OX4 3JR
☎ 0865 775476

BIRMINGHAM
Urban Wildlife Trust (Birmingham and the Black Country), Unit 213, Jubilee Trade Centre, 130 Pershore St, Birmingham. B5 6ND
☎ 021 666 7474

BRECKNOCK (Brecon)
Brecknock Wildlife Trust, Lion House, Lion Yard, Brecon, Powys. LD3 7AY
☎ 0874 625708

CHESHIRE
Cheshire Wildlife Trust, Grebe House, Peaseheath, Nantwich, CW5 6DA.
☎ 0270 610180

CLEVELAND
Cleveland Wildlife Trust, Bellamy House, UNIT 2A, Brighouse Business Village, Brighouse Road, Riverside Park, Middlesbrough, Cleveland. TS2 1RT
☎ 0642 253716

CORNWALL
Cornwall Trust for Nature Conservation, Five Acres, Allet, Truro, Cornwall, TR4 9DJ.
☎ 0872 73939

CUMBRIA
Cumbria Wildlfe Trust, Church St, Ambleside, Cumbria. LA22 0BU
☎ 05394 32476

VISITING RSPB RESERVES

DERBYSHIRE
Derbyshire Wildlife Trust, Elvaston Castle Country Park, Derby, DE7 3EP
☎ 0332 756610

DEVON
Devon Wildlife Trust, 188 Sidwell Street, Exeter, Devon, EX4 6RD
☎ 0392 79244

DORSET
Dorset Trust for Nature Conservation, 39 Christchurch Road, Bournemouth, Dorset, BH1 3NS
☎ 0202 554241

DURHAM
Durham Wildlife Trust, 52 Old Elvet, Durham. DH1 3HN
☎ 091 386 9797

DYFED
Dyfed Wildlife Trust, 7 Market Street, Haverfordwest, Dyfed. SA61 1NF
☎ 0437 765462

ESSEX
Essex Wildlife Trust, Fingringhoe Wick Nature Reserve, Fingringhoe, Colchester, Essex. CO5 7DN
☎ 0206 729678

GLAMORGAN
Glamorgan Wildlife Trust, Nature Centre, Fountain Road, Tondu, Mid Glamorgan. CF32 OEH
☎ 0656 724100

GLOUCESTERSHIRE
Gloucestershire Trust for Nature Conservation, Church House, Standish, Stonehouse, Glos. GL10 3EU
☎ 045 382 2761

GUERNSEY
La Société Guernesiaise (LSG), c/o F G Caldwell, Candle Gardens, St. Peter Port, Guernsey, C.I.
☎ 0481 725093

GWENT
Gwent Wildlife Trust 16 White Swan Court, Church Street, Monmouth, Gwent. NP5 3NY
☎ (9am-1pm) 0600 715501

HANTS & ISLE OF WIGHT
Hampshire & Isle of Wight Wildlife Trust, 71 The Hundred, Romsey, Hants. SO51 8BZ
☎ 0794 513786

HEREFORD
Herefordshire Nature Trust, Community House, 25 Castle Street, Hereford. HR1 2NW
☎ 0432 356872

HERTS & MIDDX
Hertfordshire & Middlesex Wildlife Trust, Grebe House, St Michael's Street, St Albans, Herts. AL3 4SN
☎ 0727 58901

KENT
Kent Trust for Nature Conservation, 1a Bower Mount Road, Maidstone, Kent. ME16 8AX
As from July/August 1992, Tyland Barn, Old Chatham Road, Sandling, Maidstone, Kent.
☎ 0622 753017/759017

LANCASHIRE
Lancashire Trust for Nature Conservation, The Pavilion, Ouerden Park Wildlife Centre, Shady Lane, Bamber Bridge, Preston, Lancs. PR5 6AU
☎ 0772 324129

LEICESTER & RUTLAND
Leicestershire & Rutland Trust for Nature Conservation, 1 West Street, Leicester. LE1 6UU
☎ 0533 553904

LINCS & STH HUMBERSIDE
Lincolnshire Trust for Nature Conservation, The Manor House, Alford, Lincs. LN13 9D1
☎ 0507 463468

LONDON
London Wildlife Trust, 80 York Way, London. N1 9AG
☎ 071 278 6612/3

MAN (ISLE OF)
Manx Nature Conservation Trust, Ballamoar House, Ballaugh, Isle of Man.
☎ 0624 89 7611

MONTGOMERY
Montgomeryshire Wildlife Trust, 8 Severn Square, Newtown, Powys. SY16 2AG
☎ 0686 624751

NORFOLK
Norfolk Naturalists' Trust, 72 Cathedral Close, Norwich, Norfolk. NR1 4DF
☎ 0603 625540

NORTHAMPTONSHIRE
Northants Wildlife Trust, Lings House, Billing Lings, Northampton. NN3 4BE
☎ 0604 405285

NORTHUMBERLAND
Northumberland Wildlife Trust, Hancock Museum, Barras Bridge, Newcastle-upon-Tyne. NE2 4PT
☎ 091 232 0038

NORTH WALES
North Wales Wildlife Trust, 376 High Street, Bangor, Gwynedd. LL57 1YE
☎ 0248 351541

NOTTINGHAMSHIRE
Nottinghamshire Wildlife Trust, 310 Sneinton Dale, Nottingham. NG3 7DN
☎ 0602 588242

RADNORSHIRE
Radnorshire Wildlife Trust, 1 Gwalia Annexe, Ithon Road, Llandrindod Welles, Powys. LD1 6AS
☎ 0597 823298

SCOTLAND
Scottish Wildlife Trust, (SWT), Cramond House, Kirk Cramond, Cramond Glebe Road, Edinburgh. EH4 6NS
☎ 031 312 7765

VISITING RSPB RESERVES

SHROPSHIRE
Shropshire Wildlife Trust, 167 Frankwell, Shrewsbury. SW3 8LG
☎ 0743 241691

SOMERSET
Somerset Trust for Nature Conservation, Fyne Court, Broomfield, Bridgwater, Somerset. TA5 2EQ
☎ 0823 451587/8

STAFFORDSHIRE
Staffordshire Wildlife Trust, Coutts House, Sandon, Staffordshire. ST18 0DN
☎ 088 97 534

SUFFOLK
Suffolk Wildlife Trust, Park Cottage, Saxmundham, Suffolk. IP17 1DQ
☎ 0728 603765

SURREY
Surrey Wildlife Trust, Powell Corderoy Annex, Longfield Road, Dorking, Surrey. RH4 3DF
☎ 306 743404

SUSSEX
Sussex Wildlife Trust, Woods Mill, Henfield, West Sussex. BN5 9SD
☎ 0273 492630

ULSTER
Ulster Wildlife Trust, 3 New Line, Crossgar, Down Patrick. BT30 9EP
☎ 0396 830282

WARWICKSHIRE
Warwickshire Nature Conservation Trust, (WARNACT), Brandon Lane, Coventry. OV3 3GW
☎ 0920 496848

WILTSHIRE
Wiltshire Trust for Nature Conservation, 19 High Street, Devizes, Wiltshire. SN10 1AT
☎ 0380 725670

WORCESTERSHIRE
Worcestershire Nature Conservation Trust, Lower Smite Farm, Smite Hill, Handlip, Worcester. WR3 8SZ
☎ 0905 754919

YORKSHIRE
Yorkshire Wildlife Trust, 10 Toft Green, York. YO1 1JT
☎ 0904 659570

RSNC
Royal Society for Nature Conservation, (RSNC),
The Green, Witham Park, Waterside South, Lincoln. LN5 7JR
RSNC is the national association of the Nature Conservation Trusts.
☎ 0522 544400

Sound Birding Guides from *WildSounds*

BRITISH BIRD SONGS & CALLS
109 species of the most commonly found birds in the British Isles in systematic order – each species announced
2 cassettes & booklet £14.95 + £1 p&p

MORE BRITISH BIRD SOUNDS
A further 52 species incl wildfowl, waders & lesser known species each species announced
1 cassette £6.95 + 75p p&p

SPECIAL OFFER

BRITISH BIRD SONGS AND CALLS & MORE BRITISH BIRD SOUNDS
3 cassettes £21.75 incl p&p

ALL the BIRD SONGS of BRITAIN and EUROPE on 4 Cassettes
Songs & calls of 415 species in systematic order – each announced by common name. **Ideal for use in the car.**
RRP £33.95 incl. p&p SPECIAL OFFER £29.95 + £1 p&p.

ALL the BIRD SONGS of BRITAIN and EUROPE
on 4 CDs 2nd Ed. Nov 1991
Songs & calls of of 396 breeding & migrant birds of Britain and Western Europe in systematic order
– no announcements – instant access to each species
FULL SET ONLY £49.95 incl. p&p (UK)
or individual CDs @ £12.99 + £1 p&p each

Vol 1 Divers to Birds of Prey   *Vol 2* Gamebirds to Sandgrouse
Vol 3 Cuckoos to Hippolais Warblers   *Vol 4* Sylvia Warblers to Buntings

CD is the easiest way yet to learn bird calls!

SOUNDS OF MIGRANT & WINTERING BIRDS
C Chappuis 1989. 239 cuts – mainly calls made during migration & winter – of 147 species of birds of Britain & Western Europe £13.95

AVIAN VIRTUOSOS
A NOCTURNE OF NIGHTINGALES.
The beautiful songs of 9 different and very musical Nightingales.
Available on CD @ £12.99 and cassette @ £7.95 + p&p each

WildSounds stock sound guides to other Avifaunal regions & Recording Equipment: Tape recorders, Microphones etc . . .

Prices include p&p for UK unless otherwise stated.
Please allow 21 days for delivery.
SPECIAL OFFERS valid to end of July 1992.
For orders outside UK please request a *proforma* invoice.

Enquiries & Credit Card Orders
0932 350444
(YOUR CALL MAY BE DIVERTED TO ANOTHER LINE AT NO EXTRA COST)
Please send your order with payment to

WildSounds
DEPT LG, PO BOX 309,
WEST BYFLEET, SURREY KT14 7YA

Sole proprietor of WildSounds J D Macdonald.

FOR YOUR INFORMATION, WE'RE EVERYWHERE

Across the country over 600 Tourist Information Centres are waiting to help you on your quest for the great English holiday.

You've probably got an Information Centre in your local town. Make that your first stop and they'll be happy to help with all kinds of information wherever you're heading, many can even book accommodation in advance and offer free guides and maps.

When you arrive on holiday, check out the Tourist Information Centre there for up-to-date details of current events, nearby attractions and handy local hints on the best pubs, restaurants, shops and more.

Always friendly and ready to help, find your local Tourist Information Centre and be sure of a better English holiday.

Tourist Information